Unlocking Meaning in Art Song

NATIONAL ASSOCIATION OF TEACHERS OF SINGING BOOKS

The National Association of Teachers of Singing (NATS) publishes high-quality books for singers, teachers, and other voice professionals. NATS books provide valuable and trusted resources that enhance singing pedagogy and support the important work of all singing professionals.

NATS is the leading professional organization devoted to the science and art of singing.

ABOUT THE NATIONAL ASSOCIATION OF TEACHERS OF SINGING

Founded in 1944, the National Association of Teachers of Singing (NATS) is the world's largest professional association of voice teachers and collaborative pianists with more than seven thousand members in the United States, Canada, and more than thirty-five other countries. Whether working in independent studios, community schools, elementary and secondary schools, higher education, or in the medical field, NATS members represent the diversity of today's music landscape, teaching in all musical styles. For more information, visit NATS.org.

RECENTLY PUBLISHED NATS BOOKS

Practical Vocal Acoustics: Pedagogic Applications for Teachers and Singers by Kenneth Bozeman
The Functional Unity of the Singing Voice, Second Edition Expanded by Barbara Doscher
Trauma and the Voice: A Guide for Singers, Teachers, and Other Practitioners edited by Emily Jaworski Koriath
The Singing Book, Fourth Edition by Cynthia Vaugh and Meribeth Dayme, edited by Matthew Hoch
Unlocking Meaning in Art Song: A Singer's Guide to Practical Analysis Using Schubert Songs by Beverly Stein

Unlocking Meaning in Art Song

A Singer's Guide to Practical Analysis Using Schubert Songs

Beverly Stein

ROWMAN & LITTLEFIELD
Lanham • Boulder • New York • London

Published by Rowman & Littlefield
An imprint of The Rowman & Littlefield Publishing Group, Inc.
4501 Forbes Boulevard, Suite 200, Lanham, Maryland 20706
www.rowman.com

86-90 Paul Street, London EC2A 4NE

Copyright © 2024 by The National Association of Teachers of Singing

All rights reserved. No part of this book may be reproduced in any form or by any electronic or mechanical means, including information storage and retrieval systems, without written permission from the publisher, except by a reviewer who may quote passages in a review.

ISBN 9781538187869 (cloth) | ISBN 9781538187876 (pbk.) | ISBN 9781538187883 (ebook)

To all of you with music in your hearts.

Contents

Acknowledgments ix

PART ONE: INTRODUCTION AND BASIC SKILLS

Introduction: How to Use This Book 3

1 How to Analyze the Text of Your Song 5
    What Is the Poem About? 5
    Sample Poem Analysis: "Heidenröslein" 6
    Performing a Song with a Refrain 9
    Poetic Structure 9
    Poetic Meter 10
    Rhyme Scheme 11
    Word Sounds 12
    Themes of German Romanticism 15
    Chapter Summary 16

2 What to Look for in the Musical Setting: Structure, Melody, and Rhythm 18
    Mood 18
    The Piano Part 19
    Form 22
    Phrasing 25
    Melody 26
    Motive 27
    Mid-Chapter Summary 28
    Tempo 29
    Meter and Rhythm 31
    Accents, Textures, and Dynamics 34
    Chapter Summary 36

3   What to Look for in the Musical Setting: Tonal Structure, Linear Motion, and Harmony 38
    Tonal Structure (Cadence Levels) 38
    Choice of Key 47
    Linear Motion and Motivic Parallelism 52
    Pedal Points 57
    Harmony 60
    Chapter Summary 77

PART TWO: SIMPLER SONGS TO ANALYZE

4   "Heidenröslein" 81

5   "An die Musik" 87

6   "Die Forelle" 94

7   "Gute Nacht" (from *Winterreise*) 101

PART THREE: SONGS OF MEDIUM DIFFICULTY TO ANALYZE

8   "Der Neugierige" (from *Die schöne Müllerin*) 111

9   "Der Tod und das Mädchen" 121

10 "An die Nachtigall" 133

11 "Ave Maria" (Ellens Gesang III), D. 839 139

12 "Du liebst mich nicht" (D 756b) 150

13 "Lied der Mignon" ("Nur wer die Sehnsucht kennt") 158

14 "Du bist die Ruh" 169

15 "Frühlingstraum" (from *Winterreise*) 181

16 "Gretchen am Spinnrade" 190

PART FOUR: MORE COMPLEX SONGS TO ANALYZE

17 "Erster Verlust" 213

18 "Meeres Stille" 231

19 "Die junge Nonne" 241

20 "Die Liebe hat gelogen" 257

21 "Ganymed" 271

22 "Dass sie hier gewesen!" 284

23 "Erlkönig" 298

Appendix
    Templates for Song Analysis (Long Version) 311
    Templates for Song Analysis (Short Version) 317

Bibliography 321

Glossary 325

Index 327

Acknowledgments

I am grateful for the support and inspiration I have received from so many people.

The idea for this book emerged from my twenty-five years of teaching music history and analysis at California State University, Los Angeles. Students in the graduate analysis classes inspired me to begin creating analysis guides, to help them "look under the hood" and find meaning in music, while those in my other classes cheered me on in the writing and publishing process. My thanks also go to the Cal State LA College of Arts and Letters, which afforded me a sabbatical in spring of 2020 to write many of the analysis guides and give numerous workshops on college campuses to test them out. I must necessarily thank the creators of Zoom who, when the COVID lockdown forced me to cancel all my workshops, enabled me to reschedule almost all of them online, providing useful feedback for the book. Thank you to all the faculty who invited me to give workshops, and to the wonderful students who participated with such enthusiasm!

I am particularly grateful to my many voice colleagues, who provided invaluable advice and support. Susan Kane, who taught voice for many years at Cal State LA, encouraged me from the very beginning, explaining the book-writing and editing process, and providing useful suggestions on an early draft. I had the great pleasure of presenting a talk with Alexander Hahn at the 2021 NATS Cal–Western Regional meeting and giving workshops at his campus, Cal State Long Beach, and it is to Alex that I owe the title of my book. My thanks go also to Robin Fisher, who recommended Rowman & Littlefield as a publisher and invited me to teach at the CSU Summer Arts "Romantic Lied in Germany" program in 2022, along with Alex and the inspiring collaborative pianists Peter Nelson and Hatem Nadim. Greetings to all the alums of this program!

I want to thank the music theorists Jennifer Snodgrass, Leigh Van Handel, and Jan Miyake, who welcomed me so kindly into the Society for Music Theory and provided feedback and encouragement, and my wonderful colleague at Cal State LA, the composer Sara Graef, for years of support and humor as well as detailed discussion of theory pedagogy. Thanks also to my students Alicia Morgan, who suggested using MusAnalysis for the Roman numeral analysis symbols, and Lincoln Mendel, who reviewed a section of the book.

Thank you to all the readers of the Market Survey, whose comments were invaluable; you will note that many of your suggestions have been incorporated into the book. And of course, many thanks to the editors of the NATS Books Program Editorial Board, including its chair Matthew Hoch, who recognized what I was trying to accomplish in this book and encouraged me in my efforts. Michael Tan, my editor at Rowman & Littlefield, has been unfailingly helpful and a joy to work with.

I have been inspired by Graham Johnson's writings on Schubert and Richard Wigmore's wonderful translations, as well as Richard Law's engaging and informative writing on the poetry set by Schubert. My interest in German Romanticism was ignited many years ago by a literature course at Northwestern University, and my analytical and musicological skills were honed by Michael White and Vincent Persichetti at Juilliard and Eric Chafe and Allan Keiler at Brandeis University. Susan Stockhammer, my first flute teacher and second mother, challenged me musically and analytically from an early age and introduced me to the music of Schubert.

On the personal front, I am grateful for the amazingly brilliant and wonderful Oana Tudusciuc, Sara Conley Odenkirk, and Elissa Grossman, without whose friendship I could never have navigated the past few years. I also thank my ballet teacher Francisco Martinez and my joyful ballet friends who have created such a supportive community, as well as Sarah Tayebi for her many wise words.

I was exceptionally fortunate to have been the daughter of such an intelligent, creative, and loving mother, Marlene Stein, who provided endless support and encouragement. My siblings Michael, Cathryne (my first music teacher), Howard, and Jim Stein have been incredibly supportive and loving, particularly upon the passing of our father, Herbert Charles Stein, a man of great persistence (and five children!) who knew I was writing the book, but passed in January 2024, a few months before its publication.

And finally, I would like to thank my wonderful husband, Gregory Dubois-Felsmann, and our two amazing children, Lenore and Miranda, for their patience with my long hours of writing. I am so grateful to have a partner of such extraordinary intelligence and kindness. While working on not one, but two major telescope projects (Rubin Observatory and SPHEREx) and maintaining a host of other interests, Gregory manages to be a source of stability and comfort for us all. We are proud to bring this book and these projects to the world, but our greatest gifts are our children Lenore and Miranda, who will make the world a better place by their presence.

Part 1
INTRODUCTION AND BASIC SKILLS

Introduction

How to Use This Book

The purpose of this book is to teach singers how to analyze their own music. In order to create a compelling performance, a singer needs to truly understand the meaning of the song, and this requires some analysis, as many meanings are not necessarily in plain view.

The meaning of a song goes well beyond simply understanding the words. Even music without words has a story to tell; adding words into the equation creates the rich complexity of interwoven meaning that makes art song so evocative and enjoyable. To begin with, poets employ metrical and rhetorical devices to create meaning through metaphor, structure, meter, rhyme, and sound. Adding to this, composers use musical techniques to create emotional depth, excitement, tension and release, and beauty. But music can also add additional meaning to the song, or even change it so much so that it contradicts the superficial meaning of the words. Overlook the music's comments on the text and you may miss the true meaning of the song!

Most voice teachers ask students to analyze their songs, but what exactly constitutes an analysis? And how is it possible to get into the details of analysis in a lesson or class when voice teachers and vocal coaches already have so many important aspects of singing to cover?

That's where this book comes in, providing a clear path for students and emerging professionals to learn new analytical skills, practice them, and apply them directly to their performances. The heart of this book consists of a set of twenty analysis guides that train singers how to search for meaning in their songs. While these guides are based on songs by Schubert, the techniques students learn can be applied to all types of songs.

Guided analysis questions are a practical way of teaching singers to explore their own music. In my many years of teaching music analysis, I have found that students often don't know what questions to ask, so I have created sets of analysis questions for each piece to help them through the process. While the questions are provided, students do the analysis themselves, so they feel they "own" their discoveries and can incorporate them into their performances in ways that are more personal than if they just read someone else's work. The "analysis guides" in each chapter serve as a scaffolding for developing independent analytical and interpretive skills. Not only do they allow singers to explore important ideas, but with regular practice they learn how to come up with the questions by themselves.

The book is organized into four major sections. Part I explains how to use the book, introduces techniques of text analysis, shows singers what to look for musically in a song, and reviews basic harmonic and analytical techniques that will be helpful. All of the musical examples from part I are taken from the twenty songs used in the analysis guides. Parts II through IV present analysis guides for twenty different Schubert songs, progressing in analytic complexity. Each song analysis consists of a set of questions that lead singers to discover for themselves the amazing ways in which the composer structures the music and expresses meaning.

The beginning of each analysis chapter (in parts II–IV) introduces new techniques and then takes the singer through the analysis of a song which particularly emphasizes them. Part II features songs most often sung by beginning voice students, and trains them to think about basic aspects of analysis, including form, poetic structure, the "folksong" style, simpler harmonic and tonal topics, and cadence mapping. Part III features intermediate-level repertoire and delves into more analytical depth, introducing third relationships, linear motion, circling and oscillation, mode mixture, augmented and Neapolitan sixths, ambiguous tonality, and the meaning of "flat" versus "sharp" tonalities. And finally, part IV combines many different topics to engage with some of the most challenging songs, both analytically and vocally.

This book has several intended purposes. First, it is an ideal text for a song literature course. The first three chapters introduce ways of engaging with text and music that will prepare the students for a semester of song analysis. After this introduction, each student can be assigned a different song to analyze and present to the class, or the class can study the same songs and compare their observations based on their own analyses.

The book is also helpful in the vocal studio. A teacher can assign a student to work through the guided analysis for the particular song that they are learning and come back to their next lesson with a deepened understanding of its meaning. Vocal master classes can benefit in a similar way, by having all students analyze a single song or each student pick a different song and present what they learned to the rest of the class, inspiring a robust discussion.

Teachers and collaborative pianists can also work through the analysis of a particular song themselves in order to assist a singer to understand and express the work in greater depth. Emerging artists can use the book as a way of finding the hidden meanings in order to get to the next level of interpretation. Finally, faculty in theory and analysis can assign song guides to their students, providing practice in the different analytical topics they are teaching.

Reading someone else's analysis of a work can be useful, but every singer also needs to learn how to delve into a song on their own to develop a personal relationship with the song and create a great performance. In this way they can not only effectively express the meanings originally created by the poet and composer, but also enrich them with the ideas and emotions that bubble up in themselves as a result of their own ability to more deeply explore the song.

1

How to Analyze the Text of Your Song

How does one go about discovering the meaning of a work of art? What even is meaning?

The first three chapters of this book explore the myriad ways in which meaning can be expressed by a poet and composer, and how you can uncover these different clues to the meaning of your song. Chapter 1 introduces elements of the poetry that you need to consider before examining the musical setting. The meaning of a song, however, is decidedly not limited to the meaning of the poem, and chapters 2 and 3 demonstrate the incredible variety of methods for instilling meaning through the music.

New terms will be in **boldface**, along with a definition or description, as necessary. Chapter 1 begins by describing a technique for becoming familiar with the text of your song, along with the terms you will need to know along the way. After most of the terms have been introduced, poems taken from the Schubert songs discussed in this book will be used to demonstrate the effects of the different poetic techniques, beginning with one of the simplest poems and moving to those with ambiguous meanings that require more context to understand. A short introduction to themes of German Romanticism closes out the chapter.

WHAT IS THE POEM ABOUT?

Your first perusal of the poem should be to assess its general meaning. A good way to do this is to read the poem out loud in English first to get familiar with it, and then read it again, this time doing a **dramatic reading**. Which words are particularly important? Do another reading, this time with different emphases and emotion. How many different readings can you do? (Use two different voices if it's a dialogue.)

Next, summarize the poem's general **story** or idea. Does the title tell you anything about the meaning of the poem? (Some titles are simply the first line of the poem, while others were given by the poet, and still others by the composer.)

What is the **mood** of the poem? How is the mood created? Are there any shifts in the mood? In a multi-stanza poem, see if the mood changes at any point, and how this is done. Describe the **imagery** in the poem, the pictures created in the reader's mind, particularly those that appeal to the senses. Also look for **metaphor**, the use of one object to stand in for a person or an idea.

Examine the **characters**. Who is the protagonist (the *persona*) who is speaking? Describe this person or element of nature (one character may be an inanimate object, such as the ocean in "Meere Stille"). Is there more than one protagonist? What is their relationship? Does the main protagonist change, as in "Der Tod und das Mädchen"? Be aware that you may find an **unreliable narrator**, who may not be telling you the complete truth.

Next determine the **mode of address**, who the main character is talking to, and the **subject**, who or what they are talking about. Both mode of address and the subject can be a person, an element of nature, or an emotion, among other possibilities. You may find that the mode of address shifts or becomes apparent later in the poem, as in "Der Neugierige." The addressee may not always be clear, as in "Du bist die Ruh" and "An die Nachtigall."

Structure

Look at the **structure** of the poem: How many **stanzas** (paragraphs) are set in the song? Were there any extra stanzas that the composer didn't set? If so, why do you think the composer didn't set them? Did the composer change the poem in any other way?

Does the poem have a **refrain** (a repeating line or lines)? If so, is it in each stanza or only some? How does the meaning and/or emotion of the refrain change through the poem? Does the structure of the poem tell you something about its meaning?

Summarize the **action** and **affect** (emotion) of each stanza. How does it change throughout the poem? Is there a predominant emotion or strong emotional contrasts? How are they expressed? Are there any dramatic high points or twists in the poem? Are there any **metaphors** that suggest meanings other than the superficial?

SAMPLE POEM ANALYSIS: "HEIDENRÖSLEIN"

At this point it's helpful to include some examples from the songs discussed in this book. Let's begin with what may seem to be one of Schubert's simplest songs, "Heidenröslein." This song famously sets a poem by Goethe, the German national poet who practically invented the Romantic movement. Goethe is so revered that you can ask anyone who has been educated in Germany and they will likely be able to recite one of his poems from memory!

Only sixteen measures long and setting three **stanzas** (paragraphs) of text, "Heidenröslein" is so well known that it is often thought of as a German folksong.[1] In a way, it's almost true, as both Goethe and Schubert were strongly influenced by German folksong and were each—for this poem and song at least—attempting to convey its natural style. German folksongs typically resonate with nature and/or love. Read through the three stanzas of the song text to get an idea of the story:

Heidenröslein (Goethe, translated by Richard Wigmore; bracketed words added by the author)[2]

1.	*Sah ein Knab ein Röslein stehn,*	A boy saw a wild rose,
2.	*Röslein auf der Heiden,*	Growing in the heather;
3.	*War so jung und morgenschön,*	It was so young, and lovely as the morning.
4.	*Lief er schnell, es nah zu sehn,*	He ran swiftly to look more closely,
5.	*Sah's mit vielen Freuden.*	Looked on it with great joy.
6.	*Röslein, Röslein, Röslein rot,*	Wild rose, wild rose, wild rose red,
7.	*Röslein auf der Heiden.*	Wild rose in the heather.
8.	*Knabe sprach: ich breche dich,*	Said the boy: I shall pluck you,
9	*Röslein auf der Heiden.*	Wild rose in the heather!
10.	*Röslein sprach: ich steche dich,*	Said the rose: I shall prick you
11.	*Dass du ewig denkst an mich,*	So that you will always remember me.
12.	*Und ich will's nicht leiden.*	And I [don't want to] suffer it.
13.	*Röslein, Röslein, Röslein rot,*	Wild rose, wild rose, wild rose red,
14.	*Röslein auf der Heiden.*	Wild rose in the heather.
15.	*Und der wilde Knabe brach*	And the impetuous boy plucked
16.	*'s Röslein auf der Heiden;*	The wild rose from the heather;
17.	*Röslein wehrte sich und stach,*	The rose defended herself and pricked him,
18.	*Half ihr[3] doch kein Weh und Ach,*	But her cries of pain were to no avail,
19.	*Musst' es eben leiden.*	It simply had to be borne.
20.	*Röslein, Röslein, Röslein rot,*	Wild rose, wild rose, wild rose red,
21.	*Röslein auf der Heiden.*	Wild rose in the heather.

To become familiar with the text, you would begin by reading it in English and then doing a dramatic reading of all three stanzas, noting which words are important in telling the story or expressing drama or emotion. (You will be doing this in German a little later.) Looking at the title tells us the focus of the story is the wild rose, or "little meadow rose" or "heath rose" in some translations, and this focus is emphasized by the short and long **refrains** in the poem:

6:	*Röslein, Röslein, Röslein rot,*	Wild rose, wild rose, wild rose red,
2, 7:	*Röslein auf der Heiden.*	Wild rose in the heather.

The **mood** of the poem appears to be lighthearted, a simple folksong, with nature **imagery** featuring a heath (a wild uncultivated area) and a small red rose. The main **characters** in this poem are the wild rose and the young man. A **brief summary** of the story might be the following: a young man sees a lovely rose in the meadow and picks it, even though he knows it will prick him. A summary of each stanza provides more detail:

1. A young man sees a wild rose and runs to admire it.
2. He tells the rose he will pick it; it responds that it will prick him so that he'll always remember it, and the rose doesn't want to be picked!
3. The boy picks the rose anyway ("wilde Knabe!") and the rose pricks him; her cries of pain don't help her and she has to suffer it.

The **narrator** appears to be a neutral storyteller, typical in folk poetry. But to whom is the narrator speaking (**mode of address**)? Understanding the intended audience requires more analysis, so we will return to this question a little later in the discussion.

It is helpful to examine each stanza in more detail, asking questions about the main **characters**, the **action**, and the **emotion** of each. In the first stanza the rose is described as "so jung und morgenschön" (so young, and beautiful like the morning). One begins to get the sense that we may not be talking about an actual flower; in fact, the rose is likely a **metaphor** for a young girl. We see the young boy running to look at the beautiful red rose (telling us he is impetuous), and he is full of joy at her beauty.

Next the boy makes his threat against the rose, and she responds in kind: "I will pick you" versus "I will prick you so that you will always remember me," clarifying that she does not want him to do so: "ich will's nicht leiden" means "I don't *want* to suffer it," though this is often mistranslated. The growing desire of the boy contrasts with the anger of the rose.

By the third stanza the boy is described as "wilde" (wild or impetuous); he picks the rose, and although she pricks him, she must still suffer grief and pain.

How do you feel about what has just happened? What is your emotion as you read this? If we are just talking about a boy picking a flower, this could be a charming little folk poem about nature. But by now you can tell that the flower-picking metaphor refers to the interaction between the boy and a girl. She does not want him to harm her and cause her to suffer, but he does it anyway. Now how do you feel?

Many folk poems have a superficial meaning at the story level, as well as a deeper meaning that would have been well understood by their original audience. Warnings to women to be very careful not to be seduced are numerous in traditional stories and poems. The poet and music theorist Christian Friedrich Daniel Schubart's poem "Die Forelle" is another example of this type, in which the charming story of a fish, a fisherman, and a witness who acts as the narrator becomes a moral tale on avoiding seducers.[4] In his famous musical setting, Schubert leaves out the moralistic fourth stanza, in which this warning is made explicit:

Die ihr am goldnen Quelle	You who tarry by the golden spring
Der sichern Jugend weilt,	Of secure youth,
Denkt doch an die Forelle,	Think still of the trout:
Seht ihr Gefahr, so eilt!	If you see danger, hurry by!
Meist fehlt ihr nur aus Mangel	Most of you err only from lack
Der Klugheit. Mädchen seht	Of cleverness. Girls, see
Verführer mit der Angel!	Seducers with their tackle!
Sonst blutet ihr zu spät.	Or else, too late, you'll bleed.[5]

Note how both "Heidenröslein" and "Die Forelle" overtly mention blood. Now go back to the two refrain lines in "Heidenröslein," and pay attention to the redness of the rose, which is repeated over and over.

The use of a refrain makes the poem sound very much like a traditional folksong. In fact much of Goethe's "Heidenröslein" of 1789 contains lines similar to various versions of folk poetry collected, edited, and/or written by the German philosopher and poet Herder in the 1770s. Goethe's poem is almost identical to Herder's 1779 version, but with a different moral. The refrain from line two actually appears in a poem from a 1602 collection, spelled as "Röslein auf der Heyden."[6] There's a reason it sounds like folk poetry—but poetry that has been carefully polished by a master or two!

PERFORMING A SONG WITH A REFRAIN

One of the challenges of performing a song with a refrain is that its meaning may change as you go through the song. One way to assess this is to review each refrain in the poem and write how you feel when the line is read or sung, in relation to the line that comes just before.

In the first stanza of "Heidenröslein," the single refrain line in line 2 ("Röslein auf der Heiden") follows a neutral line ("a boy saw a wild rose") so the emotion is perhaps a slight interest, while lines 6–7 of the same stanza show the lad running to see it and feeling happy, perhaps curious and full of joy. In stanza 2, the single refrain line follows his threat to the rose ("I shall pluck you!"), while the final refrain comes after the rose makes quite clear she is angered by this threat. In the third stanza, the first refrain follows the deed itself; we might all be shaking our head at that. The final refrain, however, follows the sad fact that despite the fact that the rose suffered "grief and pain," nothing could protect her from this violence.

As you can see, every one of the refrain lines can have a different **affect** (emotion). We move from curiosity and joy to fear and anger, and finally to grief. You have the opportunity to take your audience on an emotional journey, simply based on the refrains alone. Even a lighthearted performance of this poem in a charming folklike musical setting such as the one by Schubert will still convey the underlying moral tale. Those who think this is a simple song may find there is more to the story.

POETIC STRUCTURE

The structure of the poem can tell you important things about its meaning. In "Meeres Stille" (Calm Sea), Goethe imprisons the anxious sailor between two sections about the sea, physically suggesting the vastness of the ocean and the dangerous position of the becalmed sailor in the middle of it (see table 1.1).

Table 1.1. "Meeres Stille" (Calm Sea)

1. *Tiefe Stille herrscht im Wasser ,* 2. *ohne Regung ruht das Meer,*	Profound calm reigns over the waters, The sea lies motionless;
3. *und bekümmert sieht das Schiffer* 4. *glatte Fläche rings umher.* 5. *Keine Luft von keiner Seite!* 6. *Todesstille fürchterlich!*	Anxiously the sailor beholds The glassy surface all around. No breeze from any quarter! A fearful, deathly calm!
7. *In der ungeheuern Weite* 8. *Reget keine Welles sich.*	In the vast expanse No wave stirs.

The exclamation marks in lines 5 and 6 indicate they are not a mere description of the ocean, like lines 1–2 and 7–8, but an expression of the sailor's panic. Notice that the only two words that do not rhyme are the two protagonists, the water ("Wasser") and the sailor ("Schiffer"). The juxtaposition of opposites creates powerful emotion in the reader: the ocean is described using words that demonstrate its power—"herrscht" and "ungeheuern" (reigns and vast)—while in contrast, the "bekümmert[e]" (anxious) sailor beholds the "Todesstille fürchterlich" (fearful, deathly calm).

POETIC METER

Why learn about poetic meter? Poetic meter, like musical meter, is created by a recurring pattern of accented and unaccented beats. Poetic meter structures the poem like our backbone does for our body, and can influence the meaning, as we'll see in some of the more advanced analyses.

A few basics:

When you read poetry—or converse in English, for that matter—some syllables are stressed and some are unstressed. When we scan poetry, we mark the stressed syllables with a slash (/) and an unstressed syllable with a dash (-). To find **poetic meter**, you first find the basic rhythm or **foot**. A foot is simply the basic combination of accented and unaccented syllables.[7]

In the examples below, introducing some of the most common meters, emphasized syllables are in capital letters. The first word represents one poetic foot (the accent pattern); the sample text lines contain five feet (pentameter) each of trochees and iambs, and four feet (tetrameter) each of the dactyls, anapests, and amphibrachs (see table 1.2 for a chart of the basic **feet**).

Table 1.2.

Type	Accent Pattern (Foot)		Sample Text Line	Feet
Trochee:	/ -	SUN-day	MON-key BRAINS are STRUC-tured IN this MAN-ner	5
Iamb:	- /	The NEWS	I SEE, my FRIEND, that YOU and SHE must PART	5
Dactyl:	/ - -	SAT-ur-day	WON-der-ful EL-e-phants WALTZ-ing in U-ni-son	4
Anapest:	- - /	un-der-STAND	Well, I KNOW what I SEE, said the FROG to the MAN	4
Amphibrach:	-/-	ca-THE-dral	The WAN-dering SAI-lor a-BAN-doned his MIS-sion	4
Spondee:	/ /	BIG DESK	(Spondees usually appear as a break in the meter.)	

Each line of poetry will have a certain number of poetic feet. Lines in a poem may all contain the same number of feet, or the number may vary per line. We name the **meter** by combining the **foot** with the **number of feet per line**. Iambic pentameter, therefore, refers to a line of iambs (- /) with five feet to the line. Shakespeare's sonnets are often in iambic pentameter ("My MIStress' EYES are NOTHing LIKE the SUN"), as are most forms of blues songs ("I HATE to SEE that EVEning SUN go DOWN").

To scan a poem (discover its basic rhythm), read it out loud in the original language and then mark the stressed and unstressed syllables. For "Heidenröslein," the first line would look like this:

/ - / - / - / (-)
Sah ein Knab ein Röslein stehn,

Now you can determine the **foot** (main grouping of accented and unaccented syllables). In the first line we alternate accented and unaccented syllables; the foot is therefore a **trochee** (TRO-kay), which sounds like DA-da (/–). The first line has four **feet**, with the last one missing its unstressed syllable.

/ - / - / - / (-)
Sah ein Knab ein Röslein stehn,

Notice that all the weak syllables in this line have the sound "ein," creating a type of internal rhyme that creates a somewhat musical effect, appropriate for a folksong. This technique is called **assonance**, and will be discussed later in the section on word sounds.

A scan of the first stanza, along with the number of feet per line yields the following:

```
/  -  /  -  /  -  /  (-)
Sah ein Knab ein Röslein stehn,   4
/  -  /  -  /  -
Röslein auf der Heiden,            3
/  -  /  -  /  -  /  (-)
War so jung und morgenschön,       4
/  -  /  -  /  -  /  (-)
Lief er schnell, es nah zu sehn,   4
/  -  /  -  /  -
Sah's mit vielen Freuden.          3
/  -  /  -  /  -  /  (-)
Röslein, Röslein, Röslein rot,     4
/  -  /  -  /  -
Röslein auf der Heiden.            3
```

Scansion of a poem may not always be clear, but in general you should try to discover its primary meter. Some sections of a poem may use short substitutions of a different meter.[8]

If you look closely at "Heidenröslein" you can see (and hear) that some lines are shorter than others. Short text lines have a very different effect from long lines, and in this poem they mark off sections in the poem: the first section ends with the single-line refrain "Röslein auf der Heiden," the second closes the storytelling part, and the third ends the final refrain.

Another poetic choice that affects how we hear the poem is the type of ending. A **weak ending** closes with an unaccented syllable, as in the word "HEI-den," while a **strong ending** finishes on an accented syllable, as in the word "ROT." In this poem, all the long lines have stressed endings and the short lines have unstressed endings. These endings were traditionally referred to as feminine and masculine endings, respectively.[9]

RHYME SCHEME

Another important way of structuring a poem is through its **rhyme scheme**. Always study and mark the rhyme scheme, as it can tell you important things about the meaning of the poem. In "Heidenröslein" the rhyme scheme and number of feet of the first stanza are:

Sah ein Knab ein Röslein <u>stehn</u>,	a	4
Röslein auf der <u>Heiden</u>,	b	3
War so jung und morgen<u>schön</u>,	a	4
Lief er schnell, es nah zu <u>sehn</u>,	a	4
Sah's mit vielen <u>Freuden</u>.	b	3
Röslein, Röslein, Röslein rot ,	x	4
Röslein auf der <u>Heiden</u>.	b	3

Note that there are only two basic rhyme endings: "-ehn" and "eiden" (yes, "morgenschön" can rhyme with "sehn" and "Freuden" with "Heiden"). Notice that "rot" (red) doesn't rhyme with any other line, so it is labeled with an *x* and highlighted in gray.[10]

The rhyme scheme is similar in the other two stanzas, with the following rhymes:

2: dich/mich, Heiden/Leiden
3: brach/stach/ach, Heiden/Leiden

Always pay attention to which words rhyme, as they often tell the story of the poem.[11] There is an **internal rhyme** in stanza 2 between "breche" and "steche," highlighting the boy's threat and the rose's rejoinder. Below I have underlined one set of end-of-line rhyming words and outlined the other. In "Heidenroslein" they emphasize the following ideas:

1. Seeing the ⬚beautiful⬚ ⬚meadow rose⬚ standing fills the youth with ⬚joy⬚.
2. The youth threatens the relationship between "you" ("dich," the ⬚meadow rose⬚) and "me" ("mich," himself) with ⬚suffering⬚.
3. The youth broke the flower stem, the rose stuck him with her thorn, but the pain did not help her; the ⬚meadow rose⬚ still had to ⬚suffer⬚.

It is equally important to pay attention to **words that do not rhyme**. The word "rot" (marked with gray highlighting in the rhyme scheme chart above) is the only word that doesn't rhyme. It sticks out in the poem, just like the wild rose on the heath. Red, of course, is the color of blood.

WORD SOUNDS

Poets have other tricks up their sleeves besides meter and rhyme scheme. The sounds created in the poetry play an additional role in expressing meaning and emotion. Techniques that you need to understand and appreciate include alliteration, consonance, cacophony, assonance, and onomatopoeia.

Alliteration may already be familiar to you, as it is simply the repetition of the same letter or sound at the beginning of words that are next to or near each other. In "Erlkönig," Goethe laces the speech of the Erlking with alliteration, as the magical character tries to lure the young child:[12]

»*Du liebes Kind, komm, geh mit mir!*	"You dear child, come, go with me!
Gar schöne Spiele spiel ich mit dir;	Very fine games I will play with you;
Manch' bunte Blumen sind an dem Strand,	many colorful flowers are along the shore;
Meine Mutter hat manch gülden Gewand«	my mother has many golden garments."

It is possible that Goethe was imitating the sound of medieval Germanic alliterative poetry, which English speakers might recognize in *Beowulf* and *Piers Plowman* (and *The Lord of the Rings*, for that matter, as Tolkien was a medievalist), to give his Erlking an ancient, mythical sound.

The title of "Die Liebe hat gelogen" (Love has lied) is alliterative and the shared "L" sounds point out the closeness between the two words, suggesting how easily love can turn into betrayal. (In German, "gelogen" is still considered alliteration because the "L" occurs at the beginning of the root of the verb, which is "lügen.")

A similar technique in which sounds recur, but not at the beginnings of words is called **consonance**. An example is "Der ewigen Liebe getraut," from the third stanza of "Die junge Nonne," a song in which a young nun lets go of her earthly life in an ecstatic joining with her saviour. This remarkable poem makes tremendous use of alliteration, consonance, and especially **cacophony**, in which harsh sounds are created by plosive consonants such as K, G, P, B, or T, among others, to represent both the external storm raging outside as well as the internal storm to which her life had previously been subject:

Die junge Nonne
(Jacob Nicolaus Craigher de Jachelutta)

1. *Wie braust durch die **W**ip**f**el der heulende Sturm!*
2. *Es **k**lirren die Bal**k**en, es **z**ittert das Haus!*
3. *Es rollet der Donner, es **l**euchtet der **Bl**itz,*
4. *Und **f**inster die **N**acht, wie das **G**rab!*
5. *Immerhin, immerhin,*
6. *So tobt' es auch jüngst noch in mir!*

7. *Es **b**rauste das Leben, wie je**tz**o der Sturm,*
8. *Es **b**ebten die Glieder, wie je**tz**o das Haus,*
9. *Es **f**lammte die Liebe, wie je**tz**o der **Bl**itz,*
10. *Und **f**inster die **B**rust, wie das **G**rab.*

11. *Nun tobe, du **w**ilder, ge**w**al**t**'ger Sturm,*
12. *Im **H**erzen ist Friede, im **H**erzen ist Ruh,*
13. *Des **B**räutigams **h**arret die liebende **B**raut,*
14. *Gereinigt in prüfender **G**lut,*
15. *Der ewigen Liebe getraut.*

16. *Ich **h**arre, mein **H**eiland, mit sehnendem **Bl**ick!*
17. *Komm, **h**immlischer **B**räutigam, **h**ole die **B**raut,*
18. *Erlöse die Seele von irdischer **H**af*
19. *Horch, friedlich ertönet das **G**löcklein vom **T**urm!*
20. *Es lockt mich das süsse **G**etön*
21. *Allmächtig zu ewigen **H**öh'n*
22. *Alleluia!*

The Young Nun
(translated by Richard Wigmore)

How the raging storm roars through the treetops!
The rafters rattle, the house shudders!
The thunder rolls, the lightning flashes,
And the night is as dark as the grave.
So be it!
Not long ago a storm still raged in me.

My life roared like the storm now,
My limbs trembled like the house now,
Love flashed like the lightning now,
And my heart was as dark as the grave.

Now rage, wild, mighty storm;
In my heart is peace, in my heart is calm.
The loving bride awaits the bridegroom,
Purified in the testing flames,
Betrothed to eternal love.

I wait, my Saviour, with longing gaze!

Come, heavenly bridegroom, take your bride.

Free the soul from earthly bonds.
Listen, the bell sounds peacefully from the tower!

Its sweet pealing invites me
All-powerfully to eternal heights.
Alleluia!

The first stanza explodes with the harsh sounds of the storm outside, particularly in the "K" and "TS" sounds and doubled *R* and *T* of line 2: "Es **k**li**rr**en die Bal**k**en, es **z**i**tt**ert da**s** Hau**s**!" The sound of the howling wind is expressed through **onomatopoeia**, in which the word sounds like its meaning ("der heulende Sturm"), and a hint of **assonance** (the repetition of a similar vowel) may be heard in the second line: "Es r**o**llet der D**o**nner." Strong initial consonants continue in the second stanza, expressing the nun's internal storm through "B," "TS," and "F" sounds and comparing love and loss with lightning and death through **metaphor**, a comparison of two things which are not literally the same but which can shed light on their meaning.

The mood in stanzas 3 and 4 shifts from fear and pain to love and longing, as the nun affirms her belief and readiness for life beyond "earthly bonds." Yes, the plosive consonants persist (particularly in the "B" and "G" sounds), reminding us that external storms may continue, but a new sound transforms the aural landscape. The nun's ecstatic joy at uniting with her bridegroom (Christ) can be heard in the preponderance of "H" alliteration (highlighted in the text with gray), sounding like breathless sighs. Any performer of this exquisite piece must be aware of this and bring it out.

Note that most lines do not rhyme, but as we saw in "Heidenröslein," the ones that do, "Braut/getraut" (bride/betrothed) and "Getön/Höh'n" ([bell] pealing/[eternal] heights) tell the entire story: the bride is betrothed (to Christ) and the bell signals her transition to a higher realm. What Schubert does with that bell will be discussed in chapter 3.

Another expressive technique in poetry is the relationship between open and closed vowels. An example from this poem may be found in the opposition of open and closed vowels on each line of stanza 2, which extends the metaphor:

CLOSED	OPEN	
7. *Es brauste das Leben , wie jetzo der Sturm ,*		My life roared like the storm now,
8. *Es bebten die Glieder , wie jetzo das Haus ,*		my limbs trembled like the house now,
9. *Es flammte die Liebe , wie jetzo der Blitz ,*		love flashed like the lightning now,
10. *Und finster die Brust* [open]*, wie das Grab .*		and my heart was as dark as the grave.

In addition to the explosive and breathlike sounds in this poem, the galloping meter and shifting line lengths also pack a punch. Read the first stanza of the poem out loud in German to determine the primary meter:

- / - - / - - / - - / (-)
*Wie **braust** durch die **Wi**pfel der **heu**lende Sturm!*   How the raging storm roars through the treetops!

This trisyllabic meter is called an **amphibrach**, and its foot consists of an unaccented, accented, and unaccented syllable:–/ -. The first line of "Die junge Nonne" contains four feet, ending with a strong ending, meaning the final unstressed syllable is missing. Looking through the first stanza, we see three lines in this meter (amphibrachic tetrameter) followed by a shorter line ("und finster die Nacht wie das Grab"), which suddenly stops the forward motion, emphasizing the last word, "the grave." We saw in "Heidenröslein" how short lines can delineate structure in a poem, but they are also often used to highlight key words or phrases, as in this poem, where the nearness of death plays a pivotal role.

Short lines tell the story and provide clues to the meaning of "Die junge Nonne." Following the first short line is an even shorter line "Immerhin, immerhin," which can be translated as "even so," "still," "anyway," or "nevertheless." This line resonates with the idea of letting go of the external world to embrace the peace within. The short lines in stanza 3 ("purified in the testing flames, betrothed to eternal love") testify to her holy commitment as a bride of Christ. The galloping meter which suffuses this poem transforms in the final stanza into ecstatic yearning: "I wait, my Saviour, with longing gaze!" Then again in stanza 4, short lines reveal the secret in this song, that the heavenly bell (transcendence or awareness) has been pealing throughout her life and she is only now able to hear it ("Its sweet pealing invites me all-powerfully to eternal heights"), suggesting that her encounter with her savior is imminent. After the cacophony and alliteration of the four stanzas, the final "Alleluia"—the shortest line of all, and in a completely different meter—signals the end of strife and the perfection of heaven.

THEMES OF GERMAN ROMANTICISM

In order to study and prepare lieder for performance, you need to have a basic understanding of German Romanticism, a movement that developed in the late eighteenth and early nineteenth centuries. It is difficult to adequately portray this movement in all its complexity, but Romanticism, beginning with the *Sturm und Drang* (Storm and Stress) movement of the 1770s, brought heightened emotion to the literary, musical, and artistic works of the time. Notably, one of the most influential novels of the time was Goethe's *The Sorrows of Young Werther*, an epistolary novel in which the main character kills himself as a result of a love triangle, choosing the emotional over the rational.

Major themes that you should be looking for include a focus inward on the **individual**, the **wanderer** on a long journey, **nostalgia** for ancient times or evoking a more primitive style (which inspired the creation of the folksong), **ambiguity** or obscurity, **nature** (often accompanied by loneliness), **mysticism** or **holiness**, **transcendence** or **yearning for death**, and of course, **love** and other **strong emotions**, including **obsession**.[13] After the rational experiment of the Enlightenment ended in revolution, many people sought to escape the unpleasantness or mundane quality of life. The arts, particularly music, could take you to a higher state of being (as in "An die Musik") away from convention and reality. Other ways of escaping the rational mind include sleep, dreams, inebriation, the ecstasy of love, imagination, memory, magic, the senses, spontaneity, grief, anger, beauty, love, longing and desire, obsession, fantasy, insanity, the dissolution of the self (transcendence) and, of course, death.

You will find many of these themes in the songs analyzed in this book. The wanderer in "Der Winterreise" takes both a physical journey as well as an internal psychological one from a place of rejection and loss to insanity and possibly death.[14] Nostalgia plays an important role in "Erster Verlust," "Gute nacht," "Die Liebe hat gelogen," with memory flashbacks in the first two as well as in "Frühlingstraum." Ambiguity and obscurity may be found in "Die Nachtigall" and "Dass sie hier gewesen." Nature is in many songs, and can occasionally be dangerous and frightening, as in "Die junge Nonne," "Ave Maria," and "Meere Stille." Sleeping metaphors and dreams appear in "Die Nachtigall" and "Frühlingstraum," and fantasy appears in the latter as well as in "Gretchen am Spinnrade," which also includes magic. Insanity appears, of course, in "Der Leiermann," the final song of "Der Winterreise." Holiness features in "Ave Maria" and "Du bist die Ruh," with mysticism in the frightening skeleton man in "Der Tod und das Mädchen." The heart of "Die junge Nonne," "Ganymed," and "Du bist die Ruh" is transcendence, and yearning for death may be found in "Die Liebe hat gelogen" and "Die junge Nonne," with the contemplation of suicide in "Du liebst mich nicht." Lost love is seen in "Erster Verlust," "Die Liebe hat gelogen," and "Du liebst mich nicht," among others, and finally, obsession rules "Du liebst mich nicht" and "Gretchen am Spinnrade."

Be on the lookout for these themes in any of your German lieder, and you will be well positioned to develop a greater understanding of the meaning of a song.

CHAPTER SUMMARY

This chapter introduced elements of mood, imagery and metaphor, subject and mode of address, structure, poetic meter, rhyme scheme, word sounds, and themes of German Romanticism. A good way to incorporate these ideas into your song preparation is to examine each element, writing down your answers. If you are studying a particular song together in a class, your teacher may ask each student to do this for a different element and present it to the class. After reviewing all the elements, answer the following questions:

1. How has your analysis of these elements informed your understanding of the poem's protagonist and meaning? How does the mood or emotion change throughout the poem?

2. How will a deeper understanding of the poem influence your performance?

NOTES

1. John Reed, *The Schubert Song Companion* (Manchester: Manchester University Press, 1997), 257; Graham Johnson, *Schubert: The Complete Songs* (New Haven: Yale University Press, 2014), 1: 833–36; Jane K. Brown, "In the Beginning Was Poetry," in *The Cambridge Companion to the Lied*, edited by James Parsons (Cambridge: Cambridge University Press, 2004), 22–23; and Harry Seelig, "The Literary Context: Goethe as Source and Catalyst," in *German Lieder in the Nineteenth Century*, edited by Rufus Hallmark (New York: Schirmer Books, 1996), 2.

2. All translations in this book are by Richard Wigmore unless otherwise indicated, taken from his translations in the three volumes of Johnson, *Schubert: The Complete Songs*.

3. Line four of the third stanza should be "ihr" (her), as written by Goethe and Schubert and not "ihm" (his or its) as it is commonly printed. Modern German would likely use "ihm" to refer to "das Röslein," but Goethe himself used "ihr" (her), perhaps intending to suggest the rose is a metaphor for a woman. Schubert kept it in his autograph (1815), as did Diabelli in the first edition (1821). For a charming and informative discourse on all things *Heidenröslein*, see Richard Law, "Goethe's Heidenröslein," *Figures of Speech* (blog), July 25, 2017, http://figures-of-speech.com/2017/06/röslein.htm#update-3.

4. A second meaning, relating to the theorist C. F. D. Schubart's treacherous betrayal and years of terrible imprisonment, is discussed in the analysis guide for this song.

5. "Tackle" refers to the equipment used for fishing. Translation by Richard Wigmore, in Johnson, *Schubert: The Complete Songs*, 1:580.

6. On Herder and the idea of folksong, see Brown, "In the Beginning Was Poetry," 18–24. To compare "Heidenröslein" with various earlier versions of the poem, see Law, "Goethe's Heidenröslein" (blog).

7. For an enchanting introduction to meter, structure, and rhyme in poetry, see John Hollander, *Rhyme's Reason: A Guide to English Verse*, fourth ed. (New Haven: Yale University Press, 2014).

8. Deborah Stein and Robert Spillman, *Poetry into Song: Performance and Analysis of Lieder* (New York: Oxford University Press, 1996), 41.

9. Stein and Spillman, *Poetry into Song*, 48. Be aware that the composer may change the scansion; in the musical setting of the song, the word "Heiden" is now a spondee (two accented syllables in a row).

10. Law, "Goethe's Heidenröslein" (blog).

11. My thanks to Alexander Hahn (California State University, Long Beach) for calling my attention to this technique and to the opposition of dark and light vowels.

12. Translation of this stanza is by Martha Gerhart, in Franz Schubert, *100 Songs: High Voice,* ed. Steven Stolen and Richard Walters, trans. Martha Gerhart (Milwaukie, WI: Hal Leonard Corp, 2000).

13. For more on themes of German Romanticism, see Brown, "In the Beginning Was Poetry," 12–32; Seelig, "The Literary Context: Goethe as Source and Catalyst," 1–30; and Stein and Spillman, *Poetry into Song*, 3–19.

14. For discussion of the Wanderer in poetry by Wilhelm Müller, see anything written by the brilliant Schubert scholar Susan Youens, including *Schubert, Müller, and Die schöne Müllerin* (Cambridge: Cambridge University Press, 1997) and *Retracing a Winter's Journey: Schubert's "Winterreise"* (Ithaca: Cornell University Press, 1991).

2

What to Look for in the Musical Setting

Structure, Melody, and Rhythm

Now that you've engaged with the poem, assessing its general meaning through the characters, story, mood, and emotional development, and its structural and aural elements through form, meter, rhyme scheme, and word sounds, you are ready to see what Schubert added to its meaning. Composers have a point of view about the meaning of the poetry, and the music to which they set the poem is their personal commentary on it. Usually the music supports and deepens the meaning of the text, though sometimes it can tweak or even contradict the apparent text meaning, as in "Der Tod und das Mädchen," discussed in chapter 9.[1]

What is analysis and how does one go about analyzing a song? Analysis is simply noticing things, paying attention to what you hear and feel, and asking questions. The next two chapters will train you to notice aspects of your song that contribute to its meaning, giving you a general sense for what to look for. This chapter begins by exploring mood, the significance of the piano part, form, phrasing, melody, and motive. This is followed by a discussion of tempo, meter, upbeat versus downbeat phrases, rhythm, accents, texture, and dynamics. Chapter 3 will investigate tonal structure, choice of key, linear motion, pedal points, and harmony.

The analysis guides for individual songs in parts II–IV of this book will go into much more depth about each individual song. You may not be able to explore this level of detail in every song you learn, but if you do an in-depth analysis for at least a few, it will change the way you listen to, understand, and sing *any* song.

MOOD

The mood of a song is the first thing that strikes the listener and often remains with us long after a performance. After you have studied the text of the poem and understand its meaning and subtleties, listen to a high-quality performance of the song while following a translation (or text, if in English). Ask yourself the following questions:

- What is the mood of the musical setting? How do you feel while listening to the song? Does the mood change at any point, and if so, to what other mood or moods?

- How is the mood conveyed? As you are listening, try to sense in a general way what features of the setting make you feel this way: Is it the shape of the melody, the chords, the range of the melody or piano part, the rhythm, the repetition of a refrain, or something else?

- Does the mood express what you felt when you studied the poem? Are there slight changes (or even surprising differences) between the poem and the mood expressed by the music?

- Does the melody sound like the words? For instance, is the music trying to represent something nonmusical, like Gretchen's spinning wheel or the brook in "Die Forelle"? You will do a more detailed examination below, so just get a general sense for it here.

Feeling the mood of a song is an important beginning, but you must also understand how it is created. The rest of this chapter will help you to examine various parts of the song that together create the mood and express the meaning.

THE PIANO PART

In many songs, particularly in those by Schubert, the piano creates the mood and tells the story. Listen carefully to the piano part, both with and without the score, so that you hear and understand what is going on. The singer needs to know the piano part as well as they know their voice part in order to give a truly convincing performance, and likewise the pianist should sing through the vocal part to truly understand the dimensions and expressiveness of the melody and what the challenges are for the singer.

Schubert loves to include musical portrayals of nature or physical objects in his songs, situating them primarily in the piano parts. Famous examples are the stream in "Die Forelle" and "Der Neugierige," the storm in "Die junge Nonne," and of course, the spinning wheel in "Gretchen am Spinnrade." Be aware that, as in Romantic poetry, Schubert's music operates on multiple levels; these musical illustrations also express the heightened emotion of the protagonist.

The piano part may also act as an independent character in opposition to the singer. Examples appear in "Du liebst mich nicht" where only the piano arrives in the desired key of F major, and while the singer closes in the fantasy key of A major, the "true" key of A minor is confirmed at the end only in the piano part; the withholding of F major in the voice part will be discussed further in chapter 3. Similarly, the end of "Erster Verlust" shows the singer in one key and the piano in another.

Pay special attention to the prelude and postlude. In Schubert songs, the prelude often tells the entire story before the singer even takes a breath. The collaborative pianist must understand the deeper meaning of the song and convey it completely in the first four to eight bars. The audience doesn't yet know its full meaning, but the pianist's performance must be so compelling and clear that when the penny drops (when the audience finally understands the meaning of the song), they remember that innocuous little prelude and realize that the answers were already presented to them in the first few bars.

Some examples from the songs discussed in this book will demonstrate the necessity of understanding the prelude and its relationship to the meaning of the song. The first phrase of the prelude to "Der Neugierige" rises and the second falls, succinctly summarizing the story

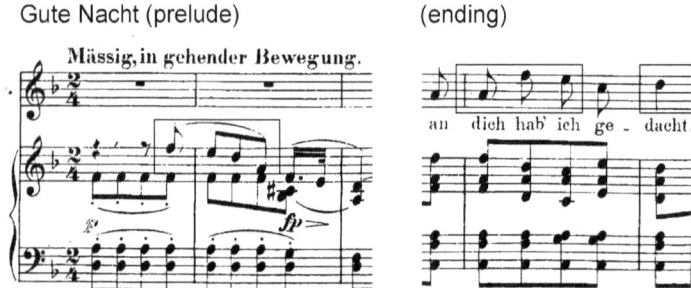

Figure 2.1. Openings to "Der Neugierige" and "Gute Nacht": The rising and falling opening of "Der Neugierige" succinctly summarizes the question of a young man trying to determine if a girl loves him or not, while the first four melodic notes of "Gute Nacht" secretly present the essence of the song (and of the entire Winterreise cycle), revealed only in the postlude to be a foreshadowing of "I thought of you" from the final verse.

of a young man trying to determine if a girl loves him (which the audience doesn't yet know) and prefiguring the dramatic point in the middle of the song in which he asks if the answer is yes or no (see figure 2.1). The opening four melodic notes of the prelude to "Gute Nacht" secretly present the essence of the song (and of the entire *Winterreise* cycle), revealed only in the postlude to be an echo of "I thought of you" from the final verse.[2]

The prelude often introduces a simple idea that is then stretched to its extreme later in the song. In "Du bist die Ruh," a song about the holiness of love, the opening rising line in the piano prelude prefigures the exquisite transformation of the melody at "The temple of my eyes is lit from your radiance alone" (m. 54) that pushes past the narrow range and key of the first two strophes to stretch up to the highest point in the song, a heavenly experience. (See figures 3.9 and 3.29 in chapter 3 under "Linear Motion and Motivic Parallelism" and "Augmented and Neapolitan Sixth Chords.") In a similar way, the left hand descends a fourth in the piano prelude, but in the later section it descends two-and-a-half octaves, creating a span of four octaves between the voice part and the bass. In "Ganymed," the octave rise in the prelude expands to fill a double octave in the six-bar postlude as the handsome youth is taken up to heaven by Jupiter (see figure 2.2).

In songs with both a prelude and postlude, compare them to see what, if anything, has changed, and then ask yourself why. "Du liebst mich nicht" contrasts the prelude's hope for love with the postlude's painful reality of rejection. The "thunder and lightning" evoked in the prelude to "Die junge Nonne" is revealed late in the song to contain the bell which signals

Figure 2.2. "Ganymed" prelude and postlude: The octave rise in the prelude expands to fill a double octave in the postlude as the handsome youth is taken up to heaven by Jupiter.

her heavenly release and which is still ringing in the postlude. The amusing semitone motive in the first measure of "Der Neugierige" is transformed into an ominous portent for the protagonist when rendered as a harmonic dissonance in the postlude. If you don't study the prelude and the postlude, you might miss something essential about the meaning of the song.

- Singers need to listen over and over to the piano part while studying the score and pianists should similarly sing through the vocal part, so that both of you can communicate and coordinate your performance.

- Make sure that you explain how you will be shaping the melody that you sing, in terms of breath, dynamics, tempo, tone quality, and mood.

- How does the piano prelude tell the story of the song? Does it present any questions or complexity? How are these developed in the rest of the song?

- Does the piano part represent a character that is independent from the voice part?

- Is there a piano interlude? What mood does it express?

- How does the piano postlude compare to the prelude? Is it the same, or are there conspicuous changes? Sometimes the true meaning of the song, the answer to the question posed in the prelude, may appear in the postlude.

- Where does the piano double the voice part (play the same notes), and where is the voice singing its own line? How will the two of you coordinate the doubled sections?

- Does the piano part feature a representation of nature or a physical object? If so, how is it expressed? What emotion might it represent?

FORM

Form can be recognized at different levels of scale. A description of how large sections of the song are put together is called "large-scale form." Each unit of large-scale form may itself be composed of smaller sections, usually a combination of musical phrases. Just as we write using sentences, paragraphs, and chapters, music is made up of phrases, and medium and large-scale sections.

There are four basic ways of proceeding in music: *repetition*, *variation*, *contrast*, and *return*. Singers and listeners will recognize that these can appear at all levels of scale. On the small scale, a phrase may repeat exactly, repeat with variation (small changes), be completely new and contrasting, or feature a return of the original phrase. On the large scale, these ways of proceeding create the song forms that we know as **strophic**, **modified strophic**, **binary**, **ternary**, **rondo**, and **through-composed**. It's good to understand the structure of a song so that you can shape it in a way that is clear and compelling for your audience. The different types discussed below will give you a general sense for form. But don't get too hung up on the name: it's more important to understand what is happening in the song than whether or not it fits perfectly into a category of form.

Strophic Songs

A strophic song, one in which each **strophe** (paragraph) of the poem is set to the same music using the technique of repetition, is the simplest type of large-scale form. If we call the musical setting "A," a strophic song could be represented as AAA, which would indicate that the music is performed three times, each time with a new text. A familiar example is Schubert's "Heidenröslein," a simple strophic song telling the story of a wild rose and an impetuous boy. This song has a refrain at the end of each verse, so the last two lines of each strophe are always the same (see discussion in chapter 4). Strophic songs often appear as a single melody and accompaniment, with the verses written below the music.

When singing a purely strophic song, ask yourself how you are going to make each strophe different. Just because the music is the same for each verse does not mean the meaning is the same, and expressing meaning is your job as a performer. Create the variety yourself by varying dynamics, articulation, emphasis, and body and facial expressions to illuminate the subtext and tell a story.

Modified Strophic Songs

Modified strophic form is a strophic song with subtle variations, small changes to allow for the expression of different words. An example can be found in "Gute Nacht" in which the first two strophes are identical (written with a repeat sign), the third adds rising runs to cadence in the upper register, and the final strophe is in the relative major. When you are performing a strophic song with variations, highlight the subtle differences of each section to your audience. The composer put them there for a reason: they give clues to the composer's commentary on the text and can help you to distinguish this verse from the last.

Binary and Ternary Forms

Contrast is used to create a dramatic shift in the mood, often inspired by a line in the poem. Both binary (AB) and ternary forms (ABA) feature a contrasting section, and through-composed form (those with no large-scale repeated sections) consists of a number of them. Binary form contrasts two sections, as in "Der Neugierige" and "Der Tod und das Mädchen." Songs may combine several ways of proceeding: "Die Forelle" begins strophically (repetition, variation), but the mood and music suddenly change when the fish is tricked into being caught (contrast). When performing a song with contrasting sections, think deeply about how you will express each section and also exactly when and how the shift will take place.

The most beloved formal device is the return, when a previously heard phrase or section recurs after a contrasting section. This is a gift to your audience, like the return of an old friend, so make sure you introduce it in a loving way, with a slight hesitation before you place the gift gently into their hands; you will hear sighs of appreciation! You must also think about what has changed since the first time the audience hears this section. Does it have the same meaning as before? If not, how will you convey that difference?

Examples of return include the above-mentioned "Die Forelle." After the contrasting middle section in which the fish's fate is sealed, we return to the familiar joyous opening music, now perhaps tinged with a little sadness. This song begins like a strophic song and winds up in a type of ternary form (AABA). Not only the fish is tricked but also the audience! Note that while Deborah Stein and Robert Spillman consider "Die Forelle" to be in ternary form, Graham Johnson describes it as modified strophic. Whichever you choose to call it, all the authors describe the surprising contrast when the fisherman muddies the water to trick the fish, and the delightful return of the refrain, with a new emotion, at the end.[3]

Other examples of ternary form include "Lied der Mignon" ("Nur wer die Sehnsucht kennt") and "Erster Verlust." "Meeres Stille" is also a type of ternary, but the return section is modified and the original cadence order is reversed. Return also plays an important role in rondo form, in which a refrain keeps returning with new musical material in between, as in "Gretchen am Spinnrade."[4]

The four techniques for proceeding in music discussed above create large-scale forms that help give shape to each song. Each form has a particular effect on the audience, of which a singer needs to be aware. A clear and easily recognizable form like strophic form makes the audience feel comfortable. After the second repetition, they know exactly what to expect and can enjoy the expression in the singer's delivery as they listen to the story being told. A strophic song with variations gives the audience the pleasure of variety, as each strophe is recognizable but contains enough changes to be enjoyable.

Through-Composed Songs

The introduction of a clearly contrasting section, on the other hand, makes listeners sit up and take notice, wondering what has just happened and why. This is where drama may flow. We are in uncharted territory and do not know where we are going. For this reason, through-composed songs (those with no large-scale repeated sections) tend to be the most dramatic, as the music keeps changing, with no familiar return. A distinctive example in this book is "Ganymed," a setting of Goethe's famous poem which depicts the handsome young man being carried heavenward to serve as the cupbearer to Zeus.

For through-composed songs, the performers should establish a clear mood or aesthetic for each section so the audience can feel that they have gone on a journey. Make sure to incorporate clear beginning and ending signs so that you do not lose the listeners.

In addition to the standard song forms, Schubert sometimes borrows from other genres such as opera. You will find dramatic recitative in "Der Tod und das Mädchen" and "Lied der Mignon" ("Nur wer die Sehnsucht kennt") and a bel canto aria in "Der Neugierige." Another formal technique used by composers is to place an important event exactly halfway through a song. In both "Du liebst mich nicht" and "Lied der Mignon" an important revelation or dramatic shift occurs at the exact midpoint of the song.

The form of a song is often an expression of the poetic form. Always compare the two; if the musical form deviates from that of the poem, you will want to know why, for the composer usually has an important reason. Rückert's poem "Du bist die Ruh" (originally titled "Kehr' ein bei mir") contains five stanzas, each of equal meter and length. In his musical setting, however, Schubert distinguishes the final stanza, in which the totality of transcendence is expressed: "The temple of my eyes is lit by your radiance alone: O, fill it wholly." It is the only stanza that is repeated, and the length of the setting takes over a third of the length of the entire song.

Make sure you have a sense for the form of your song. Even if you're not sure exactly what to call it, be able to describe the form in your own words so that you can appreciate how the audience will perceive it.

- Does your text repeat? If so, is it set to a repeat of the same or different music?

- What is the large-scale structure of the poem? What is the structure of the music? Does the music follow the structure of the poem? If not, why not? Does the change in structure add to or change the meaning of the poem in any way?

- How will the form of the song affect the audience? Is it a comforting repetitive form, a contrasting section with a return, or is it a completely through-composed song, moving ever forward?

- If strophic, how will you perform each strophe so that each is different?

- If your song is modified strophic (strophic with variations), why do you think the composer made these changes? How will that affect your performance?

- If your song features a return, is it the same as the original or are there changes? If so, why? How will you present this gift to your audience?

- If your song is through-composed, how will you distinguish the mood of each section?

- Does anything interesting happen at the midpoint of the song?

PHRASING

Phrasing is the key to engaging with your audience and telling your story. Your job is to shape the phrases and to do this, you need to put in clear "road signs," inflections that tell your listeners when you are beginning a phrase, reaching a high point, or slowing before a cadence.

How do you locate the phrases in a song? There are many hints: a composer will often conclude a phrase at the end of a text line, so look through the song to see how each line of the poem is set. The shape of the melody is another clue: melodies often begin low and rise in an archlike shape, falling at the close of a phrase. Some phrases, however, end on a high note, seemingly in the air, leaving you waiting for it to be resolved. In general, sing through each phrase with direction, moving forward through to its resolution.

Phrase endings come in different strengths. A strong ending to a phrase is a **cadence**, a resolution of harmonic instability which creates a feeling of arrival and contentment. Cadences themselves come in different strengths; you will read more about that in the section on tonal structure in chapter 3. You can think of cadence strength like punctuation, in which a comma is weak, a semicolon is medium strength, and a period is strong. A deceptive cadence, in which a cadence is promised but a different chord appears instead, creates a feeling of longing which is perfect for setting nineteenth-century poetry!

A common structure for phrases is **antecedent-consequent**, in which the first phrase asks a question and the second one answers it (see figure 2.1 for a short example). Typically the first phrase ends on the dominant and the second answering phrase ends on the tonic.

- After listening to your song many times, mark out the phrases by writing an arc over each one in your score. Small phrases are often combined to form medium-sized ones. Go through and also mark the medium-sized phrases in your score.

- How do the musical phrases compare to the text lines of the poem? Does the composer follow the structure of the poem? Take your poem and write in an arc over each text line or lines that the composer has set as a musical phrase; make a larger arc to indicate a medium section composed of two or more phrases.

- What are the shapes of each phrase? Are there antecedent-consequent phrases? How will you express these when you sing or play the song?

- For each phrase, find the most important word or words and decide how you will bring it out in your performance.

- Practice singing or playing your phrase with direction, moving forward until you find a resolution.

- Go through the phrases in your score and get a sense for which ones are the most important (containing a high point, revealing something important in the story). This will help you to build up to this point when performing the song.

- Find all the cadences in your song and circle them. Are they strong, medium, or weak? How will you express the variety? Which ones are deceptive, and how will your performance make the audience feel the pain of disappointment?

MELODY

Melody is where the performers shine, physically taking the audience on a journey through high and low, creating the mood, and telling the story. When learning a song, you will naturally want to look at the vocal **range** of the song (highest and lowest notes) as well as the **tessitura** (where the song mostly sits in your voice). Composers use range and tessitura to express the poem, so notice which words are emphasized by being set in these extreme areas. A notably wide or narrow range will also tell you something about the character, as range can correspond to emotional depth: a wide range can express extremes of emotion, while a narrow one or monotone may suggest depressive or numbed emotions; the latter is particularly true in Schubert songs, as in "Du liebst mich nicht" and "Der Tod und das Mädchen."

Within a phrase, melody may progress (end on a different note than it began), or not progress (end on the same note on which it began), which gives you important information on the shape and direction of the song.

The melody in each phrase reveals a personality. It may move forward continuously until its resolution, or may consist of shorter phrases with many rests, or a combination. Recognizing the personality of a melody will give you an additional clue to the composer's intended meaning.

A melody's personality is always expressed through the intervals within. Intervals can be narrow (semitones, whole steps, minor and major thirds) or large (fifths to an octave or more). They can also be consonant (major, minor, or perfect intervals) or dissonant (tritone, seventh, augmented second or sixth). Think about why the composer sets important words or ideas using a distinct interval, and how you will prepare to sing them expressively.

Another aspect of a melodic personality is the level of ornamentation. Learn to discern the basic melody from its ornamentation. A basic melody usually moves simply through the notes of the scale. Added ornamentation gives it beauty and complexity. Performers need to bring out the essential melody so the audience can follow. More discussion of ornamentation (neighbor and passing tones) appears in the section on harmony in chapter 3.

Finally, a melody can withhold a particular note. **Withholding**, whether of a note, a chord, or a cadence, is a technique which makes the withheld item more desirable. What doesn't appear is just as important as what appears. A good example occurs in "Heidenröslein," in which the tonic low G doesn't appear until the very last note.

- Where are the high and low points and what words do they emphasize? Why does the composer set them in these places?

- Is the range wide or narrow? How does this express the mood of the character or the text in the poem?

- What shapes does the melody create? How do they add to the drama of the song, and how will you bring them out in performance?

- Are there any unusually shaped melodies such as a monotone (melody on one note or with a limited range)?

- For each phrase, note the beginning and ending notes. Which phrases progress (end on a different note) and in which direction? Which phrases don't progress (end on the same note)? Why do you think the composer has written it this way? Which phrase or phrases have the most melodic progression (change from beginning to end of the phrase)?

- Note any particularly wide or narrow intervals and any dissonant ones. What words do they set, and why do you think the composer did this?

- Is the melody simple or is it highly ornamented? Be sure you understand how the underlying melody works and how to bring it out in performance.

- Is anything missing in the melody? Are any notes left out until later (withholding)?

MOTIVE

A musical motive is the smallest recognizable piece of a melody or rhythm. A motive can be thought of as a seed from which a whole tree (piece of music) develops. Motives appear in music from all periods, but they positively suffuse music of the nineteenth century, where the idea of all parts of a work being organically related was admired.

A motive can be melodic or rhythmic; what makes it a motive is that it is instantly recognizable. The opening motive from Beethoven's Fifth Symphony is recognizable rhythmically as short-short-short-long and melodically as a falling major third, like the sound of a doorbell. These motives recur constantly throughout the movement, building tension and pushing the music forward. Not surprisingly, musical motives may be used to express obsession, which is found in many nineteenth-century poems.

How can you determine if something is a motive? You can't, at least not in the beginning, but if a short grouping of notes or a rhythm keeps repeating throughout much of your song, it is a motive. It is up to you to discover why the composer put it in and what it means.

One of the most common melodic motives in early nineteenth-century music is the semitone motive, which can be used to express pain or sorrow. You will find this motive in "Der Neugierige," "Du liebst mich nicht," "Gretchen am Spinnrade," the first half of "Der Tod und das Mädchen," "Gute nacht," and "Dass sie hier gewesen," while "Frühlingstraum" includes both major and minor second upper neighbors as a motive. Make sure to listen carefully to the prelude or beginning of your song, as any motives will most likely first occur there.

An important rhythmic motive to recognize is the funeral march (long-short-short or variations on this rhythm). This rhythm fittingly underlies the prelude and second half of "Der Tod und das Mädchen" (see m. 22 in figure 2.3), representing the figure of Death. The funeral march rhythm also appears in "Meeres Stille," "Die Liebe hat gelogen," and the opening of

Figure 2.3. "Der Tod und das Mädchen": Upbeat rhythms for the frantic maiden contrast with strong downbeat phrases to portray gloomy Death.

"Erster Verlust." Even the triple meter song "Du liebst mich nicht" evokes a funeral march, by extending the rhythm to long-short-short-short (see figure 3.3 in chapter 3).

A related footstep motive is the tramping motive, four even eighth notes, which are repeated throughout "Gute Nacht" (see figure 2.1). When your song has a motive, be aware of any place it does not appear, and ask yourself why.

- What melodic and rhythmic motives appear?

- Are they associated with a word or idea from the poem? How will you bring them out?

- If it is a repeating motive, how will you give it shape so that it is not always the same? Sometimes even if a repeating motive represents something physical that makes a sound (like a bell ringing), you can change the dynamic level through the song to manipulate the attention that we pay to it, as in the bell in "Die junge Nonne."

- Where does the motive *not* appear and why? How will you distinguish this section?

MID-CHAPTER SUMMARY

So far you have explored the mood, piano part, form, phrasing, melody, and motive of a song. At this point it would be helpful to assess what you have learned so far. Take one song and go through each of the different musical elements discussed above, writing down your answers.

If you are studying a particular song together in a class, your teacher may ask each student to do this for a different element and present it to the class. After reviewing all the elements, answer the following questions:

1. How has your analysis of these elements informed your understanding of the song's protagonist and meaning? How does the mood or emotion change throughout the song?

2. How will a deeper understanding of the song influence your performance?

TEMPO

A key decision in preparing a song is its tempo. The tempo that is right for you is dependent on many things, but it is important to look first at the notated tempo markings, which provide information not only about how fast or slow your song should be, but also about its mood and character. The German tempo markings that appear in the Schubert songs included in this book are discussed below.

Many songs in this book feature the tempo marking **Mässig (moderate or measured)**, including "An die Musik," "An die Nachtigall," "Du liebst mich nicht," Die junge Nonne," and "Der Tod und das Mädchen." "Gute Nacht" is marked "Mässig, in gehender Bewegung," which means moderate, in a walking motion—highly appropriate for a song about walking!

Langsam (slow) appears as a tempo marking in "Die Liebe hat gelogen," "Du bist die Ruh," and "Nur wer die Sehnsucht kennt," while **Sehr langsam (very slow)** is found in "Ave Maria," and "Dass sie hier gewesen." "Der Neugierige" is marked "Langsam" at the beginning, and then "Sehr langsam" at the aria. "Meeres Stille" bears the tempo and expression "Sehr langsam, ängstlich," which means "very slow, fearful" or "anxious," and "Erster Verlust" is "Sehr langsam, wehmüthig" (wistful). **Etwas langsam (somewhat slow)** indicates that it is not as slow as *langsam*. This marking appears in "Ganymed" and "Der Leiermann," as well as many other songs.

Notice that Schubert's tempo markings tend to be primarily moderate or slow. The recitative section of "Der Tod und das Mädchen" bears the marking **Etwas geschwinder (somewhat faster)**, but only a few songs are marked **Schnell (fast)**; instead, quicker songs are marked in ways that suggest they not go too fast, such as **Etwas lebhaft (somewhat lively)** in "Die Forelle" or **Nicht zu geschwind (not too quickly)** in "Gretchen am Spinnrade." Similarly, many slower tempos are also marked with modifying descriptors, leading Graham Johnson to point out what he characterizes as the Viennese tendency toward moderate tempos.[5]

Songs may also change tempo in the middle, as in "Frühlingstraum," which begins **Etwas bewegt (somewhat moving)**, followed by Schnell, and then Langsam, marking the changes between past joys, present pain, and dreams of a magical future. A shift from Mässig to **Etwas geschwinder (somewhat faster)** at the entrance of the maiden in "Der Tod und das Mädchen" returns to the original tempo (**Das erste Zeitmass**) at the appearance of Death. Some songs don't even have a tempo marking, but rather a characteristic, as in "Heidenröslein," which is marked **Lieblich** (lovely, charming).

So how do you know how fast to perform your song? What actual tempo will make it sound "slow," "very slow," "somewhat lively," or "not too quick"? While the tempo that is right for you should be based on several elements of the music, you should begin by looking at the metronome markings. You should be aware that Schubert himself only provided metronome markings for his first seven publications by Cappi and Diabelli (published in 1821), of which six songs are discussed in this book: "Erlkönig" (op. 1, D328), "Gretchen am Spinnrade" (op. 2, D118), "Meeres Stille" (op. 3, D216) and "Heidenröslein" (op. 3, D257), "Erster Verlust" (op. 5, D226), and "Der Tod und das Mädchen" (op. 7, D531).[6] Even this limited number of songs provides us with invaluable information. One of the most important things we learn is that two songs with a marking of "Sehr langsam," for example, might be performed at different speeds. Graham Johnson compares several songs with this marking, including "Meeres Stille" (quarter note at 72 per minute) and "Erster Verlust" (54), noting that the former (marked "Sehr langsam, ängstlich") might be quicker due to the fear component vs. the "wistful" description for "Erster Verlust."[7] But I would add that even at seventy-two beats per minute, "Meeres Stille" sounds slow in performance, perhaps slower than "Erster Verlust" because the predominant rhythms in the former are half and dotted half notes, while the latter contains regular flowing eighth notes, which are four times quicker. Performers need to be aware that perceived tempo (how fast it sounds to the audience) may be more important than actual tempo (by metronome marking).

Your tempo should be based on a combination of the tempo marking, meter, mood, density of the song, and your breath capacity. The **tempo marking** generally relates to which note gets the beat. In common time the quarter note gets the beat, and in cut time (*alla breve*) it is the half note, while in compound meters (6/8, 9/8, or 12/8) the dotted quarter gets the beat. If you compare two songs marked "Langsam," one in common time and one in compound meter (12/8, for example), when performed at the same metronome marking the latter would generally sound faster, with twelve small subdivisions in the bar vs. eight in the former. In "Der Hirt auf dem Felsen," Schubert slows down the middle section by shifting from triplet to duple subdivision of the quarter note beat; the tempo has not changed, but it sounds slower.

Based on Schubert's metronome markings, Graham Johnson suggests that "Langsam" and "Sehr langsam" songs be performed with the quarter note generally between 50 and 72, "Mässig" songs between 60 and 72 beats per minute, and 76 to 84 for moderately fast songs ("Etwas geschwind") and fast songs ("Schnell"), as in "Erlkönig" at 152.[8] Of course, this is only a general background for your tempo decision. You must also consider the **density** of the song, which refers to how many levels of rhythmic subdivisions appear in it. "An die Musik" and "Der Tod und das Mädchen" are both in cut time and marked "Sehr langsam," but when played at the same metronome marking per half note, the former sounds faster, at least for the opening prelude.

A number of Schubert songs contain a funeral march rhythmic motive—long, short, short—that continues throughout the song. You should choose a tempo which feels as if you are walking slowly, as in a solemn procession. Songs from this book which contain the funeral march motive are listed in the chart below. Note that this rhythm may even be suggested in a triple meter piece, as in "Du liebst mich nicht"; in this case, the rhythmic pattern is extended to long, short, short, short.

Meter	Title	Tempo, metronome marking (main rhythm)
C	"Die Liebe hat gelogen"	Langsam (quarter, eighth, eighth)
C	"Erster Verlust"	Sehr langsam, wehmütig (half, quarter, quarter) **54**
Cut time	"Der Tod und das Mädchen"	Mässig **54** Etwas geschwinder (half, quarter, quarter)
Cut time	"Meeres Stille"	Sehr langsam, ängstlich **72** (dotted half, quarter, half, half)
3/4	"Du liebst mich nicht"	Mässig (dotted quarter + three eighths)

Your tempo decision also naturally needs to take into account the singer's breath capacity. A novice singer will need to perform a song in a more moderate tempo (that is, more quickly for a slow song and more slowly for a quick song) than an experienced singer with greater breath control and vocal technique. The most important thing is for you to find a tempo that will express the meaning and mood of the song in a way that is appropriate for your abilities.

- Does the song have tempo designation? What does it mean?

- Does it have an original (designated by the actual composer) metronome marking?

- Are there any changes in tempo? If so, what is its purpose?

- What note gets the beat?

- How many levels of subdivision do you hear? (If a quarter note gets the beat, are eighth notes common? Sixteenth notes? Or are the rhythms mostly half notes, making it sound slow?) Are there any changes in the subdivision of the beat? How does it affect the mood?

- How can you use tempo to express the mood of the song?

METER AND RHYTHM

Rhythm and meter are fundamental to the way we understand and relate to music. We come into being with a heartbeat and measure the world in this way. So naturally we are fascinated by rhythm and meter and drawn to it at a subconscious level.

Meter

Meter is simply a regular grouping of these (heart)beats marked with **accents**, emphasized notes which are louder or struck with a strong attack. The repetition of the pattern of accented and unaccented notes creates a familiarity for the listener which can be pleasant. The rhythms in the music may follow the metric patterns or break with them, waking the listener from their reverie.

Many of the songs in this book use a single meter that continues through the whole song. The exceptions use meter change to highlight a transformation of some type, as the change of address in "Der Neugierige" (shifting from speaking to himself to addressing the brook) or the change of time in "Frühlingstraum" (from the cold hard present to a longed-for future fantasy).

Dramatic shifts can occur without a meter change. The use of recitative in two bars of "Der Neugierige" at "One word is yes, the other is no" breaks completely from the aria-like motion around it to illuminate the desire of the protagonist—to know whether the girl loves him (see figure 3.23 in chapter 3). In "Lied der Mignon" ("Nur wer die Sehnsucht kennt"), Schubert interrupts the mood with seven bars of thrilling recitative accompanied with sixteenth-note sextuplets to set "I am reeling; on fire are my vitals" (see figure 3.13). And the recitative in "Der Tod und das Mädchen" shifts the emotion suddenly to panic after the gloomy funeral march prelude (figure 2.3).

Triple meters allow for a rocking sensation ("An die Nachtigall") or tender mood ("Du bist die Ruh"). Compound meters (6/8 and 12/8) can be joyful ("Frühlingstraum"), or may exaggerate this feeling to an extreme or even frightening degree, as in "Gretchen am Spinnrade" and "Die junge Nonne."

- What type of message does the meter of your song send? How does it affect the mood?

- Does the song feel like a march, a waltz, or a neutral background for a variety of rhythms? Are there changes of meter or style?

Upbeat versus Downbeat Phrase Beginnings

The meter of a poem naturally affects how it is set musically, particularly the choice of whether to use upbeat or downbeat phrases. Whether a phrase begins on the downbeat or an upbeat greatly affects the way it is perceived. Downbeat beginnings can suggest a folklike quality ("Heidenröslein" and "Der Leiermann"), a surfeit of confidence or faith ("Du bist die Ruh"), or the changeless and eternal (the ocean in "Meeres Stille"). Upbeat or offbeat beginnings, on the other hand, tend to move the song forward, particularly in 6/8 meters, as in "Gretchen am Spinnrade" in which upbeats intensify and prolong the breathless turning of the spinning wheel (and Gretchen's mind) with the stunning exception of "sein Händedruck, und ach, sein Kuss!" where the upbeats abruptly disappear and all forward motion ceases. A similar upbeat technique prevails in "Frühlingstraum," with the contrast between a cherished memory of the past and the forbidding present signified by the absence of the lilting rhythmic figure and the switch to the relative minor.

An upbeat phrase can begin with a pickup or with a rest on the downbeat, creating an emptiness that pushes the phrase forward—a long upbeat. These upbeat techniques can be found most clearly in "Gute nacht," the opening song from *Winterreise* in which the protagonist begins his weary journey to death or insanity (see figure 2.1), and in "An die Musik" in which each upbeat phrase ends on a satisfying downbeat, adding to the comfortable feeling of this song. Excluding the charming opening four bars, every phrase in "Der Neugierige" is set with a consistent upbeat rhythm, appropriate for a song in which a young man thinks about asking everyone about his love—except the girl he loves.

A common rhythmic technique used by Schubert to emphasize a change or a stronger emotion is to begin with all upbeat phrases, but then insert a contrasting middle section in which the upbeats are shifted in the bar to express a new mood. Examples may be found in "Die Forelle" where the fisherman tricks the fish, "Die Liebe hat gelogen" at "hot tears flow ever down my cheeks," and "Du liebst mich nicht" when contemplating suicide.

Schubert mixes upbeat and downbeat phrases to great effect in his songs. One main use is to juxtapose two opposite emotions, characters, or times (past versus present). The clearest example is in "Der Tod und das Mädchen," in which upbeat rhythms for the frantic maiden contrast with strong downbeat phrases to portray gloomy Death (see figure 2.3). In "Ave Maria" Schubert sets each repetition of "Hail Mary" on a downbeat while every other phrase begins on an upbeat to contrast her complete faith in the Virgin with the existential fears that beset Ellen in the dangerous place she is hiding. The vicissitudes of life versus a strong religious faith are contrasted in a similar way in "Die junge Nonne," where the only downbeats occur on the refrain "wie das Grab" (like the grave), "Immerhin" (still, nonetheless), and the "Alleluia" passages at the end.

In "Erster Verlust," a song about pining for "those fair days . . . of first love," downbeat phrases remembering the past contrast with upbeat phrases expressing lamentation and grieving in the present. "Dass sie hier gewesen" sets things that cannot be seen or pinned down (say, a fragrance) with upbeats and ambiguous harmonies, and things that can (someone or something was here, the refrain) with a downbeat and clear functional harmonies in C major. "Ganymed" expresses confidence and rejoicing in nature (and love) in the opening downbeat phrase (see figure 2.2); most of the later phrases push the music forward with upbeats, with the wonderful exception of "Mir, mir" ("To me, to me! [the subject is yearning love] in your lap, upwards . . . all-loving Father"). And in "Lied der Mignon" ("Nur wer die Sensucht kennt"), Schubert sets two sections with downbeat openings, drawing an important connection between her suffering state in text lines 1–2 and "Ah, he who knows and loves me is far away" in lines 7–8.

Noticing whether the opening of each phrase of a song begins on a downbeat or an upbeat may seem superficial, but this technique was clearly important to Schubert and other composers. Get into the habit of making a close observation, as these contrasts often point to the essential meaning of the song.

- Does your song use all upbeat phrases, all downbeat phrases, or is it mixed? Why?

- How will you bring out the characteristic of this type of song and any shift between upbeat and downbeat phrases?

Rhythm

So much of the personality of a song is created through rhythm. Simple rhythms create a folk sound, as in the repeated same eighth notes in "Heidenröslein" or the quick runs and hopping eighths at the end of "Der Hirt auf dem Felsen." Musical birds appear as dotted rhythms in "An die Nachtigall," "Ganymed," and "Frühlingstraum. Repetitive rhythms create an intentional monotony, appropriate for songs like "Meeres Stille" and "Du liebst mich nicht."

Rests are particularly important, so don't ignore their meaning. In "Der Leiermann" the sixteenth-note rests in the right hand of the piano imitate the way the hurdy gurdy sound stops briefly when switching from the melody to a chord. The rests between the notes in the prelude of "Der Neugierige" create a lighthearted mood, as though the pianist were winking at the audience and asking, "Can you believe this guy?" (see figure 2.1). Rests and grace notes in "Die Liebe hat gelogen" create sobbing and sighing at the words "Hot tears flow ceaselessly down my cheek," and the short rests between chords in "Dass sie hier gewesen" clearly set the idea of the east wind "breath[ing] fragrance into the air."

Two of the Schubert songs in this book contain a full bar of rest, signaling a complete stop in the song. When you have a measure rest in your song, you need to figure out why the composer has inserted this caesura. In "Dass sie hier gewesen" the musical phrase is cut off in m. 18 and is completed only in the last four bars of the song (compare figures 3.7 and 3.25 in chapter 3). The bar rest in "Du bist die Ruh" occurs at the absolute high point in the song (see mm. 61 and 75 in figure 3.29), as if to allow the listener to preserve the exquisite rising line to the high A♭ for just a moment before returning to earth.

A sudden rhythmic shift in "Die Forelle" calls attention to the treachery of the fisherman muddying the water to catch the fish: the babbling brook sextuplets unexpectedly cede to hammering sixteenth-note chords in mm. 38–39 with the second half of each bar completely silent. Simultaneous sextuplets versus sixteenth notes in "Ave Maria" symbolize the contrast between faith and adversity that is at the heart of this beautiful song.

Rhythm can slow or still the forward motion. A reverse hemiola near the end of "Du liebst mich nicht," in which three beats in 3/4 become two beats in 6/8, breaks down the meter as if smashing into a wall, to reiterate the painful lament "You don't love me!" The calm of the water in "Meere Stille" is suggested by a basic two-bar rhythm repeated endlessly throughout the song to evoke the monotony of a ship stranded at sea through lack of wind. And, of course, rhythm can speed up a song, as in the gradual acceleration throughout "Ganymed," in which the primary rhythms move from quarter notes, eighths, triplets, sixteenth notes, and then even faster via a "poco accelerando." This rhythmic acceleration alone expresses the essential concept of the poem, which equates rapture created through the beauty of nature (and love) with the experience of apotheosis, being carried to heaven to become a god.

- How is the personality of your song expressed through rhythm? Is it generally varied or monotonous?

- How are rests used in your song and what do they evoke?

- How are rhythmic shifts used to express contrast? What ideas or emotions are being juxtaposed?

- How does rhythm speed up or slow down sections of the song?

ACCENTS, TEXTURES, AND DYNAMICS

Accents

Pay close attention to accents in the piano part, which may emphasize important words or chords. "Erster Verlust," a song juxtaposing present grief with past joys, shifts suddenly between two keys with a strong accent and *fp* marking. The first accents in "Die Liebe hat gelogen," "Ganymed," and "Dass sie hier gewesen" emphasize striking chords, including a surprising Neapolitan chord (on beat 3 of the first measure), a dissonant appoggiatura (on the downbeat of bar 2), and a half-diminished seventh chord (on the downbeat), respectively.

Another use for accents in Schubert's music is to imitate the natural world. Accents appear in the first verse of "Die junge Nonne," which represents a physical storm, but not in the second verse, where stormy emotions are compared to the actual tempest. They also suggest the dropping of tears in "Die Liebe hat gelogen," at "Hot tears flow ceaselessly down my cheek."

Accents may express a mood or emotion. In "Die Forelle," the sextuplets representing the brook smash into an accented beat 2, suggesting the cheerful mood of the lively and impulsive trout. These accents completely disappear during the muddying of the waters, but return in the final section, perhaps only as a memory of the fish's (and observer's) past joy. On the other hand, Schubert often uses accents to create "stingers," an offbeat accent in the piano part expressing sudden pain in the protagonist. Examples appear in "Gute nacht" in combination with the semitone motive (see figure 2.1), "Du liebst mich nicht" after every one of the first five repetitions of "You don't love me," "Lied der Mignon" ("Nur wer die Sehnsucht kennt") at "Alone, cut off from all joy," and in "Der Leiermann," ostensibly to imitate the sound of the hurdy gurdy, but of course, to make us feel his pain.

Schubert even uses accents to draw attention to the piano emerging from or taking over the vocal line, as in "Ganymed" at "You cool the burning thirst" and "Dass sie hier gewesen" at the end of the first two refrains.

- What is the function of the accents in your song? Do they emphasize important words or chords, imitate the natural world, express a mood, or show the piano emerging from the vocal line?

- Did you find any "stingers"? Make sure the pianist brings them out in performance.

- How will the accents help you to express the meaning of the song in performance?

So far, this chapter has examined different aspects of tempo, meter, and rhythm individually, to demonstrate how they work and may be used to express meaning in the music. Of course, composers mix them together to brilliant effect. "An die Nachtigall" uses meter and rhythm in many of the ways described above: the triple meter combined with upbeat phrasing creates a rocking motion perfect for a song about not waking a sleeping emotion, love. The only downbeat phrases occur when the nightingale sings, marking the change of address from simple third person to the nightingale in the final couplet. And finally, the accent in the final line underlines the essential meaning of the poem: "Do not awaken my love with your singing!"

Texture

The texture of a song can tell you important things about how your audience will experience it. Does the piano part feature chords, arpeggiation, moving inner voices, or imitation? Observe the texture of your song, noting whether it stays mostly the same or changes, and if so, where and why.

A song with a similar texture throughout can feel comfortable (as in "An die Musik" or "Ave Maria"), frightening ("Du liebst mich nicht"), or even intentionally monotonous ("Meeres Stille," "Gute nacht," and "Der Leiermann") depending on the quality of what is being maintained. Changes in texture, on the other hand, tell us that something is changing or needs attention. In "An die Nachtigall," Schubert inserts a section of chords moving in contrary motion evoking a baby's cradle, before waking us with a jolt. "Dass sie hier gewesen" contrasts full chords in the verse with open octaves for the refrain, creating a distinction between things that can and cannot be seen. In "Ganymed," the texture changes constantly in each section of this song about transformation. What does the texture of your song tell you about its meaning, and how will it affect your listeners?

- Does the texture remain the same throughout the song?

- If it changes, why? How will you bring out the change?

- How will the texture affect your listeners' understanding of the song's meaning?

Dynamics

There is no such thing as an absolute dynamic level (level of loudness or softness). But composers of the nineteenth and twentieth centuries usually include dynamic markings as a way to express the general mood and approach of the song. In Schubert songs the dynamics are generally written into the piano part only. It is noticeable that most Schubert songs begin softly, generally with a *pp* notation. Many stay quite soft all the way through, with a few even including sections in *ppp* at special places as in "Die junge Nonne" at "Like the grave!" and the "Alleluia" at the end, and "Nur wer die Sensucht kennt" at "Ah, he who loves and knows me is far away."

Many predominantly soft songs still feature a dramatic change of dynamics to highlight an important word or thought, as in "Du liebst mich nicht" with a crescendo to *fff* at the dramatic rhythmic and Neapolitan motion setting "You don't, you don't love me!"; "Du bist die Ruh" with a crescendo to *f* at "The temple of my eyes is lit by your radiance alone"; "Gretchen am Spinnrade" which arrives at *f* at "I shall never, never again find peace" and *ff* at the climactic point "The pressure of his hand and, ah, his kiss!"; "Erster Verlust" with a sudden *fp* on the word "beautiful"; and "Die Liebe hat gelogen" with *f* and *ff* at "Heart, beat no more; poor heart, beat no more!" The song "Ganymed" is full of different moods, but uses the same technique, as in the big crescendo to *f* on "infinite beauty," for example. Pay attention to where the dynamics change, as it usually indicates something important is being said!

No matter what the notated dynamic level, you will need to shape each of your phrases so that they move forward and have a beginning, middle, and end. You will also need to accommodate different vowels and registers within a particular dynamic level. The point is not to achieve a perfect dynamic level, but rather simply to give the impression of *piano* or *forte*, while still supporting well and moving through to the end of your phrases.

- What is the predominant dynamic level? What is the total range?

- Are there any sudden changes or extremes of dynamic level; if so, why?

CHAPTER SUMMARY

In the second half of this chapter, you reviewed issues of tempo, meter, phrase types (upbeat versus downbeat), rhythm, accents, texture, and dynamics. To get the most out of this section, take the same song you used for the mid-chapter summary and go through each of these elements, writing down your answers. If you are studying a particular song together in a class, your teacher may ask each student to do this for a different element and present it to the class. After reviewing all the elements, answer the following questions:

1. How has your analysis of these elements informed your understanding of the song's protagonist and meaning? Does the mood or emotion change throughout the song?

2. How will a deeper understanding of the song influence your performance?

NOTES

1. Robert Schumann's "Im wunderschönen Monat Mai" provides an example in which the music sounds quite different than one might expect from the words. In general Heine's poetry abounds with irony, but while this first poem from *Dichterliebe* sounds like a positive declaration of love straight from the heart, Schumann inflects it with oscillating harmonies and ends with a dominant seventh to show the character's uncertainty about how it will be received.

2. Susan Youens, *Retracing a Winter's Journey: Franz Schubert's "Winterreise"* (Ithaca: Cornell University Press, 2013), 106.

3. Deborah Stein and Robert Spillman, *Poetry into Song: Performance and Analysis of Lieder* (New York: Oxford University Press, 1996), 200; and Graham Johnson, *Schubert: The Complete Songs* (New Haven: Yale University Press, 2014), 1:580.

4. For a discussion of rondo form and the refrain in lieder, see Stein and Spillman, *Poetry into Song*, 201–3.

5. Johnson, *Schubert: The Complete Songs*, 3:316–26, particularly 319–21.

6. Schubert did not include metronome markings in his autographs, but only in the songs from op. 1 to op. 7, "Drang in die Ferne," the *Deutsche Messe*, and his opera *Alfonso und Estrella*. Clive Brown, "Schubert's Tempo Conventions," in *Schubert Studies* (Burlington: Ashgate, 1998), 2–3.

7. "Meeres Stille" is marked in cut time, while "Erster Verlust" is in common time, but Graham Johnson suggests it is essentially an *alla breve* piece. Clive Brown notes that in slower tempos, cut time is equivalent to twice as fast as common time; although this was not always the case, his analysis of *Alfonso und Estrella* supports this interpretation. Brown, "Schubert's Tempo Conventions, 2–5; Johnson, *Schubert: The Complete Songs*, 3:322.

8. Johnson, *Schubert: The Complete Songs*, 3:321–25.

3

What to Look for in the Musical Setting

Tonal Structure, Linear Motion, and Harmony

The previous chapter explored many elements of structure, melody, and rhythm that help to create the mood and express meaning. However, no analysis is complete without an understanding of the tonal and harmonic structure of a song. This is particularly important in the music of Schubert, famous for his adventurous harmonic palette, and of the nineteenth-century composers who followed in his footsteps.

Chapter 3 introduces you to questions of tonal structure, choice of key, linear motion, pedal points, and harmony, demonstrating how each technique can express the text in a profound way. Each section contains definitions and examples, so that even if you are not experienced in harmonic analysis, you will be able to learn some common techniques that composers use to create a mood and tell a story. This chapter contains many musical examples, and it is imperative that you listen to the song to understand how the technique being demonstrated in the example expresses emotion or reveals a deeper meaning. It is recommended that for each musical example, you listen to the complete song so that you hear the technique demonstrated in context. Music is not eye music, but must be heard and felt to truly understand its implications.

TONAL STRUCTURE (CADENCE LEVELS)

Cadence Mapping

Every song has a tonal structure that guides the melody and harmony. In a way you can think of it like a map that tells you where you are traveling in the song. A great way to get a sense for the tonal structure is to create a **cadence map**. After you have listened to the song many times both with and without the music, go through and circle each cadence in your score. Use your ears to find the cadences, which should give you a sense of rest, even if only temporary. Each cadence resolves to a particular chord, which is called the **cadence level**. In most cases, a cadence brings a sense of relief, but a composer may prepare to cadence and then suddenly shift and resolve to a different chord. Such a **deceptive cadence** creates a sense of surprise or loss; in a typical deceptive cadence we are expecting a V-I cadence, but instead get V-vi.

Another type of cadence is the half cadence, a cadence to the dominant in which you still feel you are in the original key.

To create a cadence map of your song, write each cadence level in the score above each circled cadence and then write the same cadence levels (chord names) into the poem which you have analyzed. This way you can see how the cadences may express or reflect the poem, and also what type of tonal structure you are dealing with.

The choice of different cadence levels and their ordering is important in telling the story of the song. Some songs are like a warm bath, cadencing over and over to the same chord and bringing comfort and peace to the listener. A clear example of this type of song is "An die Musik" (poem by Franz von Schober) in which every text line cadences on D major (see figure 3.1 and the cadence chart below). No wonder this song is the unofficial anthem of the National Association of Teachers of Singing (NATS)!

Figure 3.1. "An die Musik": Cadencing on the same tonal level throughout the song creates a peaceful mood. In addition, the grieving semitone motive sets the mood and creates structure across the song.

	Cadence Level
Piano prelude:	D
Beloved art, in how many a bleak hour,	D
When I am enmeshed in life's tumultuous round,	D
Have you kindled my heart to the warmth of love,	D
And borne me away to a better world!	D (after deceptive motion to b in m. 17)
Often a sigh, escaping from your harp,	D
A sweet, celestial chord	D
Has revealed to me a heaven of happier times.	D
Beloved art, for this I thank you!	D (after deceptive motion to b in m. 17)
Piano postlude	D

Other songs are like a sinking ship, where the cadence levels change constantly or create distinctive shapes, as in the cadences or line closings moving by **falling thirds** in the middle of "Meeres Stille" (mm. 9–24):

Anxiously the sailor beholds	a
The glassy surface all around.	F
No breeze from any quarter!	D^7
A fearful, deathly calm!	B

or the **step-by-step descending cadence levels** in the first half of "Du liebst mich nicht":[1]

My heart is [torn apart], you do not love me!	
You gave me to know that you do not love me!	a
Though I appeared before you, entreating, wooing,	
Zealously loving, you do not love me!	A♭
You told me so, you said it in words,	G
All too explicitly, you do not love me!	G♭

Even non-musical audiences feel the anxiety in these types of songs and a singer and pianist who understand what the composer is doing can create a powerful performance.

Many songs fall somewhere in between, establishing a tonal area at the beginning (usually the key of the piece), modulating to a new tonal area or areas prepared by harmonies that make us expect a cadence in the new area, and then returning to the original key. Of course, Schubert takes us to surprising tonal areas, which is what makes his music so sublime. To really appreciate Schubert lieder, you must delight in the wandering tonality that distinguishes so many of his songs, and bring your audiences along with you.

Look at your cadence map and see if there is anything unusual. Is the first cadence in the key of the piece? If not, why not? "Du liebst mich nicht" is in A minor but cadences immediately to F major in bar 4 of the prelude. How strange! But after analyzing this piece, we learn that this shift is highly significant and tells the story of the song (discussed below). When something surprising happens in the opening of a song, there is always an important reason behind it.

Tonal Withholding

When you are studying a song and making a cadence map, you must also pay attention to where it does *not* cadence (**tonal withholding**). Composers can create wrenching emotions by preparing for a cadence and then pulling us away at the last minute (an avoided cadence) or shifting to a different tonal level than anticipated (a deceptive cadence). In addition, composers may cadence everywhere except where you expect them to land, creating a missing tonal level often associated with something that is longed for but not achieved, or perhaps a memory or desire.

An example of tonal withholding to express desire occurs in "Gretchen am Spinnrade" (see figure 3.2) where the protagonist attempts to cadence on F at the end of each refrain: a half cadence to C in m. 11 prepares for F major, but instead of this key, a quick shift to A in the bassline of m. 12 returns her to a dismal D minor, the key of her unfortunate reality. It is only later in the song, as she is dreaming of Faust, that she arrives on F at "sein hoher Gang" in m. 51.

Figure 3.2. "Gretchen am Spinnrade" (mm. 1–12): A half cadence to C major (mm. 10–11) prepares for arrival on F major (creating musical desire), but is thwarted at the last moment (mm. 12–13) by a quick return to D minor. The opening pedal point on D combined with the activity in the right hand combine to create a feeling of being stuck in an endless cycle.

You have already seen how the first half of "Du liebst mich nicht," a song in A minor, features a chromatically descending series of cadences from A to G♭ to express the sinking mood of the protagonist (see figure 3.3). Why does Schubert stop at G♭? Remember that the opening piano prelude begins in A minor but immediately cadences in F major in m. 4. Throughout the piece the singer tries many times to reach that hoped-for key and never arrives. In "Du liebst mich nicht" the piano represents fantasy and the singer reality. At the end of the song, the first three bars of the piano postlude are ever hopeful, repeating the opening of the prelude which cadenced in F major, but at the last minute, the piece closes in A minor as reality takes over.

Figure 3.3. "Du liebst mich nicht" (first half): The chromatically sinking cadence levels express the protagonist's dire mood, but never reach the longed-for key of F major.

"Meeres Stille," the C-major song setting a Goethe poem about the fearful sailor whose ship is dangerously becalmed, cadences or closes on every note of the C major scale except for the expected one—the dominant, G (see figure 3.4 and the chart below). It tries three times to cadence on G, but fails each time. Schubert even sets up a series of cadences moving by falling thirds (a, F, D^7, B)—itself a sign of a dismal outlook—whose next level would be G, but again this important tonal area is avoided. One phrase even ends on D^7, sounding like a half cadence preparing for the dominant G, but resolving instead as a German sixth, outward to $f^6_{\sharp 4}$, the tritone of the key. The mirror structure of the opening and closing cadences (C-E and E-C) demonstrates a lack of tonal progress, corresponding to the absence of windpower to move the ship. Schubert makes the hopelessness of the sailor clear through an overall structure of falling thirds C-(E)-a-F-D-B-___-E-C, lacking only the desired goal of the dominant, G.[2]

Figure 3.4. "Meeres Stille": This song about a frightened sailor cadences on every level of the C major scale (including a series of ominous falling thirds) except for the expected dominant G major.

Meeres Stille (Calm Sea)
(Goethe, translation by Richard Wigmore)

Profound calm reigns over the waters,	**C**	The sea
The sea lies motionless;	**E**	
Anxiously the sailor beholds	a	The anxious sailor = falling thirds
The glassy surface all around.	F	
No breeze from any quarter!	D⁷	Trying to get to G; doesn't resolve "correctly"
A fearful, deathly calm!	B	
In the vast expanse	**E**	The sea
No wave stirs.	**C**	

Another form of withholding occurs in "Erster Verlust" where the ostensible key of F minor (the present) keeps shifting to A♭ major (memories of the "beautiful days . . . of first love"). To preserve this ambiguity between past and present, Schubert avoids an authentic cadence on the tonic until the very last bar. In fact, the singer actually closes the song in A♭—only the piano cadences in F minor in the postlude (see figure 3.5 and the chart below; boldface letters are authentic cadences and brackets are tonal areas). In m. 2, a preparation to cadence on A♭ is thwarted on the downbeat of m. 3 with a deceptive motion followed by a weak cadence on F minor on beat 3, but only in the piano. It's as if the singer wants to go to the pleasant past of A♭ major, but the piano pulls them back to the present in F minor. The singer never cadences on the tonic; the closest they get is the half cadence to C in m. 16, preparing us for the return of the opening. In this song, the singer and the piano play opposite roles from those in "Du liebst mich nicht": while the singer in "Erster Verlust" ends in Ab major, the key of beautiful memories of the past, the piano postlude closes firmly in F minor, the key of the present sad reality.

Erster Verlust (First Loss)
(Goethe, translation by Martha Gerhart)

Ah, who will bring back those fair days,	[in f, then A♭], f [piano only]³
Those days of first love?	half cadence in A♭
Ah, who will bring back but one hour	[begins f, then A♭]
Of that sweet time?	**A♭** (voice and piano)
Alone, I nurture my wound	[in f, then b♭]⁴
And, forever renewing my lament,	[in f]
Mourn my lost happiness.	Half cadence in f
Ah, who will bring back those fair days,	[in f, then A♭] f [piano only]⁵
That sweet time?	**A♭** (voice and piano), **f** (piano only)

What to Look for in the Musical Setting 45

Figure 3.5. "Erster Verlust": This bifocal song contrasts F minor (the doleful present) and A♭ major (the fondly recalled past) and its grieving semitone motive structures the entire song.

A song which is centered in two different keys like "Erster Verlust" is considered **bifocal**. This technique is ideal for creating the ambiguity that was so desirable in Romantic artistic expression, whether in art, poetry, or music.[6]

Another example of this technique occurs in "An die Nachtigall," where the opening four lines of text (out of only six lines in the poem) alternate between C major and G major, suggesting the liminal state between sleeping and waking (see figure 3.6 and the chart below).

46   Chapter 3

An die Nachtigall (To the Nightingale)
(Matthias Claudius, translation by Martha Gerhart)

Piano prelude	in C, in G
He lies sleeping upon my heart;	in C
My [guardian] spirit sang him to sleep.	in G
And I can be merry and jest,	in C
Delight in every flower and leaf.	in G
Nightingale, ah! Nightingale, [ah!]	in g
Do not awaken my love with your singing!	in G

The first cadence is to G major in m. 8, but right up to m. 6 the piece is in C major. It would be so easy to cadence in C major on the downbeat of measure 7, but instead, a minuet-like cadence to G is appended in mm. 7–8. When the voice enters in m. 9, the harmonies of the first five bars repeat (in C), but the second half is altered to be more clearly in G. Note the rocking motion in the right hand (mm. 14–16) and the "rocking" (oscillating) harmonies in mm. 14–17.

Figure 3.6. "An die Nachtigall" (mm. 1–17): The ambiguity between G and C major suggests the liminal state between sleeping and waking.

Some songs don't even close in the same key as they begin. This is known as **directional** or **progressive tonality**, and you can find this technique in "Ganymed," which, though beginning in Ab, moves through a number of surprising keys to finally cadence in F major; you will read more about this song in the section on choice of key, below.

Creating a cadence map can reveal important things about the meaning of your song, so don't skip this step. A song all in one key creates a completely different impression than one that is constantly modulating. If your song is hiding something (trying to avoid a particular tonal area), or ambiguous (in more than one key), you need to find out why. In short, you need to be aware of how your song works in order to sing it well.

- After listening many times to your song, circle the cadences in the score.

- Now write in the cadence levels on your translation of the poem.

- What type of cadence map do you see: Is it a warm bath (cadences always on the same level), a sinking ship (cadences all over the place or else sinking stepwise), or does it follow the more typical path and tonicize or modulate to one or two other tonal levels?

- Is there a particular pattern of cadences? How would you characterize the ordering of cadences?

- Does it avoid any important cadence level?

- Are there any deceptive or avoided cadences?

- Does the song end in the same key in which it began? If not, why not?

CHOICE OF KEY

What does the choice of key tell you about a song? Quite a lot, actually, which is why you should always check to see what the original key was. In the nineteenth century, composers had clear views about the characteristics of the different keys. Although tuning was evolving more and more toward equal temperament, the idea of sharp keys having different personalities than those of flat keys was quite pronounced. This distinction between sharp and flat keys had a long history: from at least the sixteenth to the eighteenth centuries, flat keys (and often chords) had associations with love, sweetness, and softness, while sharp keys and chords could be associated with hardness, pain, or death. These ideas lingered into the nineteenth century.[7] C major was seen as the most pure, as it was the key to which a keyboard instrument was tuned. The higher up in the circle of fifths (in the sharp direction), the more brilliant the key, and the lower in the circle of fifths (in the flat direction), the more melancholy.

We have this directly from Christian Friedrich Daniel Schubart, the famous poet and music theorist who wrote the text of "Die Forelle" from the cell in which he was unjustly imprisoned. In his *Ideen zu einer Ästhetik der Tonkunst*, published posthumously in 1806, he wrote that "[t]ender and melancholy feelings [are expressed] by flat keys; wild and strong passions by sharp keys."[8] The more extreme the key (farthest away from C), the more exaggerated and sometimes negative its personality, as can be seen in the following descriptions of keys moving in the sharp direction:[9]

THE NATURAL AND SHARP MAJOR KEYS:
C major: "Completely pure. Its character is innocence, simplicity, naivety, children's talk"
G major: "Everything rustic, idyllic, and lyrical, every calm and satisfied passion, every tender gratitude for true friendship and faithful love"
D major: "The key of triumph, of Hallelujahs, of war-cries, of victory-rejoicing"
A major: "Declarations of innocent love, satisfaction with one's state of affairs, hope of seeing one's beloved again when parting; youthful cheerfulness and trust in God"
E major: "Noisy shouts of joy, laughing pleasure and not yet complete, full delight lies in E major"
B major: "Strongly colored, announcing wild passions. Anger, rage, jealousy, fury, despair."

C and G major seem close to nature, while D and A are more energetic, and E and B move to the extremes, suggesting noisy shouts and wild passions.

The flat major keys begin very sweet and loving (F, B♭, and E♭), but also descend into extremes the farther they move in the flat direction (A♭ and D♭), according to C. F. D. Schubart:

THE FLAT MAJOR KEYS:
F major: "Complaisance and calm"
B♭ major: "Cheerful love, clear conscience, hope, aspiration for a better world"
E♭ major: "The key of love, of devotion, of intimate conversations with God"
A♭ major: "The key of the grave. Death, grave, putrefaction, judgement, eternity"
D♭ major: "A leering key, degenerating into grief and rapture"
G♭ major: "Triumph over difficulty, echo of a soul which has fiercely struggled"

The natural and flat minor keys likewise descend into extreme emotions the farther down they go in the circle of fifths:

THE NATURAL AND FLAT MINOR KEYS:
A minor: "Pious womanliness and tenderness of character"
D minor: "Melancholy womanliness, the spleen and humours brood"
G minor: "Discontent, uneasiness, worry . . . bad-tempered gnashing of teeth"
C minor: "Declaration of love and at the same time the lament of unhappy love. All languishing, longing, sighing of the love-sick soul"
F minor: "Deep depression, funereal lament, groans of misery and longing for the grave"
B♭ minor: "somewhat surly . . . mocking God and the world, discontented with itself"
E♭ minor: "Feelings of the anxiety of the soul's deepest distress, of brooding despair"

There are no sharp minor songs included in the songs discussed in this book, but here are C. F. D. Schubart's descriptions for these keys:

THE SHARP MINOR KEYS:
E minor: "Naïve, womanly, innocent declaration of love, lament without grumbling"
B minor: "key of patience, of calm awaiting one's fate, submission to divine dispensation"
F♯ minor: "A gloomy key . . . resentment and discontent are its language"
C♯ minor: "Penitential lamentation . . . sighs of disappointed friendship and love"
G♯ minor: "heart squeezed until it suffocates, wailing lament . . . difficult struggle"

How well do these descriptions by the theorist and poet Christian Friedrich Daniel Schubart correspond to the composer Franz Schubert's actual practice? In some cases, quite closely. Let's examine some Schubert songs from this book which were composed in the natural and flat minor keys, beginning with the moderate keys and moving down to the extreme.

Franz Schubert sets "Lied der Mignon" ("Nur wer die Sehnsucht kennt") and "Du liebst mich nicht" in the key of A minor (described as "Pious womanliness and tenderness of character"). Both express womanliness, though we find tenderness only in the former, not in the latter. This may be because "Du liebst mich nicht" was originally composed in G♯ minor, a key whose description ("heart squeezed until it suffocates, wailing lament . . . difficult struggle") certainly matches the song!

"Gretchen am Spinnrade" and "Der Tod und das Mädchen," songs expressing obsession and horror, respectively, are both in D minor ("melancholy womanliness"). Of course, Schubert must have been familiar with Mozart's dramatic use of this key in his Requiem and in the

Queen of the Night aria from *The Magic Flute*. "Die Liebe hat gelogen" (Love has lied) is set appropriately in C minor ("Declaration of love and at the same time the lament of unhappy love. All languishing, longing, sighing of the love-sick soul"), but the key is betrayed, as every C cadence is to the major.

"Erster Verlust" (remembering a first love) and "Die junge Nonne" (transcending the storms of life) are both in F minor ("Deep depression, funereal lament, groans of misery and longing for the grave"), which suits both songs, though the former is bifocal with A♭ major, and the latter transforms to F major, the key of hope.

So far we do see a predilection for setting songs of womanly lament in the flat minor keys. In contrast, the flat major keys are associated with love, holiness, and sweetness. Although none of the twenty songs analyzed in this book are in F major, the key nonetheless plays an important role in a number of them, primarily as a goal that is hoped and yearned for, but often not met in the real world, as is the case in "Gretchen am Spinnrade" and "Der Tod und das Mädchen" (both in D minor), "Du liebst mich nicht" (in A minor), and "Die junge Nonne" (in F minor).[10] It is significant that "Ganymed," a song beginning in A♭ major but which wanders extensively through many different keys in order to express the journey and moods of the beautiful youth in his mythical travels up to the abode of the gods, achieves his heavenly goal in the key of F major.[11]

The keys of B♭ and E♭ major are very sweet: "Ave Maria" juxtaposes the harshness of Ellen's circumstances with peace of the holy Virgin in Bb major ("cheerful love, clear conscience, hope, aspiration for a better world"), while "Du bist die Ruh" presents a paean to the sacred peace and joy of love in E♭ major ("The key of love, of devotion, of intimate conversations with God").

Although Schubart (the poet and theorist) gives A♭ major a negative association ("The key of the grave. Death, grave, putrefaction, judgement, eternity"), Schubert (the composer) begins his exquisite song "Ganymed" in this key, expressing joy in nature and quickly moving through E-flat to cadence in the extremely warm keys of C♭ (at "infinite beauty") and G♭ ("press close to my heart"), then cooling off ("You cool the burning thirst within my breast") in E major to set a section of birdsong (a key described as "Noisy shouts of joy, laughing pleasure and not yet complete, full delight"), and finally reaching his heavenly destination in the lap of the "All-loving Father" in the key of F major. And why would Schubert set "Die Forelle" in D♭ major, which is described as "a leering key, degenerating into grief and rapture"? On the surface it seems strange, but below the surface, it is highly appropriate: the story of the "trout" getting hooked in the song was originally a metaphor for girls to avoid seducers, and at a deeper level the poem may have been a warning to beware of the lies that led to the poet C. F. D. Schubart's false imprisonment for political reasons (see the analysis guide on "Die Forelle" for more on this).[12] "Die junge Nonne" is in F minor moving to F major, but the point of ecstasy awaited by the bride ("I wait, my Saviour, with longing gaze! Come, heavenly bridegroom, take your bride!") is set with a transcendent and fully realized cadence to D♭ major (to set "rapture," among C. F. D. Schubart's descriptions of this key). Both "Ganymed" and "Du bist die Ruh" venture into C♭ major as the Neapolitan of the dominant, the former articulated by several clear cadences on C♭ at "infinite beauty!", "O that I might clasp you in my arms!", and "Ah, on your breast I lie languishing" and the latter slipping briefly into C♭ for a few bars at "The temple of these eyes from your radiance alone brightens" (discussed in more depth in the section on the Neapolitan sixth, below).

While C major is described by many eighteenth- and nineteenth-century theorists as the "purest" key, in the two songs in the key discussed in this book, "Dass sie hier gewesen"

Figure 3.7. "Dass sie hier gewesen" (mm. 1–16): Clear versus ambiguous harmony expresses the contrast between things that can and cannot be seen.

and "Meeres Stille," C major seems like a neutral background for some serious harmonic manipulation. "Dass sie hier gewesen" contrasts things that can and cannot be seen with clear versus ambiguous harmonies. The key of C is impossible to recognize at the opening of the song and in each slippery verse, but asserts itself strongly in the refrain, beginning in m. 13 (see figure 3.7).

In "Meeres Stille" C major is the frame key, but as we cadence or move to every other tonal level in the C major scale except the dominant (see the chart in the "Tonal Withholding" section above), this is in no way a traditional C major song!

Moving in the sharp direction, Schubert chooses G major for his "folksong" Heidenröslein ("everything rustic, idyllic, and lyrical") and D major for the grateful "An die Musik" ("The key of triumph, of Hallelujahs, of war-cries, of victory-rejoicing"). Clearly there are no war cries in "An die Musik," but triumph, Hallelujahs, and rejoicing are quietly present.

Schubert sets "Frühlingstraum" in the appropriate key of A major ("declarations of innocent love . . . hope of seeing one's beloved again when parting"), but it is a false key because it is a dream; the sad truth appears in the A minor middle section. "Der Neugierige" is in the "strongly colored" key of B major, "announcing wild passions." We don't see "anger, rage, jealousy, or fury," but we do get a suggestion of despair in both the sudden shift from B major to G major at "these two words [yes or no] contain for me the whole world" and the deceptive cadence at "Say, brook, does she love me?" (this song will be discussed in the section on third relationships below), as well as from the dissonant notes in the piano postlude which provide his answer.

In addition to noting the original key of a song, you also need to think about the question of major/minor contrast. We tend to think of major as happy and minor as sad, but you must not necessarily make this assumption in the songs of Schubert. "Du liebst mich nicht" is in A minor, but when the lines suggesting suicide repeat for the second time (in mm. 40–52), they are suddenly in the parallel major, moving from A minor to A major (see figure 3.22). A similar shift from C minor to C major occurs in "Die liebe hat gelogen" at "Alas, I am deceived, deceived by all around me" in mm. 5–6 (see figure 3.8). The nineteenth-century music scholar Kristina Muxfeldt reminds us that when Schubert shifts suddenly to major in a minor-key work, it is not necessarily a happy transformation, but often a signal of a shift to fantasy.[13]

Make sure you consider the key of your song and the other tonal areas into which it wanders. Composers such as Schubert choose these carefully to express the meaning of the text and convey particular emotions. They may also avoid certain tonal areas, so pay equal attention to what is missing from your song.

- In what key is your song?

- How does the choice of key relate to its meaning?

- If the song moves through different keys, how do they express meaning?

Figure 3.8. "Die liebe hat gelogen" (mm. 1–6): Deception is expressed through a shift to the parallel major in this funereal C minor song.

LINEAR MOTION AND MOTIVIC PARALLELISM

An important way for composers to highlight certain notes or intervals is through **linear motion**. Linear motion is essentially like a game of "connect the dots": a composer might connect two important notes in the melody or bassline with stepwise or chromatic motion. It is easy for a singer to overlook the significance of linear motion, because it is often found primarily in the piano part. However, the use of linear motion does two important things: 1) composers will tell you something important about their view of the meaning of the poem, and 2) the use of linear motion will increase the emotion expressed in the song, so you need to know where it is in order to use it effectively.

Linear motion is often used to emphasize the tonic and dominant, the two most important notes in a key, stabilizing the harmony and clarifying the key. A beautiful diatonic example occurs in the opening of "Du bist die Ruh." The **bassline descent** from $\hat{1}$ to $\hat{5}$ (E♭, D, C, B♭) clearly presents the key and sets the listener up for a cadence to tonic (see figure 3.9).

Figure 3.9. "Du bist die Ruh": (mm. 1–7): A bassline descent from $\hat{1}$ to $\hat{5}$ clarifies the key of E♭ major.

A **chromatic line** in the melody or bass can be quite dramatic, heightening the emotion of the song. In "Gretchen am Spinnrade," exciting things start to happen when she describes her lover, Faust (see figure 3.10). At "His fine gait, his noble form," the right hand of the piano prolongs the note F, but when she begins describing his mouth, eyes, and magical speech ("the smile of his lips, the power of his eyes, and the magic flow of his words") her passion increases, expressed by Schubert through rising chromatic motion (F-F♯-G-A♭-A-B♭) in the downbeats of the right hand, supported by powerful rising V^7-I motion (in octaves and fifths) in the left hand to G, A♭, and B♭. The pianist, assisted by Schubert's marking of *crescendo poco a poco*, can bring out these lines to lead into the climax at "sein Händedruck, und ach, sein Kuss!" (the pressure of his hand and, ah, his kiss!).

Of course, Schubert sometimes contravenes the listener's expectations. A rising diatonic bassline (D-E F♯-G) beginning in m. 14 of "An die Musik" (see figure 3.11) shoots past its expected arrival on A ($\hat{5}$, set with a I_4^6 chord) to arrive at B ($\hat{6}$), outlining a sixth.[14] An astute listener will recognize the interval of a sixth as one of the two main motives in this song, along with the perfect fourth; both motives appear as the first four bass notes in mm. 1–2 of the song (see figure 3.1 for the opening). The bassline now shifts from diatonic to chromatic motion (F♯-G-G♯-A-A♯-B), outlining a perfect fourth (the other motive) and supporting strong secondary harmonic motion (V_5^6/IV, $vii°^7/V \rightarrow I_4^6$, $V^7 \rightarrow vi$). What prompted Schubert to astonish the listener in this way? How else to set the "moving" and transcendent nature of music, which carries us "away to a better world!" Remember this every time you hear this extraordinary piece, and when you perform it, make sure we hear that rising chromatic motion in the bassline pushing us to exquisite heights.

Figure 3.10. "Gretchen am Spinnrade" 46–68: After a sudden shift to the third-related (and longed-for) area of F major, excitement is created by rising chromatic line and a series of V^7-I chords. Obsession, too, is expressed through the constant semitone circling around A in the right hand in mm. 60–68.

Figure 3.11. "An die Musik" (mm. 14–19): A better world is evoked through a rising chromatic line and secondary harmonies.

Sometimes composers don't want to make the key clear or may wish to convey a sense of danger by **outlining a dissonant interval**. "Meeres Stille" sets the foreboding scene of a sailor perilously becalmed at sea (see figure 3.4). Although Goethe's original poem is followed by its more optimistic companion "Glückliche Fahrt" (Prosperous Voyage), Schubert's musical setting suggests there is no happy ending here. If there were any question as to the safety of the sailor, the composer sets them to rest by strongly outlining a descending tritone (F-E-E♭-D-C♯-B) in the bass under the words "No breeze from any quarter! A fearful, deathly calm!" (see figure 3.12).[15] Chromatic basslines allow for non-functional harmonies, which can be seen in mm. 17–20 (more about these in the section on harmony below). Note, however, the right hand's rising chromatic line in contrary motion to the descending bassline in mm. 17–22 (D♯-E-F-F♯), creating tension over the static notes A and C, as if the top and bottom of the piano part were being pulled apart! Alas, F♯ is as high as the right hand can attempt; at "fürchterlich" (fearful) it subsides hopelessly back to the D♯ on which the phrase originated in m. 17.

Figure 3.12. " Meeres Stille" (mm. 17–24): The descending chromatic tritone (F down to B) bodes ill for this sailor!

Chromatic linear motion may also ascend to outline a dissonant interval. The bassline of the fiery recitative in "Lied der Mignon" ("Nur wer die Sehnsucht kennt") outlines a rising chromatic tritone (B♭-B-C-D-D♯-E) in mm. 27–33 to express the strong emotion of the text: "I feel giddy, my vitals are aflame" (see figure 3.13).

Observing linear motion ("connecting the dots") can also reveal **motivic parallelism**, the appearance of motive at different levels of scale. In the opening of the same song (see figure 3.14), the A-B-C motive from the first two bars now appears stretched out over eight measures (mm. 7–14). The singer can bring out the now slowly rising motive, heightening the tension.

Figure 3.13. "Lied der Mignon" ("Nur wer die Sehnsucht kennt"), mm. 27–33: The rising chromatic tritone expresses the strong emotion of the text.

Figure 3.14. "Lied der Mignon" ("Nur wer die Sehnsucht kennt"), mm. 1–18: In an example of motivic parallelism, the opening three notes (A-B-C) are expanded over eight measures. The pedal point in the first eight bars create a feeling of being stuck and the circling around D in the left hand creates a feeling of wandering.

A stunning example of Schubert's use of motivic parallelism appears in "Erster Verlust" (see figure 3.5). In this song of lost happiness, the composer contrasts the key of F minor (the sorrowful present) with A♭ major (the beautiful "days of first love" from the past). At the same time, the semitone motive, which appears in important places at the local level (first as the D♭-C on the downbeat of m. 3), structures the entire piece by creating large-scale "grieving" semitones across the song, based on the first note of each phrase:

C	Ach, wer bringt die schönen Tage,	Ah, who will bring back those fair days,
	Jene Tage der ersten Liebe	Those days of first love?
D♭	Ach, wer bringt nur eine Stunde,	Ah, who will bring but one hour
	Jener holden Zeit züruck.	Of that sweet time?
D♭-C	Einsam nähr' ich meine Wunde,	Alone I nurture my wound
	Und mit stets erneuter Klage	And, forever renewing my lament,
D♭-C	Traur' ich ums verlorne Glück.	Mourn my lost happiness.
C	Ach, wer bringt die schönen Tage,	Ah, who will bring back those fair days,
	Wer jene holde Zeit zuruck	That sweet time?

The most famous example of motivic parallelism occurs in "Erlkönig," where the opening "riding" motive in the left hand of the piano in mm. 2–3 expands to control the tonal structure of the entire work (see figure 3.15).[16]

tonal level:	g	B♭	C	D	E♭	D	G
mm.	1	58	87	112	117	123	131

Figure 3.15. "Erlkönig" (mm. 1–3): The opening "riding" motive in the left hand expands to structure the entire song in an astounding example of motivic parallelism.

Playing "connect the dots" with your songs can reveal important insights, so keep your eyes open for linear motion, whether in the bassline, melody, or inner voice, and make sure to bring it out in performance.

- Look for linear motion in your song. Does the composer outline any important intervals? If so, is the interval consonant or dissonant?

- Are there any surprises, where the composer moves farther than the expected interval being outlined?

- Is the linear motion diatonic or chromatic? In which direction does it move?

- What does linear motion tell you about the composer's viewpoint on the story being told?

PEDAL POINTS

Bassline motion is essential to establishing a key, modulating to a new tonal area, and cadencing there. If you are not sure about whether something is a cadence based on listening to it, you can look to see if there is a 5–1 motion in the bass. Another important technique is the **pedal point**, which occurs when the bassline stays on one note for a while, conveying a sense of being "stuck." A pedal point may create tension before a cadence just the same way as hearing the same thing over and over again causes you to wish for a change. In larger works than art song the pedal usually sits on the dominant.[17] A bassline may be embellished with neighbor or passing tones but still be considered a pedal point.

Pedal points may be used for different purposes: they may highlight an important word or idea, create a feeling of being stuck, add tension to prepare for a cadence, allow for an unusual modulation, or simply create a mood.

Among the songs in this book, the most frequent use of a pedal point is to **emphasize an important word or phrase**. In a song contrasting things that can be known with those that cannot, the pedal point on G in "Dass sie hier gewesen" highlights the most revealing line in the poem: "Beauty or love, can they remain concealed?" (see figure 3.16). The pedal point on G does not appear in the first refrain (mm. 13–18), but only at the end of the second refrain (which begins in m. 31), to prepare and set the key words "Schönheit oder Liebe, ob versteckt sie bliebe?" Sitting on the dominant makes the listener long for the answer to this question—the resolution to C major—but instead we face dissonant appoggiaturas decorating a secondary tonality, similar to those in mm. 1 and 19, but now for the first time hovering around IV instead of ii.

Figure 3.16. "Dass sie hier gewesen" (mm. 35–41): The pedal point on G highlights the most revealing line in the poem: "Beauty or love, can it remain hidden?"

As the protagonist faces her fate in "Die junge Nonne," a pedal point on F in mm. 28–33 illuminates the key word "immerhin" (nevertheless, in spite of that), which shows how faith supports her during the storms of life—and death (see figure 3.17). The pedal also emphasizes the words "like the grave."[18]

Figure 3.17. "Die junge Nonne" (mm. 27–33): A pedal point emphasizes the word "immerhin," showing how the nun's faith supports her during the storms of life—and death.

A B♭ pedal point governs the opening four bars of "Ave Maria" (see figure 3.18) presenting the idea of faith in the midst of danger, which is at the core of this moving song. While most of the chords do have a B♭ in them, the presence of the a°² (vii°²) chord poignantly demonstrates her resolve despite the difficulty of her situation.

Figure 3.18. "Ave Maria" (mm. 1–2): The pedal point suggest the idea of faith in the midst of danger.

If you ignore the presence of a pedal point, you might miss an important clue as to the central meaning of a song.

Another common use of the pedal point is to **create the feeling of being stuck**. The pedal point in the prelude of "Lied der Mignon" ("Nur wer die Sehnsucht kennt") makes clear that she is stuck in the lamenting key of A minor (see figure 3.14). The most dissonant note to the pedal is the high B♭, which sticks out in this key, suggesting something is not right, followed by a melodic descent down a major seventh to confirm it.

Schubert uses a pedal point in two different ways in "Gretchen am Spinnrade." The opening pedal on tonic D introduces Gretchen, who is stuck in this doom-filled key, her mind whirling like the spinning wheel she operates (see figure 3.2 for mm. 1–6); this pedal point of doom supports the first half of each appearance of the refrain. Later she is stuck again, but this time in the hope-filled key of F major, when she begins describing her lover (see mm. 51–54 in figure 3.10), before her excitement carries her away in a series of rising V-I motions. A second use of the pedal point is to **create tension by sitting on the dominant**. At "My poor head is crazed, my poor mind is shattered," we sit first on an E pedal (mm. 21–25) and then an F pedal (mm. 26–30)—note the expanded semitone motive here—but alas, the harmonies of V-I$_4^6$ never resolve (see figure 3.19).

Of course, the most extreme example of a pedal point is to **create a stark mood**, as in "Der Leiermann," the final song of Schubert's song cycle *Winterreise* (see figure 3.20). After journeying for so long through a bitter winter, the disappointed lover sees a half-frozen and hungry man singing to a hurdy gurdy, an ancient folk instrument that can play simple melodies over a drone. All sixty-one measures of the song are set with a pedal on A with the perfect fifth E above it. Is the protagonist looking at a vision of himself? Is the composer? Schubert had been diagnosed with syphilis by this point, which was known to lead to insanity and death; there was no cure. On the surface the song reproduces the sound of a folk instrument, but underneath we hear Schubert, the composer of the most beautiful melodies and harmonies, reduced to composing over a repetitive drone.

- Does your song have a pedal point?

- If so, why do you think the composer included it? Is it used to express a word or phrase? To create a feeling of being stuck? To create tension by sitting on the dominant? To assist in modulation? Or to create a stark or negative mood?

- How does the pedal point express the meaning of the poem?

Figure 3.19. "Gretchen am Spinnrade" (mm. 22–30): A pedal point creates tension by sitting on the local dominant.

Figure 3.20. "Der Leiermann" (mm. 1-16): The pedal point suggests the drone of the hurdy gurdy in this bleak song from Winterreise.

HARMONY

Harmony is a language that tells us where we belong. Tonic, the chord based on the first note of the scale, is our home, where we feel comfortable. The dominant, the chord based on the fifth note of the scale, leads us back home, and a dominant seventh chord creates a particularly strong pull to resolve back to tonic. The other chords are local places in our neighborhood that we may visit, but we always stop by the dominant first before we go home.

Sometimes we want to travel outside our neighborhood. We need some form of transportation powerful enough to pull us out of our community. A typical way of escaping from our home key is through tonicization or modulation, using chords that point to a different local tonic. The difference between tonicization and modulation is essentially one of degree: if the movement to a new area is relatively temporary, it is considered a tonicization and typically returns to the original tonal area. If the song continues in the new area for a while, it is a modulation.

When you start noticing new accidentals in your song, you might be moving to a new tonal area. A very clear example of movement to the dominant occurs in "Heidenröslein" (see figure 3.21). The first four bars delineate the key of G major through predominant and dominant

Figure 3.21. "Heidenröslein" (mm. 1-10): A simple tonicization of the dominant characterizes this folk-like song.

chords, creating a cadence to G. The next four bars are sprinkled with C♯, the leading tone of the new key, D. We prepare to cadence on D, but instead are surprised by a deceptive resolution to B minor in the second half of m. 8, followed by a strong cadence to D in the next two bars. Immediately after, however, we return to a clear G major, complete with two progressions to authentic cadences. The return to the home key provides a sense of comfort and familiarity to the listener.

As a singer you need to tell your audiences where you are going. Those accidentals will start pulling you to the new key, so bring them out in your performance, and let everyone feel the desire to move to a new place and the joy of arriving safely at the cadence.

One of the basic qualities of harmony is the polarity of **consonance** and **dissonance**. A consonant chord or interval creates a feeling of comfort and rest; a dissonance, on the other hand, creates a feeling of conflict or unrest that feels like it needs to be resolved. That is not to say that dissonance is somehow negative—music would be bland without dissonance, which gives it its piquancy and sense of urgency. It is very important for you to become familiar with which sections in your song are consonant and which are dissonant, so you are aware of the emotions being created in your audience.

Listen to "Du liebst mich nicht" (see figure 3.22) and notice the effect of the fully diminished seventh chords beginning in measure 29, at the first possible hint of suicide: "Would I miss the stars, the moon, the sun as much?" Dissonance can also be rhythmic. Notice how the diminished seventh chords return in mm. 34 ff., exacerbated now by dissonant rhythmic interruptions at "Du liebst, du liebst mich nicht."

Another reason to be familiar with harmony is to know which of the notes you are singing or playing are part of the essential melodic line supported by the chord and which are embellishments (passing and neighbor tones), which add spice and beauty to the melody. **Appoggiaturas** are ornaments in which an accented dissonance resolves down to a consonant note, emphasizing it.[19] A beautiful example may be found in measure 14 of "An die Musik" (see figure 3.1). Perform the appoggiatura correctly, by leaning on the dissonant note and holding it just a bit before resolving gently to the second note, and you will enrapture your audience.

- Listen to your song with the score. Where are the dissonances? What words do they set? How does this tell you more about the song's meaning?

- Listen for appoggiaturas in your song. Where do they occur? How do they make you feel? Practice performing them so that each one sounds like a musical sigh.

Roman Numeral Analysis

Some of the analysis guides in this book ask you to determine the harmonic function of the chords, often known as **Roman numeral analysis**. This type of analysis helps us to find out both where we are (our home key) and where we are going (other areas that we visit in the song), as well as the relationship between these two (or more) areas.

Why should you understand the harmonic relationships in your song? These relationships help to tell the story and express the emotions inherent in the text of the poem. Remember that the meaning of a song is not simply its text. Composers may move beyond the original meaning of the poem, adding additional meaning or even subverting it through sudden dissonances or a harmonic shift. Certain harmonies, such as diminished, augmented sixth, and

Figure 3.22. "Du liebst mich nicht" (mm. 29-40): Fully diminished seventh chords combined with rhythmic interruptions express despair.

Neapolitan sixth chords create extreme tension and you need to know their effect on your listeners. So whatever your level of theoretical expertise, listen carefully for dramatic (or mild) harmonic progressions which will help you create a memorable performance.

For those who may not feel entirely comfortable doing harmonic analysis, here are a few helpful suggestions. A useful way to find the harmonic function is to write in the chord names first. If you are having trouble figuring out their function, go to the next cadence and work backward so you can see how you got there. Of course, you will have already made your cadence map, so you will know when you are approaching a new tonal area. If the phrase is modulating, there may be a point where the chords can have two functions simultaneously. You will often find a **pivot chord**, a chord that works in both the home and the new key, which allows for easy modulation. A clear example occurs in "Lied der Mignon" (see figure 3.14). The song begins in A minor, then modulates to cadence in the relative major through the pivot chord D minor in the second half of m. 12, which functions as iv^6 in A minor and ii^6 in C major. Schubert more often uses other techniques to modulate; the simplicity of this movement to the relative major is likely related to the folksong style of much of this song, since it is supposed to be Mignon singing a traditional lament. Schubert actually used his earlier song "Ins stille Land" as the basis for this "folk song," adding a dramatic recitative in the middle.[20]

Be aware, however, that some Schubert songs such as "An die Nachtigall," have entire passages that can be understood in two keys simultaneously. Recognition of this ambiguity unlocks an important part of the meaning of this song.

Tonicization and Modulation

Tonicization and modulation are an important way of adding freshness to a song. You need to be aware of when they are happening so that you can express the feeling of motion in your performance. Practice becoming aware of tonal motion by listening for it in your song.

A common method of moving to a new key is the use of a **secondary dominant**, in which the function is already thought of in relation to the new key. The most common is V/V, which pushes us to the dominant of the new key by including a $\sharp\hat{4}$ in the key, which functions as the leading tone in the new key. We saw this in "Heidenröslein" (see figure 3.21), in which the C$\sharp$ ($\sharp\hat{4}$ in G major) leads to a tonicization of D major, the dominant. Be aware that the chord on ii in a major key is minor and ii in a minor key is diminished, so if you are in a major key and you see a major chord on the second note of the scale, it's not ii, it's V/V! Another common secondary dominant is the transformation of the tonic chord into V^7/IV by the simple addition of a minor seventh; in G major, if you add an F, suddenly you have V^7/IV.

Another sign of tonicization or modulation can be the **appearance of a I$^6_4$ chord** in a new key. "Der Neugierige" (see figure 3.23) moves to G major (mm. 35–41), then returns to tonic B major by linear motion to the I$^6_4$ chord in m. 42, preparing for the cadence in the next bar. Listen to this and other examples of this chord so that you are aware when it appears. The I$^6_4$ chord usually suggests that a cadence is about to happen.

In nineteenth-century music, the appearance of a I$^6_4$ chord is often a way of putting a floor under a new key. In fact, late in the century composers like Strauss would simply signal a new key with a I$^6_4$, and not even bother to cadence. "Erster Verlust" opens in tonic F minor, then suddenly shifts to A$\flat^6_4$ in measure two (see figure 3.5). You might wonder what a III$^6_4$ chord is doing here, but a chord in this inversion generally functions as a I$^6_4$, so bar 2 would be heard in A$\flat$ major, as a standard I$^6_4$-V^7 preparation to a cadence on A$\flat$. But instead of the expected

Figure 3.23. "Der Neugierige" (mm. 30–43): A modulation from B major to G major through voice leading magic and then back again through circling of the F♯ and the use of a I$^6_4$ chord represents the two possible words, "yes" or "no."

cadence, in measure 3 we land on a dissonant e$^{\circ 7}$ chord followed by a C$^6_5$ chord, wrenching us back to the original F minor as vii$^{\circ 7}$ to V$^6_5$. Is the F minor chord on beat 3 a cadence to tonic or a vi chord in A♭ major? Here the ambiguity is the point; the listener is pulled back and forth between the past and the present, along with the song's protagonist. If there is a cadence to F minor (though only in the piano part—the singer and the pianist do not have the same outlook on the situation), it is on a weak beat and followed immediately by an A♭$^4_3$ chord on beat 4, introducing a temporary tonicization of D♭, which is VI (in F minor) or IV (in A♭ major). Measure 5 answers this question with another I$^6_4$ chord (A♭$^6_4$), moving to a half cadence in A♭; the singer clearly wishes to stay in the key of the idyllic past, A♭ major.

Temporary tonicization, in which a few secondary harmonies highlight a new area for a brief time, are common in Schubert songs, and you should always ask yourself why the composer is paying such attention to this particular area. In "Die Forelle" (in D♭ major, see figure

Figure 3.24. "Die Forelle" (mm. 30–34): A temporary tonicization in the relative minor changes the mood when the fisherman tricks the fish.

3.24), Schubert temporarily tonicizes the relative minor (B♭ minor) when the fisherman tricks the fish ("But at length the thief grew impatient").

A not-so-temporary tonicization creates a wonderfully nebulous harmonic palette in "Dass sie hier gewesen" (see figure 3.7). Evoking wisps of memories through dissonant harmonies that are as far from C major (concrete awareness) as possible, it takes six full bars before we can tell that somehow we are searching for ii. Yes, this song in C major begins with dissonant appoggiaturas to c♯$^{o4}_3$ to set "That the east wind's fragrance breathes into the air."[21] We have no idea what key we're in, but only that we are gently blown toward something that is not very clear. It is only in bar 6 when the note E (in all voices!) resolves to D that we suddenly realize we've been looking for this chord (ii^6), after which the first text line concludes in a traditional half cadence to the dominant (m. 8). The c♯$^{o4}_3$ returns in the next line (m. 9), but this time instead of the appoggiaturas resolving to the dissonant c♯$^{o4}_3$ chord (vii$^{o4}_3$), here the c♯$^{o4}_3$ resolves deceptively to a B♭$^6_4$ chord, which is VI/ii. Another attempt to cadence is made in the next bar, with the same deceptive result. A third try (mm. 11–12) results in a successful arrival on ii^6 (setting "thereby it makes it known"). Suddenly we are in simple harmonic territory (V^7-I, V^7-I in C major) to set "that you have been here," a certainty expressed through clarity of key.

The song is strophic, so the music repeats for the second verse in mm. 19–41 ("That here tears are flowing—thereby will you know within, though it were otherwise not known, that I have been here"). After asking the question "Beauty or Love, can they remain hidden?" at the end of verse 2, the third verse in mm. 42–67 alters the C♯s to C♮s (see figure 3.25), causing the harmonies to yearn now toward F major (IV) in this verse to set "Fragrances and tears make it known that [she] has been here." Note, by the way, that in Rückert's famously ambiguous use of language, "she" (*sie* in the poem) likely refers to "Beauty or Love," as they are both feminine in German.[22] F major is often Schubert's key of love and hope, a key of sweetness and joy, as expressed in "Gretchen am Spinnrade," "Du liebst mich nicht," "Ganymed," and "Die junge

Figure 3.25. "Dass sie hier gewesen" (third verse, mm. 42–67): A gradual clarification of the temporary tonicization of IV expresses the poem's contrast between things that can and cannot be seen. The final two bars resolve the refrain melody that was cut off in m. 18 (see figure 3.7).

Nonne." After alighting briefly on F major in mm. 46–47, we arrive instead on F minor in m. 50 to set "make it known"; is the news perhaps a surprise or does it call up a wistful memory? After a brief tonicization in A♭ major (mm. 51–54), we finally arrive on F major at the repeat of "Fragrances and tears make it known." Once things are "made known," they are out in the open, in a standard tonal level, in this case, the desired IV that has been sought for eighteen bars. As before, the refrain follows in simple V^7-I motion, as the wispy clouds, mere signs, are blown away amid the certainty of knowing.

One more comment on this song. The C major refrain is cut off suddenly in m. 18 (see figure 3.7). It is not until the last two bars in the piano postlude that the melody is finally resolved (figure 3.25).

- Look at your cadence map to see where your song travels.

- In a modulating passage, look for a pivot chord, a chord that works in both keys.

- Keep an eye out for secondary dominants. Remember that in a major key the chord on $\hat{2}$ is minor and in a minor key it is diminished; if this chord is major, it is probably functioning as V/V, not II.

- Another sign of modulation is a I^6_4 chord in a new key; the appearance of a I^6_4 is often a way of putting a floor under a new key; it wants to move to V and then to cadence on I.

- Look for temporary tonicizations, in which a few secondary harmonies highlight a new area for a brief time. Ask yourself why the composer is moving into this area (hint: check the text!).

Augmented and Neapolitan Sixth Chords

Nineteenth-century composers are famous for their use of delicious chromatic chords, expressing strong emotions and thrilling the listener. Two types that you should be familiar with are **augmented sixth chords** and the **Neapolitan sixth**. Augmented sixth chords move by semitone in contrary motion to the octave, typically resolving to a I^6_4 or V chord. Composers use them to push very strongly, usually to the dominant of a new area, and they create a wonderful feeling of urgency and desire.

Semitone motion to one note creates a tendency tone, a strong push to that note. Two of these—going in opposite directions no less—create a very strong push to the octave, emphasizing that tonal area (whatever note is doubled at the octave).

Go to the piano and play an octave. Now shrink it by a semitone on the top and bottom and you have an augmented sixth. Play it and resolve it by opening to the octave. Do this several times and listen to the sound it makes. How does it make you feel? Pay attention when you hear contrary motion to the octave!

How do you check for an augmented sixth chord? Ask yourself the following questions:

1. Is there an octave created in the arrival chord?
2. If so, is one note arrived at by rising semitone and the other by descending semitone? If the answer is yes, you've got yourself an augmented sixth chord.

How to determine which type of augmented sixth chords you are dealing with is easy if you imagine them as different types of hot dogs. You can think of the bun opening flat (moving in contrary motion by semitones to the octave) as the augmented sixth moving to the octave. Now drop in the hot dog (a major third above the bass note) and you have an Italian sixth. If you add some sauerkraut (a perfect fifth above the bass note), you get a German sausage—that is, a German sixth. This chord sounds like a dominant seventh chord, but instead of moving to tonic, it resolves outward like an augmented sixth chord. Romantic composers love to fool listeners who think they are getting a dominant seventh resolution, but are then surprised when the chord suddenly shifts in a new direction. Finally, if instead of sauerkraut (a perfect fifth above the bass), you add Grey Poupon (a tritone above the bass)—*voilà*, you have a French sixth! The French sixth has that *je ne sais quoi*, a delicious shimmering dissonance that makes it sound wonderfully colorful. Practice playing each of these augmented sixth chords and their resolutions at the piano so that you can hear the urgency and deliciousness created through these harmonies. The most important harmonic analysis is the one you do with your ears.

Schubert often makes use of the German sixth chord to move to the dominant or a I_4^6 chord. Among the songs discussed in this book, you can find this chord in "An die Nachtigall," "Erster Verlust," and "Meeres Stille" (see figure 3.26). In "Die junge Nonne," we find a

Figure 3.26. German sixth chords in Schubert songs: "An die Nachtigall" (to I_4^6), "Erster Verlust" (to V), "Meeres Stille" (to i_4^6), and "Die Junge Nonne" (direct to I).

common-tone augmented sixth chord, in which the German sixth of the dominant moves directly to the tonic chord, without a dominant or I_4^6 in between. In this case the German sixth chord in mm. 69 and 71 embellishes the tonic chord (mm. 70 and 72), with the notes B♮ and D♭ moving in contrary motion to C (though with no direct semitone motion from D♭ to C3 in the lower voice), with the F held as a common tone, keeping the "bell" ringing in the bass.

The Neapolitan sixth is another chord that pushes strongly toward the dominant and thus pulls mercilessly at the listener's heartstrings. Based on the ♭2, this chord usually appears in first inversion, hence its name. In this chord the twinge of the ubiquitous melodic semitone motive is expanded to a harmonic level, increasing its power. In "Die Liebe hat gelogen" (see figure 3.27), the pain of betrayal in love is signified in the funeral march prelude with a huge Neapolitan sixth (accented and marked *fp*), followed shortly by a tasty French sixth to close on a half cadence.

Figure 3.27. Die Liebe hat gelogen (mm. 1–2): The pain of betrayal in love is signified in the funeral march prelude with a huge Neapolitan sixth (accented and marked "fp"), followed shortly by a tasty French sixth (mm. 1–2) to close on a half cadence.

In "Frühlingstraum" from *Winterreise*, a Neapolitan sixth (over a pedal A) mirrors the upper neighbor motive that runs throughout the song (see figure 3.28). Note the French sixth "stinger" in m. 24 (marked *fz*), which adds a kick to this passage.

The Neapolitan can be also expanded to a temporary tonic. In "Du liebst mich nicht" (see figure 3.22 in mm. 29–38), two similar phrases are set a minor second apart, one implying A minor and the other B♭ minor, the level of the Neapolitan. But that apparently wasn't enough for Schubert, who wrenches the listener back and forth between these two areas in mm. 36–40.

You might find composers moving to the Neapolitan of the dominant. "Du bist die Ruh" and "Ganymed" both feature this technique in the local key of E♭ major, shifting to the area of C♭ major. The piano prelude and first half of "Du bist die Ruh" feature a rising fourth motive of B♭-E♭ (see figure 3.9). To set the final stanza of poetry, "The temple of these eyes from your radiance alone brightens," Schubert stretches this motive to twice its original length in the vocal part (figure 3.29). At the same time, he works magic with the harmony: the E♭ in m. 54 slides into the region of C♭ (mm. 55–57) by linear motion (the G moves down to G♭ and the B♭ up to C♭), temporarily suspending us in this extremely flat area, in a holy and at the same time sensuous place. But just as quickly (m. 68) we slide down a semitone to B♭ and then, astonishingly to E♭^{7} leading to a heavenly IV chord in m. 60. It turns out that the faraway key of C♭ was merely the Neapolitan of the dominant in E♭ major, so perhaps anyone can find this transcendent realm!

Figure 3.28. "Frühlingstraum" (mm. 22–26): A Neapolitan sixth (over a pedal A) mirrors the upper neighbor motive that runs throughout the song.

Figure 3.29. "Du bist die Ruh" (mm. 54–65): A brief shift to the Neapolitan of the dominant to set "The temple of these eyes from your radiance alone brightens" creates a transcendent moment.

What to Look for in the Musical Setting 71

"Ganymed" lingers in the warm key of C♭ for a much longer time, setting appropriately passionate texts (see figure 3.30). Frequent key changes throughout this song express different moods experienced by the handsome youth during his journey up to the heavens. Figure 3.30 shows the movement from love's joy in E♭ (m. 20) to "infinite beauty" in C♭ (m. 31). Here we have well and truly modulated to C♭, staying quite a while in this excessively flat key before moving on to G♭.

Figure 3.30. "Ganymed" (mm. 20–56): A long immersion in the Neapolitan of the dominant (and very warm key of C♭) sets the youth's ecstatic joy at nature's "endless beauty," followed by an enharmonic shift to allow for the cooler key of E major at "You cool the burning thirst of my bosom, lovely morning breeze!"

(continues on next page)

Figure 3.30. *Continued*

Although the I$_4^6$, augmented sixth, and Neapolitan chords all tend to push toward the dominant, the latter two, with their strong semitone motion, create a much more powerful and urgent feeling. As a performer, you need to be aware of how strongly you are swaying your listeners' emotions in these passages.

- Does your song contain augmented sixth or Neapolitan chords? Listen for a sixth opening up to the octave through semitones in contrary motion (augmented sixth). Listen also for a chord based on ♭$\hat{2}$ (Neapolitan). Both chords are flavorful and push to the dominant. Look to see what words are set to them; the composer is trying to tell you something important!

Enharmonic Shift

Nineteenth-century composers may cross from a flat key to a sharp key or vice versa in order to make an emotional point. You have already learned about the theorist C. F. D. Schubart's system of key characteristics and how seriously Franz Schubert, the composer, among others, took his selection of key. Crossing from one side to the other had a special meaning, and you need to be alert to this possibility when it appears.

An enharmonic passage is one in which the same chord may be spelled differently, as in G♭ major and F♯ major. These two spellings of the chord in "Ganymed" allow for a smooth transition from the flat key of G♭ to the sharp key of E major (see figure 3.30). Cadences to the passionate keys of C♭ and then G♭ major in mm. 28–46 set "infinite beauty! O that I might

Figure 3.31. "Die junge Nonne" (mm. 61–74): After a rapturous cadence to the third-related D♭ major to set "Come heavenly bridegroom, take the bride!" Schubert moves briefly through an enharmonic passage at "Release my soul from earthly bonds!" in mm. 67–68, setting up a minor plagal bell-like oscillation before returning to the flat side.

clasp you in my arms! Ah, on your breast I lie languishing, and your flowers, your grass press close to my heart." At this point an enharmonic shift from G♭ to F♯ occurs (mm. 45–46); note the use of the pedal point on F♯ to stabilize the new key and allow for the easy modulation from F♯ and B major to the cool key of E major at "You cool the burning thirst within my breast, sweet morning breeze!" (m. 50).

After a rapturous cadence to the third-related D♭ major in "Die junge Nonne" (in F minor/F major) to set "Come heavenly bridegroom, take your bride!" Schubert moves briefly through an enharmonic passage at "Free the soul from earthly bonds!" in mm. 67–68, setting up a minor plagal bell-like oscillation between f♯6 and C♯ before returning to the flat side (see figure 3.31).

- Does your song have an enharmonic shift, in which the same chord is spelled differently? If so, what is its purpose?

Sudden Shift to a New Key

While Classical period composers typically modulated gradually, nineteenth-century composers often simply stepped right into the new key, so that a phrase might end in one key and begin in another. The emotional effect is of stepping into a new thought or feeling. A well-known example in Schubert songs is the sudden shift from A minor to F major in

"Gretchen am Spinnrade," at the point where she fixates on her lover, Faust ("His fine gait, his noble form"), another example of F major as the key associated with love and hope (see figure 3.10). Listen to the song with the score. The second verse (beginning "nach ihm nur schau ich") begins in A minor with cadences on mm. 46 and 50, expressing her yearning and actions: "I look out of the window only to seek him, I leave the house only to seek him." But the minute she starts describing his person, we shift directly into F major: "His fine gait, his noble form" (mm. 51–54), followed by the rising V/I bassline motion as she becomes more excited. The shift to a chord a third away in m. 51 is easy to achieve through voice leading: the E in the A minor chord simply moves up a semitone to F. (More third-related harmonies are discussed below.) Of course, it helps that the relentless clicking sound of the spinning wheel treadle (or heartbeat, if you will) ceases abruptly at this point, so that we can submerge ourselves in this gorgeous new key.

- Does your song feature any sudden shifts to a new key, and if so, why? Practice recognizing a sudden harmonic shift in your songs; eventually you will be able to hear it even without a score.

Third Relationships and Chromatic Mediants

Third relationships and chromatic mediants are important in nineteenth-century music, appreciated for the fresh quality they bring to the harmonies. A **chromatic mediant** is a third-related chord that has been altered in some way; in the key of C major, for example, a chord on E major would be a chromatic mediant, as G♯ does not appear in C major. While eighteenth-century composers tended to modulate to the dominant, nineteenth-century composers often moved to the chromatic mediant or other third-related area. A famous example in the piano repertoire is Beethoven's *Waldstein* sonata, which modulates from tonic C major to the chromatic mediant, E major.

A moving example in song appears in "Der Neugierige" (see figure 3.23) in which a young man tells everyone else about his feelings for the girl he likes—except for her. The song is in B major, and at the point where he desperately wants to know if her answer is "yes" or "no," Schubert emphatically tells us the answer by a sudden shift to G major, a third away, on the word "no," achieved through smooth voice leading. After a cadence to B major in m. 32, the recitative begins in the next bar on F♯ major (V in B), shifting to an A♯ diminished seventh chord (vii°7 in B) accomplished by a simple shift from F♯ to G, highlighting the semitone motive introduced in the first bar. The slide to a G major chord in m. 35, on the word "no" is just as simple: this time the G natural remains and the C♯ and F♯ move up a semitone to D and G. We continue in G major until m. 41, after which a similar type of voice-leading magic returns us in the next bar to a I$_4^6$ chord in B major.

You have already seen the exquisite shift down a major third (E♭ major to C♭ major) in "Du bist die Ruh" at the line "the temple of my eyes is lit by your radiance alone" in the "Augmented and Neapolitan Chords" section (above). "Die junge Nonne" also expresses holiness and sensuality through the third relationship (see figure 3.31). The first two strophes rumble with lightning and thunder in F minor to express the storms of nature and life, while peace and love in the third strophe transform the key to F major. In the fourth strophe, however, the ecstasy anticipated through the young nun's union with her "heavenly bridegroom" overwhelms the simpler key of F major (merely the key of love and hope), transforming through simple voice-leading to D♭ major, the key of rapture. As in earlier examples, F major shifts

Figure 3.32. "Die Liebe hat gelogen" (mm. 7–13): "Die Liebe hat gelogen" (in a funereal C minor) shifts from a cadence to C major (a false key) at m. 7, to a measure each in B♭, A♭, B, and A, expressing the protagonist's agitation.

easily to D♭ major through voice leading: the C moves up a semitone to D♭, and the A moves down a semitone to A♭ to arrive at D♭^{6} in m. 63.

Although direct movement a third away is common, Schubert also moves directly to other tonal areas, as well. "Die Liebe hat gelogen" (in a funereal C minor) shifts from a cadence to C major (a false key) at m. 7, to a measure each in B♭, A♭, B, and A, respectively (see figure 3.32). Listen to the song from the beginning. How does this shifting passage express the protagonist's agitation? How will you perform passages like this?

- Does your song contain chromatic mediants (a third-related chord that has been altered in some way) or a shift to a third-related key (such as C major to E major)? How does it sound, and why do you think the composer sets the text this way?

- Are there other direct shifts to a different tonal level? How does this affect the way you perform it and the audience's experience of the song?

Oscillation and Circling

Musical **oscillation** is when a note or chord goes back and forth between two or several notes, resulting in a static or hypnotic quality. Why might a composer use this technique, and why should you care? Oscillation and circling are often an important way of underlining the essential meaning of the poem, so pay attention when you see this in your song.

Some examples will clarify the necessity of recognizing this technique. The alternation between tonic and dominant near the end of "An die Nachtigall" combines with contrary motion in the piano part (mm. 30–34) to create a rocking sensation, lulling the listener—or more importantly, "Love"—to sleep (see the top example in figure 3.26).

In "Der Neugierige," the two key words "yes" and "no" seem to oscillate back and forth in the piano part in mm. 35–36 (see figure 3.23). Oscillation also sets the saddest line in "Lied der Mignon" ("Nur wer die Sehnsucht kennt," see figure 3.33), "Ah, he who loves and knows me is far away," suggesting she may be rocking herself to find some solace (mm. 23–26).

Circling is a way of emphasizing an important note by ringing it with an upper and lower neighbor. You may have seen this called a "double neighbor," "changing tones," or a "neighbor group." These are particularly powerful when they are semitones to the circled notes: if you are familiar with the power of tendency tones, this technique is twice as effective at pushing toward a note. In m. 41 of "Der Neugierige" (see figure 3.23) Schubert circles the note F♯ by upper and lower semitone neighbors (G-F♯-E♯-F♯) in order to emphasize the arrival of the I$^6_4$ in B major, after the oscillating passage in the third-related key of G major.

The prelude to "Lied der Mignon" ("Nur wer die Sehnsucht kennt") opens with a static drone on the tonic note A, creating a feeling of numbness (see figure 3.14). At the same time, Schubert circles around the note D in the inner voice of the left hand in mm. 1–4 (C-D-D♯-C-C♯-D). Why is the composer emphasizing the D ($\hat{4}$) if we are in A minor? This song is about longing and trying to find those close to you, and this inner voice seems to be wandering around. The arrival on iv in measure 4 after the secondary dominant in measure 3 makes it feel like some kind of arrival, though not an actual cadence. Notice that due to the pedal on A, this lamenting song contains no satisfying V-I motion in the bass, either in the prelude or the postlude.

Obsession, too, may be expressed through melodic circling, as in "Gretchen am Spinnrade" (see figure 3.10). Gretchen's excitement at the thought of her lover, Faust, is apparent in the climbing V^7-I motion and rising chromatic line (F-F♯-G-A♭-A-B♭) in the downbeats of the right hand (mm. 54–60). At this point she is positively transfixed, as revealed by the obsessive circling around the note A in the right hand throughout mm. 60–68, using the semitone motive first heard in m. 3 (B♭-A, B♭-A-G♯-A, B♭-A-G♯-A, B♭, G♯, A-B♭) at "His hand clasp and ah, his kiss!" This circular chromaticism leads to the climax which inspired my favorite joke: "How do you resolve a dissonance in the nineteenth century? With an even greater dissonance!" Here a strong push to a dissonant chord (V$^6_5$) "resolves" to an even more dissonant one (vii°^{7}), using the famous semitone motive. Perfection!

Figure 3.33. "Lied der Mignon" ("Nur wer die Sehnsucht kennt"), mm. 23–26: Oscillation in the bassline at "Ah, he who loves and knows me is far away" suggests that Mignon is rocking herself to find some solace.

- Do you find any **oscillation** in your song? What is its purpose?

- Is there any **melodic circling** in your song? If so, what is it suggesting about the meaning of the text?

CHAPTER SUMMARY

Getting a sense for the harmonic structure of your song is crucial for deepening your understanding of its meaning. Always look at and listen for the tonal structure, choice of key, linear motion, pedal points, and different harmonic techniques used to express the story and emotion of the text.

To put what you learned into practice, take the same song you used for the summaries in chapter 2 and go through each of these elements, writing down your answers. If you are studying a particular song together in a class, your teacher may ask each student to do this for a different element and present it to the class. After reviewing all the elements, answer the following questions:

1. How has your analysis of these elements informed your understanding of the song's protagonist and meaning? How does the mood or emotion change throughout the song?

2. How will a deeper understanding of the song influence your performance?

* * *

Now that you have learned how to examine both the poem and its musical setting in chapters 1 to 3, you are ready to do a close analysis of a song. Parts II–IV of this book present individual guided analyses of songs, using Schubert lieder as examples. You or your teacher may select songs from whichever section seems most appropriate; in general, they move from the simplest in structure and analytical techniques to the most complex; a list of the techniques discussed in Parts II–IV appears in the introduction of this book. For each song analysis you will need a **score of the song** as well as the **text and translation**.[23]

Although the songs specifically discussed in this book are all Schubert lieder, the techniques for analysis presented here can be used for any song. May your deep engagement with these and other songs give rise to inspired and memorable performances!

NOTES

1. English translation by Richard Wigmore, with my alteration in brackets.

2. "Die Liebe hat gelogen" in C minor, features cadences on C, B, B♭, A, A♭ (not in this order), but none on the dominant, G major.

3. The weak cadences to F minor in mm. 3 and 19, more examples of the piano staying in the present while the singer lingers in the past, will be discussed below in the section on harmony.

4. Note the temporary tonicization to iv (B♭ minor) to set the word "wound" in the fifth line of the poem.

5. Brackets denote tonal areas visited, but without a cadence. The cadences to F minor in mm. 3 and 19, more examples of the piano arriving at the desired cadence without the singer, will be discussed below in the section on harmony.

6. According to Matthew Steinbron, approximately 13 percent of Schubert's songs are polyfocal (containing more than one tonal center). Matthew Steinbron, "Polyfocal Structures in Franz Schubert's Lieder," PhD diss. (Louisiana State University, 2011), 19.

7. These associations originated from the durus-mollis contrast, or the difference between soft B (B♭ or "B-moll") and hard B (B♮ or "B-dur"). See Rita Steblin's chapter "The Sharp-Flat Principle," in Rita Steblin, *A History of Key Characteristics in the Eighteenth and Early Nineteenth Centuries* (Ann Arbor: UMI Research Press, 1983), 103–33; Eric Chafe's discussions of Monteverdi's *Orfeo* in Eric Chafe, *Monteverdi's Tonal Language* (New York: Schirmer, 1992), 126–58 (see especially p. 141) and of Bach's *St. Matthew Passion* in Eric Chafe, *Tonal Allegory in the Vocal Music of J. S. Bach* (Berkeley: University of California Press, 1991), 390–423; and Beverly Stein's commentary on Carissimi's *Jephte* in Stein, "Between Key and Mode: Tonal Practice in the Music of Giacomo Carissimi" (PhD diss., Brandeis University, 1994), 244–320.

8. The poet and theorist Schubart is referred to in this book by his first names or initials to distinguish him from the composer Schubert, whose name may appear similar. Christian Friedrich Daniel Schubart, *Ideen zu einer Ästhetik der Tonkunst* (Vienna: Degen, 1806), reprint, ed. P. A. Merbach (Leipzig: Wolkenwander-Verlag, 1924), quoted in Steblin, *A History of Key Characteristics*, 124–25.

9. These are edited for length. The complete descriptions by C. D. F. Schubart may be found in Steblin, *A History of Key Characteristics*, 121–24. This agrees in general with several other key charts from the period, including those by Georg Joseph Vogler (teacher of Weber and Meyerbeer), Andre-Ernest-Modeste Grétry, and Francesco Galeazzi. Steblin, *A History of Key Characteristics*, 103–33.

10. In "Die junge Nonne" as in "Gretchen am Spinnrade," the joy they experience may be a result of fantasy, not reality.

11. Based on his observations in Schubert songs, John Reed describes F major "a pastoral key, often associated with evening, autumn, the stars, hope and consolation; also with sleep." John Reed, *The Schubert Song Companion* (Manchester: Manchester University Press, 1997), 487.

12. Graham Johnson, *Schubert: The Complete Songs* (New Haven: Yale University Press, 2014), 2:911–13.

13. Kristina Muxfeldt, *Vanishing Sensibilities: Schubert, Beethoven, Schumann* (Oxford: Oxford University Press, 2011), 173.

14. I am using the older term I_4^6 in this book; readers will recognize that this chord generally has a dominant function. When followed by V, the cadential motion involving this chord is often also written as V_{4-3}^{6-5}, suggesting a V chord with a double suspension.

15. Note the brief flirtation with the lower neighbor A♯ which suggests and then rejects a perfect fifth descent.

16. Charles Burkhart, "Schenker's 'Motivic Parallelisms,'" *Journal of Music Theory* 22 (1978), 160. Other motivic parallelisms along with distinct motivic and key associations with each of the four characters are discussed in chapter 23.

17. The longer the dominant pedal, the more tension created. In the first movement of Beethoven's *Pathétique* sonata, almost the entire second half of the development section sits on a dominant pedal (mm. 167–94); the proportion is thirty bars of development, followed by twenty-eight bars on the dominant to prepare for the thrilling recapitulation.

18. Note that this is the first time the Angelus bell, which has been ringing since the piano prelude, appears on F.

19. Technically appoggiaturas are approached by leap and resolved by step, versus an escape tone which is approached by step and resolved by leap. The other types of non-chord tones have a similar effect, and so for the purposes of this book I'm referring to any embellishing tone on a downbeat as an appoggiatura.

20. Johnson, *Schubert: The Complete Songs*, 1:96–98 and 2:208–11.

21. Translation is by Martha Gerhart, in Franz Schubert, *100 Songs: High Voice,* ed. Steven Stolen and Richard Walters, trans. Martha Gerhart (Milwaukie, WI: Hal Leonard Corp, 2000).

22. For an engaging discourse on Rückert's poem see Richard Law, "'Dass sie hier gewesen' D 775: Rückert and Schubert," *Figures of Speech* (blog), January 16, 2019, http://figures-of-speech.com/2019/01/hier-gewesen.htm.

23. If you don't have a Schubert song collection, you may search for your song online at the International Music Score Library Project at https://imslp.org/wiki/Main_Page. Texts and translations may be found on the LiederNet Archive at https://www.lieder.net.

Part 2
SIMPLER SONGS TO ANALYZE

4

"Heidenröslein"

In this book, each analysis chapter begins with an exploration of the text. However, since that was already included in the introduction to poetry analysis in chapter 1, this analysis will begin with the music.

Learning to shape musical **phrases** is key to a moving performance. This chapter shows how **cadences** work and the effect they can create on your audience. There is also a useful trick for figuring out **chord progressions**, and simple **modulation** to the dominant is explained. The concept of **form** is also introduced.

Finally, you will become more aware of the implications of **vocal range**, **withholding** (an effective tool to pique the listeners' desire), and the **piano postlude**.

* * *

POEM

Please review chapter 1 for an analysis of the poem "Heidenröslein."

MUSICAL SETTING

Mood

1a) Listen to the song and describe the mood. What makes it sound this way? How do the repeated eighth notes add to the mood? _____
_____
_____

1b) The key of G major is described by the poet and theorist C. F. D. Schubart as "everything rustic, idyllic, and lyrical, every calm and satisfied passion, every tender gratitude for true friendship and faithful love."[1] Which elements of this description do you think are expressed by the song? _____

Form

2) How to set this poem to music? The pseudo-folk poem "Heidenröslein" is set here in **strophic form**, a folklike style in which each stanza of the poetry is set to the same music. How will you differentiate each strophe in your performance? _____

_____
_____
_____

Phrasing

3) How many phrases do you hear in each strophe (verse) of the song? _____ For each phrase, list the numbers of the lines of the poem which appear in it. The first phrase is done for you:

Poetic lines:

1. 1–2

2. ___ – ___

3. ___ – ___

Phrase 1 (mm. 1–4)

4a) Compare the first and last notes of phrase 1. What do you notice? How does that make you feel? _____
_____
_____

4b) In what key is the piece? _____

4c) Write down the first and last *chords* of phrase 1 (mm. 1–4): ___ ___
Note that even though the first phrase ends on a high G (m. 4) and leaves you hanging in the air, the *chord* underneath it makes you feel right at home, returning to the key of the piece, which was the first chord in m. 1.

> Understanding whether the chords are consonant and make you feel like you are at home vs. dissonant or in a different key will help you to understand what mood the composer is creating.

Cadences and figuring out chord progressions

The easiest way to do this is to:

1. **Listen for and find the cadence of the phrase:** in this case it occurs between mm. 3 and 4, from a D_5^6 and D^2 in m. 3 (which is V_5^6 and V^2 in G major) to a G^6 and G root position chord (I^6 and I in G major).

2. **Go backward from the cadence!** We have just solved mm. 3–4; now look at m. 2. The chord in m. 2 is an a_4^6 chord in the right hand. The **function** (Roman numeral) of this chord in G major can be ii_4^6 (if you think of the G in the bass as a pedal) or ii^2 (if you consider the G as part of the chord).

3. **Now you understand the harmony:** It's a simple I, ii, V, I progression, which is guaranteed to make the listener feel relatively comfortable. Of course, that rising melodic line that leaves you hanging in mid-air combined with the eighth-note rest lets you know that something needs to follow—you can't end here.

Phrase 2 (mm. 5–10)

The first phrase began on a B and rose to a high G. The second phrase (mm. 5–10) does the same, but ends on a D. Let's see how they're the same or different.

5a) Compare m. 2 with m. 6 (the second bar of phrases 1 and 2, respectively). What melodic note changes in m. 6? _____ How does that change the chord? Name the *chord* (letter name) and its new *function* (Roman numeral, in terms of the key of the piece): _____ _____

5b) Just like mm. 3–4, mm. 7–8 contain a cadence. Write down the *chord* in the first half of m. 8, along with its *function* (Roman numeral) in G major: _____ _____

To what chord do we want to resolve? _____ What chord do we get instead? _____ What is the name for a cadence which goes to a different place? _____ _____ How does this type of cadence make you feel? _____ Write down the words in stanzas 2 and 3 of the poem that are highlighted by this surprising motion (in German and English): _____

_____

In a strophic setting the harmonies remain the same and only the words change. Why do you think Schubert ended his setting of line 4 of the poem with a deceptive cadence?

_____

How does knowing the last verse change your understanding of the use of the deceptive cadence in line 4 of stanzas 1 and 2 of the poem?

_____

_____

5c) The deceptive cadence is remedied in mm. 9–10, with a cadence to D major. Write the *chords* (letters) in mm. 9–10 and put the *functions* (Roman numerals in terms of D major) below the chords.

   ____ - ____ - ____ → ____

D: ____ - ____ - ____ → ____

5d) Notice that the tritone in m. 10 gives expression to and brings out the word "Freuden." Write down the German and English words in m. 10 in the second and third verses:
_____

What do you notice about the words in m. 10? _____ Why do you think Schubert emphasizes these two words (from verse 1 and verses 2–3)?
_____
_____

Tonicization

We just tonicized D major, which is the dominant in the key of G. Moving to the dominant is a very traditional thing to do in a folk song setting, so it is not at all surprising. The chordal functions of phrase 1 (mm. 1–4), can be written out simply in G major. Phrase 2 (mm. 5–10), however, modulates to D major. How do we know? Try writing the functions in the original key (G major) for mm. 5–10 and you get the following (vertical lines represent barlines):

G: I | V^2/V | V^6- vi^6 | V^7/V - vi/V | V^6- V^2/V | V^7/V → V

Writing it in the key of D you get:

D: IV | V^2 | I^6- ii^6 | V^7- vi | I^6- V^2 | V^7 → I

When you start seeing lots of secondary chords (i.e., vi/V and V/V), then usually you have tonicized a new area! When you have two possible ways of writing the function of the chords (see below), choose the simplest way of writing it, and use that key.

G: I | V^2/V | V^6- vi^6 | V^7/V - vi/V | V^6- V^2/V | V^7/V → V
D: IV | V^2 | I^6- ii^6 | V^7- vi | I^6- V^2 | V^7 → I

The key of D is simpler, so we shift in the functional analysis. Write both keys in until you get to the **pivot chord** (the chord that functions in both keys), highlighted here in gray:

G: I |
D: IV | V^2 | I^6- ii^6 | V^7- vi | I^6- V^2 | V^7 → I

Once you have shifted to the new key, you generally don't need to continue writing in the chords in the original key. (Of course, sometimes Schubert is intentionally ambiguous in his modulations; we'll discuss this much later in this book.)

To recap: phrase 1 is in G major and phrase 2 tonicizes D major. Let's see what happens in phrase 3!

Phrase 3 (mm. 11–14)

6a) Compare the melody of mm. 11–12 with that of mm. 3–4; what do you notice in terms of beginning and ending notes and general shape? _____
_____

What do lines 2 and 6 of the poem have in common? _____
_____

6b) Now compare the harmony of mm. 11–12 with that of mm. 3–4. Do you see they are almost exactly the same?

mm. 3–4:   G: V_5^6 - V^2 | I^6 - I

mm. 11–12: G: __ - __ | __ - __

6c) Just as before, we are left hanging in the air on a high G, even though we are on the tonic chord (G major). Last time we modulated to the dominant. What does Schubert do harmonically in mm. 13–14? Write the chords and functions for these two bars below:

__ - __ | __ - __ - __ |
__ - __ | __ - __ - __ |

6d) Write down the highest and lowest notes in the vocal part in mm. 13–14: ___ ___

What interval do they create? _____ How do you feel when you hear or sing this quick octave descent combined with a standard cadence? _____
_____

6e) Look through the vocal part of the entire piece: Which note only appears in the last measure? _____

> When you are studying a song, make sure to notice what the composer is leaving out or withholding from the listener. Often this makes the listener want that note (or chord or rhythm, etc.) all the more.

7) In this case Schubert is teasing us by completely leaving out the tonic until the last bar of the vocal line! How does that make you feel? How can you use Schubert's little trick in your performance? _____
_____

Piano Postlude

> ****ALWAYS PAY ATTENTION TO A PIANO PRELUDE OR POSTLUDE!****
> Schubert often tells the story of the song in the prelude, if there is one, and a postlude conveys the final word on the subject, what Schubert wants the listener to remember about the song.

The postlude in "Heidenröslein" is deceptively simple: the piano rushes in to add its two cents (with a pickup of sixteenth notes) and repeats the vocal part from mm. 13–14 in parallel tenths, but this time with snappy grace notes as if winking at the audience. Is it all a bit of a joke, or do the grace notes reveal a little pain? You decide!

* * *

8) What have you learned about the meaning of the song from your analysis? _____
_____
_____
_____
_____

9) How will you express it through your performance? _____
_____
_____
_____
_____

NOTE

1. Christian Friedrich Daniel Schubart, *Ideen zu einer Ästhetik der Tonkunst* (Vienna: Degen, 1806), reprint, ed. P. A. Merbach (Leipzig: Wolkenwander-Verlag, 1924), quoted in Rita Steblin, *A History of Key Characteristics in the Eighteenth and Early Nineteenth Centuries* (Ann Arbor: UMI Research Press, 1983), 124–25.

5

"An die Musik"

What do cadences have to do with the mood and expression of a song? This chapter shows you how to make a **cadence map** in order to understand how the composer organizes cadences to create meaning in a song. The **appoggiatura** is a musical sigh, so you need to be able to recognize appoggiaturas in your songs and perform them with expressive tenderness. **Linear motion** is simply melodic motion in one voice (melody, bassline, or inner voice); it often outlines an important interval in the key, such as a perfect fourth or fifth and, if chromatic, can introduce some spectacular harmonies.[1] Composers often use linear motion to tell the story of the song, so you need to be on the lookout.

Secondary harmonies occur when the song temporarily moves through a new key, providing a fresh sound to the listener. Another way to freshen the sound is through the use of a **harmonic surprise**, which can delight or move the audience; you need to be aware of these and use them to create a stunning performance. And finally, **motive** (a recurring and recognizable melodic fragment) is a device which may in itself create a certain mood; in addition, its frequent repetition can express comfort (as in this song) or, when taken to extreme, even obsession!

* * *

TEXT

1) What is the subject of the poem and its main point?
   _____
   _____

2) What elements of Romanticism do you find in the poem? Underline all words that show Romantic expression. _____
   _____
   _____
   _____

3) How many stanzas (paragraphs of text) are there? _____

4) What is the rhythmic meter of the poem? (There are weak beats and strong beats; how many strong beats do you find per line?) _____

5) What is the rhyme scheme? _____

6) Does each stanza follow the same meter and rhyme scheme? _____ (Unfortunately, we don't know if Schubert or Schober added the fifth line; my bet is on Schubert.)

7) What do you think of when you read this poem? Write down any similar experiences you have had, or anything this poem brings to your mind: _____
_____
_____
_____
_____

MUSIC

8) Listen to the song while following the score in which you have added your translation. How does this song (as opposed to just the poem) make you feel? Write down a few adjectives: _____
_____

9) Which words in the poem do you think Schubert has brought out in general? _____
_____

Tessitura

10) Look at the vocal range of mm. 5–9. What is the text here, and why do you think Schubert sets the text in this register? _____
_____

What happens to the range in mm. 11–17, and what are the words? Why do you think Schubert changes the tessitura? _____
_____
_____

Piano Prelude

11a) Listen to the piano prelude (the opening to the downbeat of m. 3): describe the rhythm and texture in the right hand: _____

How does this make you feel? _____

"An die Musik"

11b) The key of D major is described by the poet and theorist C. F. D. Schubart as "the key of triumph, of Hallelujahs, of war-cries, of victory-rejoicing."[2] Which, if any, of this description do you think accords with the mood of this song? _____
_____

Motive

12) Describe the left-hand motive in mm. 1–2 (to beat 2 of m. 2)—in other words, how would you recognize it later? (two intervals and the rhythm): _____
_____

You will find these two intervals all through this piece! (See m. 18, for example, for the falling sixth.)

13) What words is the piano "saying" in m. 1? _____

14) Does this motive begin on the downbeat? _____ Why do you think Schubert does this? _____

Find all the other instances of this **rhythmic** motive and write down the bar numbers (e.g., mm. 1–2, etc.): _____
_____

15) Now look at the rhythm in the right hand of the piano in m. 5: it is the rhythmic motive in diminution (twice as fast). How does it add to the mood? _____
_____

Where else do you find this quicker rhythm in the piano part? List the measure numbers in which you find it. The first one is done for you:

Measure numbers: *Length of pattern:*
mm. 15–16 (1st half only)   (1½ bars)
mm. _____   (_____ bars)
mm. _____   (_____ bars)

Compare the length of the pattern through the piece by looking at your chart above: What do you notice? _____ Why do you think Schubert does this? (Hint: What do the final text lines express?) _____
_____
_____
_____
_____

16) Before we leave motive, look at the left hand of the piano in mm. 20–21 and 21–22. What do you notice? _____
_____

Appoggiaturas

17) Listen to the postlude (piano part at end of song). Circle all the appoggiaturas in the postlude. (An appoggiatura is a musical sigh.) How does Schubert mark them to make them stand out? Why do you suppose he concluded this song with four clear musical sighs? (Hint: reread the text.) _____

_____

Cadences and Harmonic Journey

A **cadence** is a resting place in a musical phrase. Cadences can make you feel secure or can disappoint you when you don't get what you expect. They can also be used to express desire!

Cadence ordering helps to express the meaning of the song: they are a road map for where you're going! Here are three types of **cadence maps**, each expressing a different meaning.

- Stability and comfort: cadences appear at the same level throughout the song (for example, all on F major):

  — — — —

- Negative affect (depression): cadences appear on descending tonal levels:

  —
      —
          —
              —

- Feeling bereft, creating desire: cadences may suddenly be yanked to a different key (as if you are being offered delicious cookies, but then they are suddenly pulled away!)

      ‾
  — _/

  or the song may keep trying to reach a certain key and be unsuccessful, **withholding** that cadence level completely.

In this next section you will write out the **cadence map** for this song, and determine how the composer's choice of cadence order conveys the mood of the piece.

18) In what key is this piece? (Hint: check the final chord of the piece, in general.) ____

19) For a tonic cadence, what chords would you expect to see? ____–____

20) Where is the first cadence? (A cadence is a brief resting place, like a period in a sentence. It makes you feel temporarily satisfied.) Listen to the piano opening and raise your hand when you hear it. Write down the measure and beat of the cadence, along with the note (chord) it cadences to. (If you have trouble with bass clef, read it up a third.) _____

_____

21) How does the bassline set up the cadence in m. 2, beats 3 and 4? _____

How does this make you feel? _____

"An die Musik"

What aspect of the poem is expressed by the piano prelude and why? _____
_____

What can the pianist do to set up the mood of this song? _____
_____

22) Listen to the song and raise your hand each time you get to a cadence (circle it). Now go back and figure out what note the cadence went to. List the measure numbers and cadence levels (e.g., G or f).

CADENCE CHART:

m. _____ _____
m. _____ _____
m. _____ _____
m. _____ _____
m. _____ _____
m. _____ _____

23) Do you feel like the tonic key is clear in this piece? (Are at least the first and last cadences on tonic or is this a song where we are modulating constantly, cadencing in different keys and getting confused?) _____

24) Now think about the meaning of the text and explain why you think Schubert planned his cadences on these levels. What does it say about Schubert's feeling about music?
_____
_____
_____

BASSLINE MOTION

25) Look at the bassline in mm. 8–9: What important interval of the key does it outline?
_____

26) Compare the bassline in mm. 10–11 with mm. 12–13: What do you notice? _____
_____

What octave is outlined in each two-bar phrase? _____ How does this relate to the key of the piece? _____

27) Look at the bassline in m. 15 to beats 1 and 2 of m. 16: What interval is outlined, and how does it function in the key? _____ How does it make you feel to hear this strong motion twice? _____

28) What happens in the bassline on beats 3–4 of m. 16, and where does it go? _____
_____

HARMONIC FUNCTION

29) Listen to the opening to bars (to the first cadence). Write down the names and functions of the chords:

	m. 1, beat 3	m. 2, beat 1	m. 2, beat 3	m. 3, beat 1
names:	___	___	___	___
functions:	___	___	___	___

30) How typical of a chord progression is this? _____

31) How does it make you feel? _____ Why? _____
    _____

32) Listen to mm. 6–9. Write down the names and functions of the chords from mm. 7–9:

	m. 7, beat 1	m. 7, beat 3	m. 8, beat 1	m. 8, beat 2	m. 8, beat 3	m. 9, beat 1	m. 9, beat 3
names:	___	___	___	___	___	___	___
functions:	___	___	___	___	___	___	___

33) To which chord does a V^7 usually move? To which chords does this one move? How do you feel on the fourth and fifth chord? What is the text at this point? How can this emotion be brought out by the pianist? _____
    _____
    _____

34) Listen to mm. 14–19. Write down the names and functions of the chords (hint: first start with the letter names, then analyze backward from m. 19 so that you can see where the chords are moving to):

	m. 14			m. 15		m. 16		m. 17		m. 18		m. 19
	bt 1	bt 3	bt 4	bt 1	bt 3	bt 1	bt 3	bt 1	bt 3	bt 1	bt 3	bt 1
n:	___	___	___	___	___	___	___	___	___	___	___	___
f:	___	___	___	___	___	___	___	___	___	___	___	___

Every time you have a secondary dominant (including vii chords) resolving, put an arrow between them, as in V/V → V.

What do the arrows tell you? _____
_____
_____

35) How is the chord progression in mm. 6–9 similar to that in mm. 14–19? How is it different? Why do you think Schubert puts this spectacular progression at this place in the song? _____
_____
_____
_____

36) What have you learned about the meaning of the song from your analysis? _____
_____
_____
_____
_____

37) How will you express it through your performance? _____
_____
_____
_____
_____

NOTES

1. A detailed analysis of the linear motion in this song may be found in Deborah Stein and Robert Spillman, *Poetry into Song* (New York: Oxford University Press, 1996), 149–52. "An die Musik" is used to explain the concept of a "compound line" in linear analysis, where instead of one primary tone, a piece may have several. The three important tones (and registers) noted in this song are low D-F♯, middle A, and high D. The top two merge beginning in m. 12, and all are then connected in the postlude beginning in m. 19 to the end.

2. Christian Friedrich Daniel Schubart, *Ideen zu einer Ästhetik der Tonkunst* (Vienna: Degen, 1806), reprint, ed. P. A. Merbach (Leipzig: Wolkenwander-Verlag, 1924), quoted in Rita Steblin, *A History of Key Characteristics in the Eighteenth and Early Nineteenth Centuries* (Ann Arbor: UMI Research Press, 1983), 124–25.

6

"Die Forelle"

What tricks do poets use to entrap the reader? This chapter shows how even the most "folk-like" poems may contain highly sophisticated techniques for enchanting the reader. In analyzing "Die Forelle" you will learn how **opposite vowel patterns** mirror a **chiastic** structure in the poem, and how **enjambement** can be used to stir up trouble, creating tension in the line and requiring the composer to use new music.

Schubert's **folklike musical style** seems to mirror the folklike story—or does it mirror the simple person who gets "caught"? You will have the opportunity to decide for yourself!

In this piece we can hear the characters literally **represented in the music**: the gurgling of the brook, the darting and later flapping of the fish, and the galumphing and then sneaking steps of the fisherman—all but the silent observer who observes the scene and its vexing finale.

The song seems so simple, yet it conceals additional layers of meaning. Ostensibly telling the story of a fish and a sneaky fisherman, the poem is one of many which reminded girls (in this case, through a fishing metaphor) to avoid seducers. At an even deeper level, the poem may be a warning from the poet C. F. D. Schubart to beware of the lies of powerful aristocrats, lies which led to the poet's harsh ten-year imprisonment for political reasons.

Even the form may be less clear than it first appears. Most of "Die Forelle" sounds like a simple strophic song, in which each repetition of the music sets a different stanza of the poem. A sudden contrast appears about two-thirds of the way in, followed by a return of opening material, revealing itself to be in ternary form, or at least not quite the simple form we expected. This song is full of deceit—it is not just the fish that is tricked, but also the listener!

TEXT

1) What is the subject of the poem and its main point? _____
   _____

2) What is the main affect (emotional state) of each strophe (stanza) and why? What words express the feeling? _____
   _____
   _____

3) With what specific words is the fish described? The fisherman? _____
   _____
   _____
   _____

4) How are the emotions of the two humans (fisherman and the poet) specifically contrasted? (in German and English) _____
   _____
   _____

   How would you bring this out in a performance? _____
   _____

5) The original poem (C. F. D. Schubart, 1782) had a fourth strophe, a cautionary moral:

Die ihr am goldnen Quelle	You who tarry by the golden spring
Der sichern Jugend weilt,	Of secure youth,
Denkt doch an die Forelle,	Think still of the trout:
Seht ihr Gefahr, so eilt!	If you see danger, hurry by!
Meist fehlt ihr nur aus Mangel	Most of you err only from lack
Der Klugheit. Mädchen seht	Of cleverness. Girls, see
Verführer mit der Angel!	Seducers with their tackle!
Sonst blutet ihr zu spät.	Or else, too late, you'll bleed.

   What meaning do you think the poem has now? _____
   _____
   _____

Are you surprised by the language of the final line? This poem joins a long line of those warning girls about the danger of seducers.

One cannot attempt to understand the meaning of the poem, however, without recognizing the context of its creation. Christian Friedrich Daniel Schubart, the poet and music theorist, got in trouble with the Duke of Württemberg by writing critically about the aristocrat in *Die deutsche Chronik*, Schubart's weekly newspaper. Though living outside the duke's realm, Schubart was somehow invited back in and made the mistake of returning, at which point he was snatched up and put into prison for ten long years. It was during this period that he composed the poems that were eventually set by the composer Schubert a few decades later.[1]

The "muddying of the waters" by the sneaky fisherman, then, may be an allegory of the entrapment of Schubart by the Duke of Württemberg. The addition of the fourth stanza, which seems so different from the other three, may have been added as a cover to protect Schubart, just as he had done with his poem *Die Fürstengruft*. However, Schubert (the composer), did not omit the fourth stanza, as by the time he came into contact with it in the posthumous Viennese edition of Schubart's poems, "Die Forelle" was printed with only three stanzas; it is likely that the poet's son removed the final stanza for this publication, which was selected and introduced by the son.[2]

6) What is the rhythmic meter of the entire poem and what mood does it convey? (There are weak beats and strong beats; how many strong beats do you find per line?) Why do you think the poet chose this meter? _____
_____
_____

7) What is the rhyme scheme? Does each strophe follow the same meter and rhyme scheme?
_____

The key of D♭ major is described by the poet and theorist C. F. D. Schubart as "a leering key, degenerating into grief and rapture."[3] While that may seem a strange description for a song about a fish, you know by now that this song has multiple meanings, and as a warning for girls to avoid seducers, it fits quite well, as does the next level of meaning, a warning against being caught by political treachery.

MUSIC

8) Listen to the song while following the score in which you have added your translation. How does this song (as opposed to just the poem) make you feel? Write down a few adjectives: _____
_____

9a) The music to strophes 1 and 2 are the same, yet the text is different. How can you project the different circumstances in your performance of strophe 2? _____
_____
_____

9b) Why do you think Schubert changed the music for the third strophe? _____
_____
_____

9c) All of the phrases in this song begin on upbeats over the barline except for one short section. In which measures does this occur, and why do you think Schubert shifted the placement of the upbeats at this point? _____
_____
_____

How can you bring this out in performance? _____
_____
_____

10a) What do you notice about the rhythm of the outer voices in the piano prelude (mm. 1–5)? Why do you think Schubert includes this to set the poem? Which character in the poem might this represent? _____
_____
_____
_____

How do the inner voices contrast rhythmically? Which character might this represent?
_____
_____
_____

10b) Note the two different right-hand piano gestures: one is more stepwise with a little chromaticism (in the prelude and then mm. 14–29, which includes the interlude) and the other is arpeggiated (mm. 6–13). What happens in the poem in m. 14 to trigger the change? _____
_____
_____
_____

11) Now go back to the poem: In the first two strophes, what is the function of the first four lines and then of the second four lines? _____
_____
_____

12) In what way does the melody of mm. 6–21 reflect the mood of the poem? How can you bring this out in your performance? Why do you suppose Schubert repeats the last line with variation? _____
_____
_____
_____

13) What key is this piece in? (Hint: look at final chord and key signature.) Write out the chord names for I, V, and V/V: _____

Now write in the chord functions (Roman numerals) for mm. 6–9 (one chord per measure):

____-____-____-____

Is this simple or complex harmony (diatonic or chromatic?) _____

Why do you think Schubert writes such simple harmony (and melody, for that matter) for this opening section? _____
_____
_____
_____
_____

14) Do the same for mm. 10–13 (except use two chords for m. 12):

____-____-____ ____-____

What kind of cadence is this? _____ Is this a surprise or expected?
_____

The rest of the setting is similar in complexity.

15) How and why does the melody change in the setting of the third strophe (m. 31)?
_____
_____
_____

How could you perform these to bring out the changes in the melody? _____
_____
_____

16a) How and why does the mood change harmonically in the setting of the third strophe?
_____
_____

In mm. 31–34 we briefly tonicize another key; what key is it? (Write down the names of the chords in mm. 31–36, one per bar, and then write down the function of each chord in the key of the piece.)

_____-_____ _____-_____

_____-_____ _____-_____

16b) What happens to the right-hand pattern (i.e., compare m. 31 to m. 6)? Why do you think it is different? _____
_____

17) Look at the bassline in mm. 35–37: What is happening, and how does it express what is happening in the poem? _____
_____

18) Write out the notes of the bassline from mm. 38–44. Some measures have more than one:

____–____–____ ____–____ ____–(____)–____–____

(M. 42 is in parentheses because it is a lower neighbor and the last two are the same.)

What is the interval, and what does it say about the view of the onlooker toward the trout's fate? _____

19) Why do you think Schubert brings back the music from mm. 18–21? _____
_____
_____

20) How do you think the listener is supposed to feel at the end of the song? How can you express this feeling in your performance? _____
_____
_____
_____

21) What have you learned about the meaning of the song from your analysis? _____
_____
_____
_____
_____

22) How will you express it through your performance? _____
_____
_____
_____
_____

NOTES

1. Graham Johnson, *Schubert: The Complete Songs* (New Haven: Yale University Press, 2014), 2:912.
2. Richard Law, "Christian Schubart: The Trout," *Figures of Speech* (blog), February 7, 2016, http://figures-of-speech.com/2016/02/die-forelle-5.htm; and Lucia Porhansl, "Schuberts Textvorlagen nach Friedrich Wilhelm Gotter und Christian Friedrich Daniel Schubart," *Schubert durch die Brille*, 10 (1993): 69–74.
3. Christian Friedrich Daniel Schubart, *Ideen zu einer Ästhetik der Tonkunst* (Vienna: Degen, 1806), reprint, ed. P. A. Merbach (Leipzig: Wolkenwander-Verlag, 1924), quoted in Rita Steblin, *A History of Key Characteristics in the Eighteenth and Early Nineteenth Centuries* (Ann Arbor: UMI Research Press, 1983), 124–25.

7

"Gute Nacht" (from *Winterreise*)

Memory or **nostalgia** is at the core of so many nineteenth-century works and is particularly resonant in the **song cycle** *Winterreise*. (A song cycle is a musical setting of poems that are related by story, mood, character development, or theme; the songs themselves may be linked by motive, key structure, by sharing the same beginning or ending note, or even by being connected, as in Beethoven's *An die ferne Geliebte*.)

In Müller and Schubert's setting, a man who has been rejected by his lover goes on a long journey in the frozen winter. But as in so many Schubert songs, the external story reveals a **metaphorical meaning**: it is actually an interior monologue experienced as a result of his alienation from the world; his journey is one on the way to death or insanity. Müller's cycle must have been particularly evocative for Schubert, who was suffering from a resurgence of symptoms of syphilis, at least while writing the second part.[1]

"Gute Nacht," the first song in the cycle, not only sets the scene dramatically but hints at the never-ending journey through real and metaphorical darkness and ice. In this song you will discover how Schubert modifies the strophic form in order to contrast the **present and past**. Two **motives** play a key role in setting the scene, and Schubert contrasts **static and moving lines** throughout; one represents the present and one, the past—but which? Schubert's famous **stingers (accents)** appear in the piano part to taunt the wanderer, just when he is remembering his love in a **sweet key**.

* * *

TEXT

1a) One of the most compelling features of Müller's *Winterreise* poems is their intermingling of past memory and present struggle. Go through each line in your text and translation and indicate "past" or "present" to the right of each line (see next page).

1b) What do you notice about lines 1 and 2? _____
_____

1c) Do you see how Müller introduces one of the main subjects of his cycle in the first two lines: the juxtaposition of the past and present?

1d) Now write the line numbers for past and present from line 3 to the end of the first stanza (line 8).

PAST: lines 3 – ____

PRESENT: lines ____ – 8

1e) What affect (mood or emotion) is associated with each time period (past and present)?
_____
_____

1f) How will an understanding of the juxtaposition of time shape your interpretation of this song? _____
_____
_____

Fremd bin ich eingezogen,	I arrived a stranger
fremd zieh' ich wieder aus.	a stranger I depart.
Der Mai war mir gewogen,	May blessed me
mit manchem Blumenstrauss.	with many a bouquet of flowers.
Das Mädchen sprach von Liebe,	The girl spoke of love,
die Mutter gar von Eh',	her mother even of marriage.
nun ist die Welt so trübe,	Now the world is so desolate,
der Weg gehüllt in Schnee.	the path concealed beneath snow.
Ich kann zu meiner Reisen	I cannot choose the time
nicht wählen mit der Zeit,	for my journey;
Muss selbst den Weg mir weisen	I must find my own way
in dieser Dunkelheit.	in this darkness.
Es zieht ein Mondenschatten	A shadow thrown by the moon
als mein Gefährte mit,	is my companion,
und auf den weissen Matten	and on the white meadows
such' ich des Wildes Tritt	I see the tracks of deer.
Was soll ich länger weilen,	Why should I tarry longer
dass man mich trieb hinaus?	and be driven out?
Lass irre Hunde heulen	Let stray dogs howl
vor ihres Herren Haus;	before their master's house.
Die Liebe liebt das Wandern,	Love delights in wandering
Gott hat sie so gemacht,	God made it so;
von Einem zu dem Andern,	from one to another,
fein Liebchen, gute Nacht!	sweetheart, goodnight!
Will dich im Traum nicht stören,	I will not disturb you as you dream;
wär schad' um deine Ruh',	it would be a shame to spoil your rest.
sollst meinen Tritt nicht hören,	You shall not hear my footsteps—
sacht, sacht die Türe zu!	softly, softly the door is closed!
Schreib' im Vorübergehen	As I pass I write
an's Tor dir: gute Nacht,	"good night" upon your gate,
damit du mögest sehen,	so that you may see
an dich hab' ich gedacht.	that I thought of you.

"Gute Nacht" (from Winterreise*)*

2a) To whom is the wanderer speaking in each stanza? _____
_____

When does it change? _____
_____

2b) What positive and negative images are contrasted in the first stanza? _____
_____

2c) What negative images appear later in the poem? _____
_____

2d) How is loneliness expressed in the poem? _____
_____

2e) How does the wanderer feel in stanza 2 and why? _____
_____
_____

2f) What does the line "Love delights in wandering" mean (stanza 2)? _____
_____
_____

2g) How does the wanderer feel in stanza 3 and why? Do you think he's serious about not wanting to disturb her? _____
_____
_____

3a) What is the poetic meter? _____ What is the pattern of endings (e.g., weak vs. strong)? _____

3b) Note that this pattern continues throughout all the verses. Read several lines of the meter saying "DA" for the accented syllables and "dee" for the unaccented syllables.

What is the effect of the same meter being repeated over and over again? _____

Why do you suppose the poet does this? _____
_____

Below we will see how Schubert expresses this mood through his music.

MUSIC

Piano Prelude (mm. 1–6)

Remember that Schubert's preludes often tell the entire story before a word is sung.

4a) The first notes we hear are a repeated F; how many times is the note repeated in the first two bars? _____

4b) How does this set the scene of an endless journey through ice and despair, especially when accompanied by the same rhythm in the left hand? _____
_____

4c) This repeated figure has been called the **"tramping" motive**; can you see why? Notice that it is marked *staccato*; each note is separate from the others. Pay close attention to its appearance throughout the song: Does it ever disappear? _____ Observe the contrast of **static vs. moving lines** in all the voices.

4d) What direction does the melodic line go in mm. 1–3? _____ What is the interval and how rapidly does it move? _____

What does this suggest about the mood of this song? _____

Of the cycle? _____

4e) Listen to the prelude again and circle any dissonances in your score. Why do you suppose Schubert marks them with an *fp*? _____

What do these dissonances convey about the person tramping through the snow and singing this song? _____

4f) Marching through snow all night would make anyone cold. Do you hear the piano shaking from cold at any point? _____

4g) The first two notes in the top voice introduce the **semitone motive**. Earlier in this book you discovered how Schubert often uses this motive to express a character's anxiety and to create tension. We will encounter this motive later in the song!

Strophes 1 and 2 (mm. 7–38)

The challenge of writing a strophic song is that the same music has to fit the meaning of several verses. The music for strophes 1 and 2 is written with a repeat sign and thus is identical; let's look at how Schubert manages to make the music fit both verses.

5a) Compare mm. 7–11 with mm. 11–15; what do you notice? How does this repetition reflect the idea of a long journey? _____
_____

5b) The descending melodic line from the prelude returns in the voice part. How many descending lines do you hear in mm. 7–15? _____

5c) Do you find the semitone motive anywhere in mm. 7–15? Put a box around it where it appears in your score and write down in which measures it appears: _____

5d) On what note does each text line cadence in mm. 7–15? _____

6a) How does the direction of the melody change in mm.16–23? _____

What notes and what interval does Schubert outline from the downbeat of m. 16 to the highest note in m. 22? _____

How does this express a change in the mood at this point? (Note that the text lines 5 and 6 are repeated.) _____

6b) Which motive appears in m. 16 in the vocal part? _____

Note the countermelody in the right hand of the piano: In what direction does it move? _____ Why, do you think? _____
_____

Note the direction to the pianist ("ligato," a German spelling of "legato" or connected); again, why do you think Schubert made this indication? _____
_____

How does it compare with the articulation of the "tramping" motive? Notice how the "tramping" motive jumps to the voice part in this bar, while the piano gets something special! What happens in the left hand of m. 18? _____
_____

Make sure to bring out these rising lines.

6c) Compare mm. 16–19 and mm. 20–23: What do you notice? On what note is the cadence in m. 19? ____ In m. 23? ____ How do these cadences compare to those in mm. 1–15?
_____
_____

Why do you think Schubert moves there?[2] (Hint: check out the section on key characteristics in chapter 3 and write in the descriptions of these two keys.) _____
_____
_____
_____
_____

6d) How does Schubert rip us from this sweet reverie of love or beauty in mm. 24–26? (Hint: look at the right hand.) Do you recognize this motive and its purpose? _____
_____

And see how Schubert exacerbates this pain with the *fp*. What makes Schubert shift the mood so suddenly? _____
_____

6e) Compare mm. 26–29 and mm. 30–33: How are they the same? _____
_____

How are they different? _____
_____

Why do you think Schubert made the change, and how does it affect the mood?
_____
_____

Notice the appearance of the semitone motive in m. 32, which is not present in m. 28.

7) Which text lines in strophes 1 and 2 are set to mm. 16–23 (list line numbers)? _____
_____

What is similar enough in these lines that Schubert sets them with the same music? Note that lines 13 and 14 are repeated in the modulatory section, as in strophe 1.

Strophe 3 (mm. 39–71)

8a) Compare the setting of strophe 3 with that of strophes 1–2. Circle all changes. How do the changes in mm. 39–47 affect the emotion expressed? Why does Schubert do this?
_____

How do the changes in mm. 58–66 reflect the text? _____
_____

How will you express this in your performance? _____
_____
_____

Notice how the melody and piano part at "Love likes to wander" is the same as that setting "The girl spoke of love" from stanza 1, linking them musically. As a result the words at first seem lighthearted (mm. 47–55), but then anger seeps in through the descending dotted rhythms (mm. 57–66). This is one of many ways in which a composer can add additional meaning to a text.

8b) Notice that in strophes 3 and 4, Schubert sets the last four lines to the modulatory section of mm. 48–55 (here in F and B♭), instead of just the two lines as in strophes 1 and 2. What about the text of each stanza caused Schubert to make this change, do you think? _____
_____

Strophe 4 (mm. 72–end)

9a) How does Schubert transform the final strophe? _____

What does that tell us about the emotion of the speaker here? _____

_____

Notice that with this change the semitone motive becomes less painful whenever it appears. Despite the possible self-pity of the first few lines of text, Schubert keeps it musically very earnest.

9b) To what keys does the modulatory section now cadence (mm. 81–88)? _____
_____

Why does Schubert not move to the flat areas of F and B♭ here? _____
_____

(Notice the extra "wandering" countermelody in m. 84!)

9c) Compare mm. 97–98 and mm. 99–100: What do you think has happened in the protagonist's mind to cause this change? _____
_____

How will you express this in your performance? (Schubert has helpfully included *un poco ritardando* to call attention to this moment.) Where do you think we are now: in the past or in the present? _____

Notice how mm. 96–98 ("I thought of you") repeat the same music as mm. 64–66 ("sweetheart, goodnight!"). Schubert has been varying the endings of this strophic song throughout, but in this case intentionally links these two lines of poetry through reuse of the music. Note further how this short melody echoes the very opening of the song, the falling line in the right hand of the prelude. As usual, Schubert suggests the entire story (and that of the *Winterreise* cycle) in the prelude, revealing its full meaning—"I thought of you"—only at the end of the song.

9d) Listen for the melody from mm. 99–100 as it appears in the piano postlude. Is it clear or hidden? _____

What do you think this tells us about his memory of her? _____

Schubert was famous for being a sensitive interpreter of poetry, but as can be seen here, he could also manipulate it to serve his purposes, deepening the meaning to create a memorable work of art.

10a) What have you learned about the meaning of the song from your analysis? _____

_____
_____
_____
_____

10b) How will you express it through your performance? _____

_____
_____
_____
_____

NOTES

1. Susan Youens, *Retracing a Winter's Journey: Schubert's Winterreise* (Ithaca and London: Cornell University Press, 1991), xiii, 24–25, 51–58.

2. Not only are they major keys, but they are also very "sweet." See chapter 3 under "Choice of Key" for a summary of the attributes of flat vs. sharp keys.

Part 3
SONGS OF MEDIUM DIFFICULTY TO ANALYZE

8

"Der Neugierige" (from *Die schöne Müllerin*)

Yes or no? As in many Schubert songs, the **piano prelude** in this song tells the entire story before the singer even opens his mouth. Again we hear Schubert making use of a folklike style, perhaps with a nudge and a wink, before launching into a lyrical aria, complete with its own recitative.

In this analysis you will become aware of how **changes in poetic address** inspire a musical transformation from low to high art, from folksong to bel canto aria. In addition, you will learn how to identify a **motive**, whose frequent appearance can often represent obsession in nineteenth-century song; here the youth's anxiety is expressed by the **semitone motive** and dissonance. Another feature idolized by nineteenth-century composers is the harmonic freshness created by the **third relationship** (movement to the chromatic mediant).[1]

Other techniques introduced in this chapter include **melodic circling** (a way of emphasizing an important note in the key), **mode mixture** (mixing major and minor chords to enhance the color), **oscillation** (back and forth movement between two or more chords), and the emotional power of a **deceptive cadence**.

* * *

"Der Neugierige" is the sixth song in Schubert's twenty-song cycle *Die schöne Müllerin*, set to poetry by Wilhelm Müller. A young miller leaves his own mill to wander in nature, following a little brook. When he comes across another mill complete with a beautiful miller's daughter, he decides to stay and work there, feeling that his "dear little brook" has brought him there. "Der Neugierige" means "the curious one," but Graham Johnson suggests its meaning is actually somewhat more akin to "greedy for something new," which reflects the insatiable desire to find out the answer to his question.[2]

POEM

1a) Who is speaking, and what is he trying to determine? _____

1b) What lover's game does this remind you of? _____

(Apparently the poet himself actually played a game like this by writing "yes" and "no" on pieces of paper to try to ascertain whether a certain young lady liked him.)[3]

2a) Describe the following for each of the five strophes:

a) to whom is he speaking? b) what do we learn about the speaker?

1) _____

2) _____

3) _____

4) _____

5) _____

2b) Where does the speaker change his address? _____

To whom does he ask this important question? _____

What does the brook represent? _____

Poetic Meter

The poem is set in relatively short lines of three feet each (iambic trimeter = three accents per line) alternating weak and strong endings; a weak ending has an unaccented beat at the end; a strong ending ends with the accented beat:

-/-/-/-
-/-/-/

3) Read the poem out loud in German so that you can hear the meter and accents of the poem.[4]

"Der Neugierige" (from Die schöne Müllerin)

MUSIC

At first "Der Neugierige" gives the impression of being set in a simple folksong style, setting a traditional game of "she loves me, she loves me not." Of course, Schubert excels at the outward impression of folk musical traditions while secretly manipulating the form to express subtler and sometimes quite unfolklike styles and meanings, as we will see in this piece.

4a) Listen to the song while following the score in which you have added your translation. How does this song (as opposed to just the poem) make you feel? Write down a few adjectives:

   _____
   _____

4b) B major is described by the poet and theorist C. F. D. Schubart as "strongly colored, announcing wild passions. . . . Anger, rage, jealousy, fury, despair . . ."[5] Which of these might apply to the mood of this song? _____
   _____

4c) Which phrases begin on an upbeat and which on a downbeat? (Include the entire song, including the prelude.) _____

   Why do you think this is? _____

   How is the mood created by phrases with eighth-note pickups different from that with quarter-note pickups? _____
   _____

Piano Prelude

> Always pay close attention to the piano prelude, as Schubert usually tells you what the entire song will be about in just these few bars!

5a) How many bars long is the piano prelude? _____

5b) Into how many phrases is it subdivided? _____

5c) In what direction does the first phrase move? _____ The second? _____

5d) Why do you think Schubert introduces this poem with such opposing musical phrases?
   _____
   _____

5e) How are these phrases similar? _____

Motive

> A motive is a very short rhythmic and/or melodic interval or few notes that are easily recognizable. How do you know if it's a motive or just a few random notes? It's a motive if it occurs in the beginning of a piece and keeps recurring. The frequent appearance of a motive often signals obsession on the part of the protagonist, a key Romantic trait!

6a) Circle the semitone motive in the first four bars. Don't forget the left hand!

6b) What does the rhythm suggest and why? _____
_____

6c) What is the tempo marking? _____

6d) What mood does the tempo combined with the rhythm suggest? _____
_____

7a) Where is the high point and what note is it? _____

This note really sticks out! Circle it. Now look through the piano part up to m. 22: there is only one place in the right hand that goes higher. Write down the measure number, and circle it in your score. _____ We will return to this later.

7b) Does each phrase end on a consonant or a dissonant chord? _____

How does consonance or dissonance of the final chord affect the mood of each phrase?
_____
_____

7c) Why do you suppose Schubert set up two such conflicting phrases in his piano prelude?
_____
_____

8a) Look at the left hand in mm. 2 and 3: Do you find the motive there? In what notes?
_____

8b) How does the rising direction of mm. 1–2 and high note in m. 2 make you feel?
_____

8c) If the song is in B major, what is the chord and function of m. 2? _____ _____

8d) How does the sudden sounding of this chord make you feel, and what in the poem does this express? _____
_____

9) Go through the **entire piece** and circle the semitone motive wherever you can find it—it's everywhere!

"Der Neugierige" (from Die schöne Müllerin*)*

Cadences (Tonal Structure)

> Always look for cadences—they are like a road map to tell you where you are traveling in the song.

10) Listen to the entire song again and circle cadences in your score. Now write in the cadence levels (e.g., C major, A minor) on your translation, to give yourself a **tonal map**. Are there any deceptive, evaded, or avoided cadences? Note this on your score and translation! Nineteenth-century composers commonly use these to create feelings of longing and desire, often by frustrating the listener!

First Section (the "scena," stanzas 1–2, mm. 5–22)

11a) What key is the piece in? _____

11b) Write down the cadence levels for V and V/V: _____

11c) On what tonal area (chord) does the piano prelude cadence? _____

  Is this expected? _____

11d) To what tonal area does the piece tonicize in m. 12? _____

  Is this expected? _____

11e) To what tonal area is the cadence in m. 20? _____

  Is this expected? _____

> **Appogiaturas**: Pay attention to how you perform appoggiaturas—they are the musical expression of a sigh! The first note is usually an accented dissonance which the second note resolves. This song is full of them (the semitone is motivic!) and they need to be performed sensitively. The first note of an appoggiatura is gently stressed and the second note releases a bit. (In m. 6, for example, Schubert sets the appoggiatura so that it follows the correct accents on the word "Blume" [flowers]: pronounced as Blu-me.) We should hear the miller's sighs (subtly) throughout this song!

12a) What happens to the cadence in the piano interlude? (mm. 20–22)? _____
_____

12b) Notice how in m. 21 the piano right hand imitates the vocal melody of m. 19. What's different harmonically? (i.e., Where does it want to cadence?) _____
_____

12c) Why do you suppose Schubert cuts it off? _____
_____

12d) What do you hear for most of m. 22? _____

12e) Look at the first two lines of stanza 3: Why do you think Schubert sets m. 22 in this way?
_____

116   *Chapter 8*

You may also recognize this technique from **bel canto arias** in which the orchestra plays the entire melody except for the last chord, stops, and starts again to allow the soloist to sing the complete aria. Schubert has created somewhat of a *scena ed aria* for his humble miller, giving the lie to the simple folksong he is ostensibly uttering.

Section 2A (stanza 3, beginning of the "aria," mm. 23–32)

13a) To whom is the miller now singing? _____

13b) Why do you suppose Schubert changes the tempo at this point? _____
_____

13c) What happens in the left hand, and why? _____
_____

13d) To whom should he actually be singing to ask if she loves him? _____
_____

13e) Compare the melody in mm. 23–24 with that in m. 5. What similarity do you notice?
_____

Circle the **motive** in each of these four bars.

14a) How do you think the miller feels about the brook remaining silent ("stumm" = mute)? Naturally Schubert tells us through his music: what is surprising harmonically in m. 25?
_____

14b) Why do you think Schubert does this? _____
_____
_____

14c) In m. 26 notice the C♯ on beat 2 (in the right hand of the accompaniment). This comes right after the harmonic effect of m. 25; why do you think Schubert adds it? _____
_____

14d) What interval do you find in the bassline of m. 26 and why? _____
_____

14e) What can the pianist do to bring out the "commentary" in m. 26? _____
_____

Notice the piano C♯ echoes the word "stumm" (mute); ironic that the brook actually does appear to speak to him, but he doesn't understand its meaning.

15a) To what tonal level (chord) is the half cadence on the downbeat of m. 26? _____

Does this make sense in the key of the song? _____

15b) To what tonal level (chord) is the full cadence on the downbeat of m. 30, repeated in m. 32? _____ Does this make sense in the key of the song? _____

Section 2B (stanza 4, recitative and oscillation, mm. 33–42)

This glorious aria is suddenly interrupted by a true recitative as the miller considers the two possibilities of "yes" or "no."

16a) What makes this section (mm. 33–34) sound like a recitative? _____
_____

16b) Why do you think Schubert does this? _____
_____

16c) Compare the activity of the piano setting the word "yes" (m. 33) and "no" (m. 35):
_____
_____

17a) What chord introduces the recitative on the word "yes" in m. 33 (chord name and function)? _____ _____

17b) What chord appears on the word "no" in. m. 35 (chord name and function)? _____ _____

17c) What is the interval between the roots of these two chords? _____

Do you see how Schubert has expressed the melodic semitone motive in a harmonic way (two chords related by semitone, instead of two notes)? This is an example of **motivic parallelism**, where a motive appears at different levels of scale, in this case, melodic and harmonic. These two chords contrast the word "yes" in m. 33 with the word "no" in m. 35, demonstrating that in this song, the semitone motive represents the essential question posed by the protagonist: she loves me, she loves me not?

17d) Since these two chords (downbeats of mm. 33 and 35) are a semitone apart, how does Schubert move from one to the other? Write the notes for the chord in the correct inversion on the downbeat of m. 33, the second beat of m. 34, and the downbeat of m. 35.

m. 33   m. 34   m. 35
          (2nd beat)

_____   _____   _____
_____   _____   _____
_____   _____   _____

Notice how some notes are prolonged, and some move up by semitone. Circle any movement by semitone. In performance, pianists can bring out the semitone movement—after all, it's motivic!

Do you see how the magic of linear motion smooths the way to a tonal area (G) that is a chromatic mediant away? (A chromatic mediant is a third-related chord that has been altered chromatically, as it does not appear naturally in the key.) Chromatic mediants add freshness and wonder to a song, so keep your eyes open for them! In "Der Neugierige" they impart to this "indecision" recitative a sense of fantasy and imagination.

> In the nineteenth century, it is not unusual for a melodic motive to be expressed harmonically as well. The appearance of a motive at different levels of scale is known as **motivic parallelism**. Beethoven does it all the time, so keep an eye out for it in nineteenth-century music. By temporarily shifting the tonal center by a motivic semitone in this passage (mm. 35–41), Schubert foreshadows the eventual negative outcome and its importance to the miller: "**No**, both words contain (lock up) for me the entire world."

Musical Oscillation

> Musical **oscillation** is when a note or chord keeps going back and forth between two or several notes, resulting in a static quality.

Notice the musical oscillation beginning in the piano part in m. 35 (the four chords in beats 2 and 3).

18a) To what words is it set in m. 36 (pickup to 36 + beats 1 and 2)? _____

18b) What is Schubert suggesting by having the music go back and forth like this? _____

(Notice what the melody line does when the oscillation releases on the downbeats of m. 37 and m. 40.)

Modulation

> Always ask yourself how we got to a new key and how we get back to the original key of the song.

After the cadence in m. 41 we quickly shift back to the original key of the song for a return of the aria theme. How do we get from the key of m. 41 to that of m. 43?

19a) Write the bass note of the following: m. 41: ____ m. 42: ____

19b) What is this interval? _____

19c) Write the chord name and function (related to B major, the key of the song) in m. 42 (beat 1): ____ ____

19d) Write in the top notes in the left hand of the piano in m. 41: ____ ____ ____

19e) What motive do you see? _____

> **Circling** is way of emphasizing an important note.

20a) What is the important note being circled in m. 41, and what is the chord's function in the key of the piece? _____ _____

> In modulation, the appearance of a I_4^6 is a way of putting a floor under a new key. This is very common in nineteenth-century music; in fact, late in the century composers like Strauss just signaled a new key with a I_4^6, and often didn't even bother to cadence!

20b) What two chords (and their functions) follow the I_4^6 on the downbeat of m. 43?

___–___, ___–___ This is why the return of the aria theme in m. 43 feels so welcome!

Section 2C (stanza 5, return of the aria, mm. 43–52)

21a) Compare mm. 43–46 with mm. 23–26; what do you notice? _____

21b) In which bar does the melody change? _____ Which note is different? _____

21c) In which bar does the left hand of the piano change? _____

How does Schubert set "liebt sie mich" and why? (See questions 22a–e.)

22a) *Melody*: What happens on the word "liebt" and why? _____
_____
_____

22b) *Harmony*: What harmony do we expect on the downbeat of m. 50? _____
_____

What harmonies and functions do we get instead? _____
_____

What kind of cadence is this? _____ On what word is this cadence and why?
_____
_____

22c) *Bassline*: Write in the following three notes: last beat m. 49, 1st beat m. 50, 2nd beat m. 50: ___ ___ ___ Recognize this? _____ Find and circle this same interval pattern in the voice part (hint: look in mm. 48–49).

22d) What do you think Schubert is suggesting by setting "liebt sie mich" this way? _____
_____
_____

22e) Now that you understand what is going on musically in mm 48–50, how would you perform this passage? _____
_____
_____

Piano Postlude (mm. 52–55)

23a) To what level (chord) is the cadence in the downbeat of m. 52? ___ Is this satisfying; is it all's well that ends well? _____

23b) Is there a dissonance in m. 53 to suggest that things may not be resolved? _____
_____
_____

Have you seen these two notes earlier in the piece (hint: look in the first bar of the piano prelude!)? Do you see that it's the notes of the original semitone motive, now appearing as a harmonic dissonance? That cute little motive now has something to tell us about the protagonist's fate. What could it be? _____
_____

23c) What could the pianist do to allow the audience to understand that the question has not really been answered? _____
_____

24a) What have you learned about the meaning of the song from your analysis? _____
_____
_____
_____
_____

24b) How will you express it through your performance? _____
_____
_____
_____
_____

NOTES

1. Discussion of the chromatic third relationship in this song, as well as the question of tempo in this song is addressed at length in Deborah Stein and Robert Spillman, *Poetry into Song* (New York: Oxford University Press, 1996), 77–78 and 126–27.

2. Graham Johnson, *Schubert: The Complete Songs* (New Haven: Yale University Press, 2014), 2:825 (translation by Richard Wigmore, 824–25).

3. Susan Youens, *Schubert: Die schöne Mullerin* (Cambridge: Cambridge University Press, 1992), 5; and Johnson, *Schubert: The Complete Songs*, 2:825.

4. As it happens, Schubert added the word "alle" in line 3, which slightly shifts the accents from "Sie **kön**nen **mir** nicht **sa**gen" to "Sie **kön**nen mir **al**le nicht **sa**gen," which still works as three feet but with a slight shift to dactyls (/"). Johnson, *Schubert, The Complete Songs*, 2:284.

5. Christian Friedrich Daniel Schubart, *Ideen zu einer Ästhetik der Tonkunst* (Vienna: Degen, 1806), reprint, ed. P. A. Merbach (Leipzig: Wolkenwander-Verlag, 1924), quoted in Rita Steblin, *A History of Key Characteristics in the Eighteenth and Early Nineteenth Centuries* (Ann Arbor: UMI Research Press, 1983), 124–25.

9

"Der Tod und das Mädchen"

In lieder, as in life, things may not always be what they seem. In your analysis of "Der Tod und das Mädchen" (Death and the Maiden) you will find that awareness of the context of a poem and how a composer may manipulate its meaning are both crucial to a convincing performance of this song. Clues to the meaning of the poem may be found in its **poetic meter**, **line length**, and **vowel contrasts**. Important musical elements include **choice of key and tonal areas**, **contrasting vocal ranges and genres, monotone, rhythmic and melodic motives, linear motion,** and **unstable harmony and dissonance.** A word to the wise: don't believe everything you hear!

TEXT

1a) Summarize the dramatic scene in this poem: _____
_____
_____

1b) What emotion is expressed by the maiden, and how can you tell? _____
_____

1c) What emotion is expressed by Death, and how can you tell? _____
_____

1d) How does the contrast in emotion between the poem make you feel? _____
_____

The poem, published in 1775 by Matthias Claudius, expresses the *Empfindsamkeit* aesthetic as in his "An die Nachtigall." Claudius was the son of a pastor who produced a wide range of poetry and other writings, often in a folklike style. In the collected editions from which this poem is drawn, the poet underscores the importance of death by including as the frontispiece a skeletal figure with a sickle (a harvesting tool), calling him "Freund Hain." (Freund Hain was a traditional German metaphor for death, who we call the Grim Reaper, in use since at least the seventeenth century.)[1]

2) Given the poet's background, what do you imagine is his eighteenth-century view of death and why? _____
_____

Why do you suppose Claudius put the maiden first and followed her with Death instead of the other way around? _____
_____
_____

The subject of "death and the maiden" goes back to the Middle Ages and was often depicted visually through art. In understanding this song, you need to know that in many Germanic representations, death is shown as a male skeleton, often pursuing a nude or seminude maiden. The depiction of "death and the maiden" thus often resulted in an erotic painting or sketch.[2]

3) Given this context, reread the poem. How does the poem express eroticism? _____
_____
_____
_____

Do you see that there can be two possible meanings to this poem, a metaphor for a peaceful death or a sexual engagement on the part of Death?

Poetic Meter

Four common types of poetic meter are **iambic** (unstressed-stressed = ' /), **trochaic** (stressed-unstressed = / '), **anapestic** (unstressed/unstressed/stressed = ' ' /), and **dactylic** (stressed-unstressed-unstressed = / ' ').

4a) What is the poetic meter of strophe 1, spoken by the maiden? _____

How many feet (strong beats) are there per line? _____

Why do you think Claudius chose this poetic meter for the maiden? _____
_____

4b) What is the poetic meter of strophe 2, spoken by Death? _____

How many feet are there per line? _____

Why do you think the first line has a different number of feet than the rest of this strophe; what is different about it? _____
_____

"Der Tod und das Mädchen" 123

4c) Why do you think strophes 1 and 2 have a different number of feet? _____
_____
_____

4d) What is the rhyme scheme? _____

Is it the same in both strophes? _____

4e) Speak the last word of each line out loud. What sound (the vowel and whether it is long or short) is on the accented beat of each final word? Compare the two strophes and write in the vowel; circle whether long or short in German. The first two are done for you:

_i_ short/[long]   __ short/long
_a_ [short]/long   __ short/long
__ short/long   __ short/long
__ short/long   __ short/long

What is the relationship between the rhyme schemes of the two strophes and why?
_____
_____

4f) In poetry, when a line ends on an accented syllable, it is said to be "strong"; conversely, when a line ends on an unaccented syllable, it is called "weak." Read the poem out loud and determine the ending type of each line of poetry: write "S" or "W" at the end of each line. The first two are done for you:

_W_   ____
_S_   ____
____   ____
____   ____

Compare the pattern of strong and week endings in strophe 1 with strophe 2; what do you notice? _____

How does this compare with the length of vowel sounds used on the last syllable of each line of strophe 1 vs. strophe 2 (see 4e)? _____
_____

4g) Why do you think the poet contrasts the two strophes in these three ways: feet per line (4a and 4b), short and long vowel patterns (4e), and structure of strong and weak endings (4f)? _____
_____

4h) How will these discoveries affect the way you express the words in your performance?
_____
_____
_____

MUSIC

Key, Range

5a) In what key is this piece? (Hint: look at the final chord and key signature.) _____
Mozart's Requiem is also in this key, as is "Der Hölle Rache" from his opera *Magic Flute*, in which the Queen of the Night is the embodiment of evil when she demands that her daughter kill her father! The theorist C. F. D. Schubart describes this key as "Melancholy womanliness, the spleen and humours brood."[3] Do you see why Schubert may have written "Der Tod und das Mädchen" in this key?

5b) How clear is the key at the beginning of the piece, and how do you know? _____
_____
_____

6a) What is the vocal range for the first strophe? _____

Highest note and measures: ___ _____ Lowest note and measures: ___ _____

6b) What is the vocal range for the second strophe? _____

Highest note and measures: ___ _____ Lowest note and measures: ___ _____

6c) Why do you think Schubert made this choice? _____
_____

How will you bring out this contrast in your performance? _____
_____
_____

Piano Prelude

7a) Look at the bassline in the prelude (mm. 1–8): Which note is the most frequent and how many times does it sound? ____ ____

7b) Why do you think he keeps sounding that tone? _____
_____

7c) What is the significance of the cut time signature, do you think? _____
_____

7d) Write down the rhythmic motive in each bar of the prelude: _____
Schubert uses this long, short, short rhythm in many of his songs to suggest a funeral march. (See "Motive" in chapter 2 for other examples.)

7e) Listen to the melody in the right hand (mm. 1–8). Schubert was famous for the beauty of his melodies. Why do you think this melody is so limited in shape? _____
_____

How many semitone intervals do you find (count up and down as separate)? _____

Why do you think Schubert emphasizes this interval? _____
_____

7f) How does Schubert vary the tonic in m. 1, beats 3 and 4? (Hint: look at the top note of the left hand.) _____

What should the pianist keep in mind when performing this section? _____
_____

7g) How would you describe the register and spacing of the prelude chords? _____
_____

What effect does this have? _____
_____

The Maiden

Rhythm

8a) How does the rhythm of the piano part change in mm. 9ff.? _____
_____

What is the effect of the off-beat entrances? _____
_____

What range of the piano are we now in and why? _____
_____

How will you bring out the rhythmic and registral change in your performance? _____
_____

Do you hear Beethoven's 5th symphony? Nineteenth-century composers all had the weight of Beethoven on them, so this rhythm was not likely accidental.

8b) How does the rhythm of the piano part change again in m. 16, and what does it imply?
_____
_____

How can you express this in your performance? _____
_____

8c) Note that Schubert sets the iambic lines of the maiden with upbeat phrases. How does this express her mood? _____
_____

Melody and Linear Motion

9a) In what direction is the vocal melody moving in mm. 9–13 and why? _____

_____

To what word is the highest note set and why? _____

What is the interval between the maiden's first note and the highest note, and why?

_____

9b) What is the purpose of the appoggiaturas in mm. 8 and 9, and how will you bring this out in your performance? _____

_____

9c) Draw an imaginary line from the high E♭ in m. 13 to the next highest note, the D in m. 15, and continue following the line. In which direction is the vocal melody moving now and why?

_____

What is the interval from her highest note in m. 13 to her final note in m. 19? _____

What does this suggest? _____

9d) Why do you think she repeats "und rühre mich nicht an" twice, the second time at a lower level? _____

What is the melodic interval created by her second utterance of the phrase, and what does it tell you? _____

9e) Find three descending melodic fourth passages in mm. 16–21. Write the three sets of descending intervals: ___ to ___, ___ to ___, ___ to ___ What is the highest note at the beginning (m. 16)? ____ What is the lowest note (in the piano right hand) in m. 21? ____What's that interval, and what does it bode for the maiden? _____

Have we seen this descending interval before? _____

_____

9f) How does the rhythm of the vocal melody change in mm. 16–19, and where does the rhythm originally appear? (Hint: look at the piano rhythm.) _____

_____

What does this suggest about the situation? _____

_____

9g) Has Schubert included a hint of sexual frisson between the two characters of Death (male) and the maiden (female)? Examine the text and shape of the maiden's melodic line.

_____

_____

Harmony

10a) What is the harmony in m. 10 (chord and function)? _____

How close is this chord to tonic? (How do you move from tonic to this chord?)
_____

10b) What is the harmony in mm. 11 and 12 (chord and function)? _____ , _____

_____ , _____ Why do you think he set "wilder Knochenmann" to these harmonies?
_____
_____

10c) What harmonies (chord and function) set mm. 13–14 and why? _____ , _____

_____ , _____ _____

10d) Compare the harmonic functions of mm. 11–12 with 13–14; what is similar and how does it affect the mood? _____
_____
_____

10e) What harmonies (chord and function) set mm. 15–17 (first half)? (Assume the key of the phrase is a temporary tonic.) _____ , _____ , _____ _____ , _____ , _____ The half cadence suggests she is striving to reach a particular tonal level (key). So what lovely key is she striving to reach? _____ Does she cadence there; does she get her wish? ____

F major is not only the relative major of D minor, but also has positive attributes, described as "complaisan[t] and calm" by the theorist C. F. D. Schubart. Schubert the composer uses F major as a key of hope in this song, as well as in "Gretchen am Spinnrade" (also in D minor) and "Du liebst mich nicht" (in A minor); in all three, the protagonist strives to reach the key of F major, but fails.

10f) What harmonies (chord and function) set the repeat of the phrase in the second half of mm. 17–19? (Assume key of the phrase is a temporary tonic). _____ , _____ , _____ _____ , _____ , _____ Note that her attempt to reach that hopeful key has been replaced by transposition to a much darker key! Why do you think Schubert juxtaposes these two keys in this way? _____
_____

What does it tell you about her chances? _____
_____

10g) What harmony appears on the downbeat of m. 20—surprise!—and what do you think is its significance? _____

On what chord does this phrase end (m. 21), and what does this suggest? _____
_____

Death

11a) Compare the piano part of mm. 22–25 with mm. 1–4: What is the same and what is different? What element of music is missing and why? _____
_____
_____

11b) Notice the iambic lines of Death are not set with upbeat phrases, as were the maiden's, but with downbeat phrases. How does this help to portray his character? _____
_____
_____

11c) What is the key of mm. 22–25, and is it clear? _____
What type of cadence does Schubert use this time and why? _____
_____

11d) What happens to the melody in mm. 22–27? _____
_____

Schubert is known for his exquisitely beautiful melodies; when he composes a dull melody, a monotone, it is always to express something very specific. Why do you think Schubert writes this long monotone? (Hint: think who is speaking.) _____
_____

Some people think that the Devil is actually speaking through the maiden; others, that the singer must represent two separate characters. Which do you think is the case, and how will you express this transformation in your performance?

11e) Look at the vocal melody in mm. 22–29: Which note is the most frequent, and how many times does it sound? ____, _____ Where have we heard this before? (Hint: see question 7e.) _____
_____

11f) An old tradition in ringing funeral bells was to signify the age of the departed by the number of rings. In this case, what would have been the age of the maiden according to Schubert? _____

11g) How will you personify Death and suggest the sound of ringing funeral bells in your performance? _____
_____

12a) On what chord do we cadence in m. 29? _____

12b) What do you think is the significance of arriving at this level? _____
_____
_____

12c) Write in the harmony (chords and function) for mm. 26–29; circle the cadential chord.

_____, _____ _____, _____, _____

_____, _____ _____, _____, _____

12d) Look at the bassline in mm. 26–28 and write in the notes and the interval created between the first and last notes: ___ ___, ___ ___, ___ Interval: _____

Compare this motion with the vocal melody in mm. 16–17 and mm. 18–19, and the piano right hand in mm. 20–21: _____

What might Schubert be suggesting by this inversion? _____

_____

12e) Compare the bassline of mm. 20–21 with mm. 27–28: What do you notice about the direction, intervals, and function of the last chord? _____

_____

What might this express? _____

_____

12f) What chord appears on the word "Freund" (friend)? _____ Is this chord consonant or dissonant? _____ What do you think Schubert was trying to suggest about Death's character through the use of this chord on "friend"? Would you trust this person?

_____

13a) What note is repeated in the vocal melody in mm. 30–34, and how many times is it repeated? _____

13b) What two basic harmonies (chord and function) alternate in mm. 30–31?

chords: _____ and _____ function: _____ and _____

If we are still in the key we confirmed with the cadence in m. 29, what is the relationship between these two chords (hint: see question 11b about the type of cadence)?

_____

13c) What two harmonies alternate in mm 32–33? Write the chord names first:

_____–_____ Now write their function: _____–_____

13d) Which area is now being emphasized in mm. 32–33? (What chord does he keep moving to?) _____ This key is described by the theorist C. F. D. Schubart as "Cheerful love, clear conscience, hope, aspiration for a better world."[4] B♭ also had long-standing associations with sweetness and softness. Clearly Death is trying to persuade the maiden that he will be gentle, and Schubert therefore sets Death's sweet-talking lines with very sweet chords.

130   *Chapter 9*

13e) In what way is Schubert using these associations in mm. 32–33? _____
_____

What does it tell you about the character of Death? _____
_____

13f) What happens harmonically (chord and function) on the word "sanft" (soft)? _____
_____

Is this chord consonant or dissonant? _____ Does this chord sound "soft" to you? _____ Is this chord near or far in the circle of fifths from the chord of m. 33? ____

How near or far (how many steps = fifths away)?[5] _____

What is the melodic interval between B♭ and E? _____

Do you think Schubert intends us to believe what Death is saying? Why or why not?
_____

How will you convey this in your performance? _____
_____
_____
_____

14a) To what tonal level (chord) does the phrase end at the cadence in m. 37 (downbeat)?
_____ Is this a surprise? _____ Why do you think the cadence has been transformed? What could this imply? _____
_____

14b) Listen to the harmonies for m. 34 to the downbeat of m. 40. Does this sound like strong or weak motion to a cadence and why? _____ What do you think Schubert intends to show by this harmonic progression? _____
_____
_____

14c) Whether or not you plan to sing the low D at the end, what do you suppose is the effect of this extremely low note in performance? _____
_____

Why do you suppose Schubert would close this work with it? _____
_____

14d) Where does the tolling bell return in the vocal melody at the original level of D? _____

_____ How many separate D's are sung from mm. 33–38? _____ Add the number of F's in mm. 30–33 to the D's in 33–38 and what do you get? _____ What is the likely significance of this number? _____
_____

14e) Has Schubert included a hint of sexual frisson between the two characters of Death (male) and the maiden (female)? Examine the text and harmonies of Death's speech:
_____
_____
_____

15a) Carefully compare the piano postlude beginning at m. 37 to the end with the prelude in mm. 1–8. What is similar? _____
_____

What is different harmonically? _____

What is different melodically and why? _____
_____

Which inner melody remains almost the same? (Hint: it begins in m. 1 on F in the piano left hand.) _____

Why do you suppose the A in m. 38, beat 4 becomes a D and F♯ in m. 38, beat 4? ___
_____

15b) Compare the length of the two passages (piano prelude and postlude): How many bars are each? _____ _____ Which is shorter? _____

How is this accomplished (which bar is changed)? _____
_____

15c) Beginning with the second half of m. 37, how many chords are struck until the end? _____ Now why do you think Schubert may have altered the postlude? ___
_____

16a) Schubert is known for sometimes putting his own spin on the poetry he sets, even going so far as changing the original meaning—no wonder Goethe was suspicious of artistic settings of his poetry. In what way has Schubert changed or deepened the meaning of the poem through his musical setting? _____
_____
_____
_____

16b) Now summarize your views on the emotion and psychology of each character and what sets them apart. How will you express them in your performance of this song? Be specific.
_____
_____
_____
_____
_____

17a) What have you learned about the meaning of the song from your analysis? _____
_____
_____
_____
_____

17b) How will you express it through your performance? _____
_____
_____
_____
_____

NOTES

1. Graham Johnson, *Schubert: The Complete Songs* (New Haven: Yale University Press, 2014), 3: 344–45.

2. See particularly Hans Baldung's "Der Tod und das Mädchen" painting (Kunstmuseum, Basel) and drawing (Staatliche Museen zu Berlin, Perußischer Kulturbesitz) as well as similar works by Niklaus Manuel Deutsch, Hans Schwarz, and Barthel Beham, among other German sixteenth-century artists.

3. Christian Friedrich Daniel Schubart, *Ideen zu einer Ästhetik der Tonkunst* (Vienna: Degen, 1806), reprint, ed. P. A. Merbach (Leipzig: Wolkenwander-Verlag, 1924), quoted in Rita Steblin, *A History of Key Characteristics in the Eighteenth and Early Nineteenth Centuries* (Ann Arbor: UMI Research Press, 1983), 124–25.

4. Rita Steblin, *A History of Key Characteristics in the Eighteenth and Early Nineteenth Centuries*, 121–24.

5. While flat chords had associations with softness, sweetness, femininity, and life, chords on the sharper side (a, d, e) were often used to express hardness, death, and lamentation. These associations originated from the **durus-mollis contrast**, or the difference between soft B (B♭ = B-moll) and hard B (B♮ = B-dur). See discussion of the sharp-flat contrast in the "Choice of Key" section in chapter 3 of this book.

10

"An die Nachtigall"

How can a composer express that delicious state between sleeping and waking? In this chapter you will explore Schubert's use of **key ambiguity** and learn how a phrase can be in two keys at once! You will learn how the composer creates a **dreamy** mood and how you can bring it out in performance. If you are not familiar with **augmented sixth chords**, this chapter will serve as an introduction. While this poem may admit of several meanings, your close examination of the music will help to reveal the most likely intent. And finally, you will ask yourself what Schubert could possibly be telling us in his lighthearted piano postlude!

TEXT

1) Who or what is sleeping and must not be woken up? _____

   By whom? _____

   What is this poem actually about? _____
   _____
   _____

2) The poem was written in 1771 by Matthias Claudius and expresses the aesthetic of *Empfindsamkeit* (the sensitive style). How do you feel by the time you reach the end?
   _____
   _____

   Why? _____
   _____

   How is this poem different from a typical Romantic poem? _____
   _____
   _____

134 Chapter 10

3) Note that this poem consists only of a single stanza. What is the rhythmic meter of the poem? _____ (There are weak beats and strong beats; how many strong beats do you find per line?) _____ Is there an exception? _____
_____

4a) What is the rhyme scheme? _____

4b) What happens in the last two lines, and how does it make you feel to hear it? _____
_____
_____

5) Read the poem carefully. Who is the "Er" and "ihn" (He/him) in lines 1 and 2? Do you see the answer in line 6? _____
_____

6) Based on your answer to question 5, who do you think is singing this? Describe this character and why they may feel the way they do: _____
_____
_____
_____
_____

MUSIC

7a) What key is this piece in? (Hint: look at the final chord and key signature.) _____

7b) What key does this piece appear to start in (look at first chord)? _____

7c) Hmmmn. . . . How clear is the key at the beginning of the piece? _____

7d) What else makes the key unclear besides the first chord? (Hint: it's a note.) _____

7e) The poet and theorist C. F. D. Schubart describes C major as "completely pure. Its character is innocence, simplicity, naivety, children's talk" and G major as "everything rustic, idyllic, and lyrical, every calm and satisfied passion, every tender gratitude for true friendship and faithful love."[1] In what ways are these two keys appropriate to express the text of the poem?
_____
_____

7f) What is the vocal range? Highest note, measures: _____
lowest note, measures: _____ How would you characterize the vocal range, and why do you think Schubert made this choice? _____
_____

8) Look at the top line in the right hand from mm. 1–8:

   a) What interval is outlined between the first and last note? _____

   b) Does the top line move stepwise or by leap? _____

   c) In what direction does it move? _____

   d) Why does Schubert do this? _____

   e) Compare mm. 9–17 (where the voice first comes in) with the piano prelude (mm. 1–8). Where is it similar, and in which bar does it diverge? _____
   _____

9a) Where is the first cadence? Listen to the piano opening and raise your hand when you hear it. Write down the measure and beat of the cadence, along with the note (chord) it cadences to.
   _____

9b) How does the bassline set up the cadence in m. 7? _____

9c) How does this make you feel? _____
   _____

9d) Listen to the song and raise your hand each time you get to a cadence (circle it). Now go back and figure out what note the cadence went to. List the measure numbers and cadence levels. The first one is done for you.

   CADENCE CHART:
   m. 8:   G
   m. ___   ___
   m. ___   ___
   m. ___   ___
   m. ___   ___
   m. ___   ___
   m. ___   ___

9e) What do you notice about all the cadences in this piece? _____

9f) Why do you think Schubert chose to set his piece this way? What does it tell you about how he viewed the poem? _____
   _____
   _____

10a) Write the chords for mm. 1–8 in your score (one per bar except for mm. 6 and 7); then analyze the harmonies in both C and G and write them in the score. (Hint: to help you figure out the chords, note that Schubert uses suspensions throughout this phrase, and also includes a cambiata in mm. 2 and 4, which means the functional chord is not reached in the right hand until the third beat.) The first two chords are done for you.

$$C - G^4_3-$$
$$C: \quad I - V^4_3-$$
$$G: \quad IV - V^4_3/IV-$$
_____ _ _____ _ _____ _ _____ _ _____ _ _____
_____ _ _____ _ _____ _ _____ _ _____ _ _____
_____ _ _____ _ _____ _ _____ _ _____ _ _____

10b) What kind of chord appears in m. 2, and where does it want to go? _____

Does it go there? If not, where does it go instead? _____

How does the deceptive cadence make you feel? _____

Mm. 3–5 sit in this key (A minor), which works well in both C and G. Are we sleeping or waking? _____

10c) How far can you get in the key of C (include measure numbers)? _____

Can you see how easily Schubert could have cadenced to C in m. 7? How does it feel when we shift from the dreamy descent of mm. 1–6 to the sudden strong and articulated cadence to a different key in mm. 7–8? _____

10d) As usual, Schubert tells the entire story of the song in the piano prelude: we are dreaming along in one key, when suddenly we are rudely awakened in another! Notice that the primary key for text lines 1 and 3 is C, while the primary key of lines 2 and 4 is G. Am I awake or asleep?

11a) Why do you think Schubert selected a triple meter to set this poem? _____

11b) Look at the right hand of the piano in mm. 14–17 and 18–21: What rhythmic pattern do you see? _____

11c) What text line does it set? _____

11d) Why do you think Schubert used this rhythmic pattern for this particular text? _____

12a) What rhythmic pattern appears in the right hand of the piano in mm. 22, 24, 26, and 28? _____

12b) What do you think it represents? _____
_____

12c) How can the pianist bring this out? _____
_____

12d) Is there a similar representation in the voice part? Which measures? _____
_____

12e) How can the singer bring it out? _____
_____

12f) Why do you think the singer sings a single note from mm. 30–35? _____
_____
_____

12g) Write the chords of mm. 22–25: ____ ____, ____ ____ What is the primary key in this passage? _____ What function (Roman numeral) is this in the key of the piece?
_____

12h) Where else does IV play an important role in this piece? Next to each line of poetry at the top of your score, write the main key in which the line is set. What do you notice? ____
_____

Why do you think Schubert spends so much time in the subdominant in this song?
_____
_____

13a) Look at the rhythm and direction of the piano parts in mm. 30–34: What is happening?
_____
_____
_____

13b) What do you think it represents? _____
_____

13c) How can the pianist bring this out? _____
_____
_____

14a) What happens harmonically in m. 30? _____
_____

14b) Why do you think Schubert does this? _____
_____

Schubert sets the word "Amor" (Love) in m. 35 with a very special chord, an augmented sixth chord. Here we have a German sixth chord, which sounds like a dominant seventh chord (E♭ G B♭ C♯) but is written differently because the top note moves up, not down. Augmented sixths move strongly to an octave by contrary motion, with a semitone move up to the top note and a semitone move to the bottom note. Augmented sixth chords usually move to a I_4^6 or V chord; in this case the C♯ moves up to high D and the E♭ moves down to low D to create G_4^6 (I_4^6). Because they move so strongly in contrary motion, augmented sixth chords are very passionate chords—why else do you think Schubert used them to set "Amor"?

14c) What happens harmonically in m. 36? _____

_____

14d) How does it make you feel? _____

14e) What is the mood of the piano postlude and how is this created? Compare mm. 37–38 with mm. 39–40: what has changed, and how does it [slightly] affect the mood? _____

_____

_____

_____

15) How will you express the liminal experience of hovering between sleeping and waking in your performance? _____

_____

_____

16a) What have you learned about the meaning of the song from your analysis? _____

_____

_____

_____

_____

16b) How will you express it through your performance? _____

_____

_____

_____

_____

NOTE

1. Christian Friedrich Daniel Schubart, *Ideen zu einer Ästhetik der Tonkunst* (Vienna: Degen, 1806), reprint, ed. P. A. Merbach (Leipzig: Wolkenwander-Verlag, 1924), quoted in Rita Steblin, *A History of Key Characteristics in the Eighteenth and Early Nineteenth Centuries* (Ann Arbor: UMI Research Press, 1983), 124–25.

11

"Ave Maria" (Ellens Gesang III), D. 839

Schubert's "Ave Maria," the beautiful hymn to the Virgin, is beloved around the world. But not everyone understands its original context, or how this "simple" strophic song contains a powerful message rendered by Schubert through **choice of key**, **emphasis on a significant chord function**, and use of **pedal points, deceptive cadences,** and **stable or restricted linear motion**. Other elements you will find in this analysis are **augmented chords, suspensions,** and **surprise harmonic motion**.

As in "Der Tod und das Mädchen," two very different forces are opposed in this song. Do the analysis to figure it out, and you will have a greater understanding that will allow you to bring depth and meaning to your performance of this piece.

* * *

TEXT

The text is taken from Sir Walter Scott's long poem *The Lady of the Lake*, which contributed to Romanticism's overall fascination with the Scottish Highlands. The poem takes place during a clan rebellion against King James of Scotland. Schubert called it "Ellens Gesang" after the main character, whose father was a former advisor to the king but had been exiled. The king travels incognito and meets Ellen and falls in love. During this scene Ellen and her father are hiding in a cave because they do not support the rebellion against the king, and Ellen sings a prayer to the Virgin Mary.

1) To understand the context of this poem, it is helpful to be familiar with the ancient Latin prayer to the Virgin, *Ave Maria gratia plena* (see below). Begin by reading it out loud. Notice that it is in three parts: the first two originate from the Gospel according to Luke and represent a greeting and praise of Mary. The third line was added in the Renaissance and is a request for Mary's intercession and protection: "pray for us sinners now and at the hour of our death."

140 *Chapter 11*

Ave Maria, gratia plena	Hail Mary, full of grace,
Dominus tecum.	the Lord is with thee.
Benedicta tu in mulieribus,	Blessed art thou amongst women,
Et benedictus fructus ventris tui, Iesus.	and blessed is the fruit of thy womb, Jesus.
Sancta Maria, Mater Dei,	Holy Mary, Mother of God,
Ora pro nobis peccatoribus,	pray for us sinners,
Nunc et in hora mortis nostrae. Amen.	now and at the hour of our death. Amen.

2) Now read Scott's "Hymn to the Virgin" (below). Underline the sections that represent greeting and praise of the Virgin. Circle the sections that request assistance. With respect to the two functions (greeting/praise of Mary vs. request for intercessions), how is Walter Scott's poem structured? (Where is the praise/greeting and where the requests?)

_____

Which function predominates? _____

Why? _____

Sir Walter Scott's "Hymn to the Virgin"

Ave Maria! maiden mild!
Listen to a maiden's prayer!
Thou canst hear though from the wild,
Thou canst save amid despair.
Safe may we sleep beneath thy care,
Though banish'd, outcast, and reviled;
Maiden! Hear a maiden's prayer—
Mother, hear a suppliant child!
Ave Maria!

Ave Maria! undefiled!
The flinty couch we now must share
Shall seem with down of eider piled,
If thy protection hover there.
The murky cavern's heavy air
Shall breathe of balm if thou hast smiled;
Then, Maiden! hear a maiden's prayer;
Mother, list a suppliant child!
Ave Maria!

Ave Maria! stainless styled!
Foul demons of the earth and air,
From this their wonted haunt exiled,
Shall flee before thy presence fair.
We bow us to our lot of care,
Beneath thy guidance reconciled;
Hear for a maid a maiden's prayer,
And for a father hear a child!

3a) Compare the first stanza of Walter Scott's original with Storck's German translation. (The English translation in the score is not the original Walter Scott poetry excerpted from *The Lady of the Lake*, but is a retranslation into English of Storck's translation from the original poem into German.)[1] Next to each line of the Storck translation, write down 1) the rhyme scheme for each, and 2) whether the ending is strong (ends on accented syllable, indicated by "S") or weak (ends on unaccented syllable, indicated by "W"). The endings and the rhyme scheme for the first stanza of the original Scott poem are provided for you.

Walter Scott's original (first strophe)			**Storck's German translation**		
Ave Maria! maiden mild!	S	a	Ave Maria! Jungfrau mild,	__	__
Listen to a maiden's prayer!	W	b	Erhöre einer Jungfrau Flehen,	__	__
Thou canst hear though from the wild;	S	a	Aus diesem Felsen starr und wild	__	__
Thou canst save amid despair.	W	b	Soll mein Gebet zu dir hin wehen.	__	__
Safe may we sleep beneath thy care,	W	b	Wir schlafen sicher bis zum Morgen,	__	__
Though banish'd, outcast and reviled	S	a	Ob Menschen noch so grausam sind.	__	__
Maiden! hear a maiden's prayer;	W	b	O Jungfrau, sieh der Jungfrau Sorgen,	__	__
Mother, hear a suppliant child!	S	a	O Mutter, hör ein bittend Kind!	__	__
Ave Maria!			Ave Maria!		

3b) What is distinctive about the **rhyme scheme** of the Scott version? _____
_____

What happens to the rhyme scheme in the second quatrain (group of four lines)? ____
_____

> The poetic structure of the original Scott poem is **chiastic**: the second half is in reverse order compared to the first half. (The noun is "chiasm.") In a way it is similar to an arc in architecture.

3c) Does Storck's German translation preserve the rhyme scheme? _____
_____

3d) What is distinct about the endings of the Scott version (e.g., strong vs. weak)? _____
_____

3e) Does Storck's German translation preserve the ending pattern (strong vs. weak)? _____
_____ So the endings of the Storck translation are chiastic.

3f) Underline any **negative words** in lines 3–8 in Scott's poem. Now circle any **positive words** in the same poem. What do you notice? _____
_____
_____
_____

3g) Now do the same for Storck's German translation. How does the Storck structure differ from that of the Scott original? _____

Does it still show opposition between faith and despair? _____
_____

Poets often use the technique of juxtaposing opposite ideas in order to elicit a strong emotion in the reader/listener. Do you see how Scott opposes the ideas of **faith** and **despair** in this poem? Keep your eyes and ears open for this juxtaposition expressed not only through text, but also through harmony!

3h) Below is a literal English translation of Storck's German translation of the original Scott poem.[1] Underline any negative or despairing words and circle any positive words implying faith. What do you notice?

Storck's translation used by Schubert	**Literal translation of Storck's translation**
Ave Maria! Jungfrau mild,	Ave Maria! maiden mild!
Erhöre einer Jungfrau Flehen,	Listen to a maiden's entreaty
Aus diesem Felsen starr und wild	From this wild unyielding rock
Soll mein Gebet zu dir hin wehen.	My prayer shall be wafted to you.
Wir schlafen sicher bis zum Morgen,	We sleep safe until morning,
Ob Menschen noch so grausam sind.	However cruel men may be.
O Jungfrau, sieh der Jungfrau Sorgen,	O Maiden, behold a maiden's cares,
O Mutter, hör ein bittend Kind!	O Mother, hear a suppliant child!
Ave Maria!	Hail Mary!
Ave Maria! Unbefleckt!	Ave Maria! undefiled!
Wenn wir auf diesen Fels hinsinken	When we sink down upon this rock
Zum Schlaf, und uns dein Schutz bedeckt	To sleep, and your protection hovers over us,
Wird weich der harte Fels uns dünken.	The hard rock shall seem soft to us.
Du lächelst, Rosendüfte wehen	You smile, and the fragrance of roses
In dieser dumpfen Felsenkluft,	Wafts through this musty cavern.
O Mutter, höre Kindes Flehen,	Oh mother, hear a child's entreaties
O Jungfrau, eine Jungfrau ruft!	Oh Virgin, a maiden cries out!
Ave Maria!	Hail Mary!
Ave Maria! Reine Magd!	Ave Maria! Purest Maiden!
Der Erde und der Luft Dämonen,	Demons of the earth and air,
Von deines Auges Huld verjagt,	By the grace of your eyes expelled,
Sie können hier nicht bei uns wohnen,	Cannot dwell with us here.
Wir woll'n uns still dem Schicksal beugen,	Let us silently bow to our fate,
Da uns dein heil'ger Trost anweht;	Since your holy comfort touches us;
Der Jungfrau wolle hold dich neigen,	Incline in grace to a maiden,
Dem Kind, das für den Vater fleht.	To a child that prays for its father.
Ave Maria!	Ave Maria!

"Ave Maria" (Ellens Gesang III), D. 839

4a) What do lines 1–2 and 7–8 express in each poem? _____

_____

_____

What do the middle four lines (lines 3–6) express? _____

_____

_____

4b) How can you tell what she is feeling as she sings the words of her prayer? _____

_____

How can you express the feeling of prayer in your performance? _____

_____

_____

4c) To whom is the song addressed? _____

How do you know? _____

Where does the exhortation appear in each strophe? _____

_____

Why? _____

4d) Who is the speaker? (Review the story by Sir Walter Scott, summarized at the beginning of this chapter.) _____

What is she praying for? _____

Where is she spending the night? _____

What dangers does the speaker fear? _____

_____

How does the Virgin's blessing protect the speaker? _____

_____

Think of a time when you have been in a fearful situation and write down how you felt and what you did to protect or console yourself: _____

_____

_____

_____

4e) What two relationships to the Virgin does the speaker highlight in lines 7 and 8 of the first two stanzas? _____

What changes in lines 7 and 8 between the first and second stanza? _____

_____

_____

144 Chapter 11

How do lines 7 and 8 differ in stanza 3? _____

_____

For whom is she praying? _____ Why? _____

MUSIC

5a) Note the difference in phrase type between the downbeat setting of the refrain "Ave Maria" at the opening of each strophe and the upbeat setting of all the other lines of poetry. Why do you think Schubert creates this contrast? _____

_____

_____

_____

5b) In what key is this piece? Look up the description of this key in chapter 3 in the section called "Choice of Key" and write it below. Why do you think Schubert chose this particular key? _____

_____

_____

5c) What happens in the bassline (left hand) of the first two bars? _____

What is this technique called? _____ What positive attribute related to prayer could this technique possibly represent? _____

5d) Write in the chords of the first two bars: _____

_____

Now write in the function of these chords in Roman numerals. (Note that the chord in the right hand of the second beat of m. 2 does not accord with the left hand; how is this possible?) (Hint: see question 5c.)

_____

5e) The use of a secondary dominant points to a particular tonal area through a V-I motion. Which tonal level (Roman numeral) is emphasized in bars 1–2 by a secondary dominant? _____ Why do you think Schubert highlights this area to set a prayer? ___

_____

5f) Look at the shape of the right-hand arpeggios. What shape is created by the top notes across the two bars? _____ Why do you think? _____

_____

How can the collaborative pianist bring this out? _____

_____

"Ave Maria" (Ellens Gesang III), D. 839

6a) What two things finally happen in m. 3? (Hint: Which part enters, which part finally moves?) _____
_____

6b) Write in the chords and function (Roman numerals) for m. 3 and the downbeat of m. 4:

_____-_____-_____-_____ , _____

_____-_____-_____-_____ , _____

6c) What does m. 3 prepare for, and how is it done? _____
_____

What chord do we expect on the downbeat of m. 4? _____ Do we get it? _____ If not, what do we get instead? _____ What kind of cadence is this? _____

What emotion do you think the speaker feels? _____
_____

How do you feel? _____
_____

How do you want your audience to feel here? _____
_____

Why do you think Schubert does this? _____
_____

Does the phrase end here or does it continue? _____

6d) Write down the chords and function in the rest of m. 4 and the downbeat of m. 5:

_____-_____-_____ , _____

_____-_____-_____ , _____

What do we get on the downbeat of m. 5? _____

How does it make you feel? _____

Does the phrase end here? _____

6e) If you were to hold the first note of m. 3 and connect it to the downbeat of m. 4, what long note do you get? _____ What if you connected this note to the downbeat of m. 5: What very long note would you get from m. 3 to the downbeat of m. 5? _____ So the melody of these two bars is essentially what note? _____

7a) What happens in the bassline in m. 5? _____

146   Chapter 11

7b)   Write in the chord names in m. 5: ___–___–___–___ What is the chord on beat 3?
      _____ Is this chord consonant or dissonant? (Hint: Could you imagine sitting on it
      for a while, or does it feel like it needs to resolve somehow?) If you recognize the quality
      of the chord, write it here: _____

      How does it make you feel when you hear it? _____

      Why do you think Schubert puts this in? _____
      _____
      _____

      Can you see that this dissonance is created by the F♯ passing tone from F to G in the
      piano right hand? Your audience will be moved by this dissonance if you bring it out.

7c)   In m. 5, follow the note F in the right hand; what does it become on beat 3? _____

      Where does it move on beat 4? _____ Beat 3 is a characteristic example of
      nineteenth-century music in which chromatic voice leading is more important than the
      function of the chords. But it does contribute to a compelling sound: What chord does
      this chromatic motion create on beat 3, and what emotion does it express? _____
      _____

      What emotion do you find in line 2 of each verse? _____
      _____

      Write one word from each line that expresses this emotion or idea: _____
      _____

7d)   Look at the voice leading in the soprano line from m. 5 to the downbeat of m. 7. What
      note is sung on beat 3 of m. 5? _____ What note is sung on the downbeat of m. 6?
      _____ Do you see how this note is carried over? Where does it move on beat 2 of m. 6?
      _____ On beat 3? _____ What note do you get on the downbeat of m. 7? _____

      What pattern are you starting to see? _____

      What note appears on beat 4 of m. 7? _____ What note appears just before it? _____

      Where does the note on beat 4 of m. 7 reappear in m. 8? _____

      To what note does it land on beat 3? _____ Do you see how the whole section from m.
      5 to m. 8 represents a long melodic descent?

7e)   Regarding the cadence in m. 8: what Roman numeral would this represent in the origi-
      nal key of the piece? _____ Is this an expected key to cadence in? _____

      Why do you think Schubert moves to this area in this piece? (Think about the emotions
      created by expected/desired movements vs. those that are unexpected.)
      _____
      _____

If you write out the harmonies and analyze their functions, you can see that Schubert moves through three chords related to D minor (m. 5, beat 4 to m. 6, beat 2), three to G minor (m. 6, beat 3 to m. 7, beat 1), and then six in F (m. 7, beat 2 until the cadence in m. 8 on beat 3). The short sections of tonal instability add to the feeling of worry and pleading, but they are resolved through the clear and thorough cadential progression in mm. 7 and 8.

7f) On what note and in what measure is the high point of mm. 3–8? _____

Notice how close the high point is to the cadence; Schubert puts the point of greatest tension just before its resolution. How will you bring this out? _____
_____

7g) What idea does this high point set in stanza 1? Write down the line in English:
_____

How does this relate to line 4 in stanzas 2 and 3? _____
_____
_____

Do you see why the line rises so high here?

7h) Now go back to m. 1, in the beginning of the song. What do you notice about the direction of the piano arpeggios in the right hand, and what do they symbolize? _____
_____
_____

8a) In mm. 9–14, where is the high point (measure and beat), and what are the two notes?
_____
_____

8b) What is it called when the downbeat is a dissonance that resolves to a consonance? _____ What is the emotional result of this technique? _____
_____

Notice the *fp* marking exactly at this spot, which adds to the expression.

8c) A similar technique appears on beat 1 of m. 12 which links the two words ("Sorgen"/"Mutter," "Flehen"/"Jungfrau," and "neigen"/"Kind"). Translate these word pairs here: _____
_____
_____

9a) Name the two chords in m. 9 (beats 1–2 and beats 3–4): _____–_____ Now write down the chord functions (Roman numerals) in the keys of B♭ and in F:

B♭: _____–_____

F: _____–_____

Which key makes the most sense for this measure? _____

9b) Name the two chords in m. 10 (beats 1–2 and beats 3–4): _____–_____ Now write down the chord functions (Roman numerals) in the key of B♭:

B♭: _____–_____.

What kind of cadence is this, and how does it make you feel? _____

Which aspect of the poem does it suggest? _____
_____

10) Look at the right hand of the piano in m. 11 at the F – F♯–G motion on beats 1, 2, and 3. Compare this with the same motion in m. 5 (beats 2–4); do you see how Schubert uses linear motion to push the song forward and allow for colorful harmony? As in m. 5, linear motion overrides the purely functional: we move from F to D to c, which could be B♭: V–V/vi – ii (unusual but beautiful); after this follows a functional passage: a half cadence on beat three followed by a cadence progression to tonic in mm. 13–14. How can the pianist bring out this important chromatic motion? _____
_____

11a) In the voice part in m. 9, which is the main note in beats 1–2? ____ In beats 3–4? ____ In m. 10 for beats 1–2 and 3–4? ____–____

11b) Now do the same for mm. 11–14: m. 11, beat 1: ____ beat 2: ____ beat 3 (both eighth notes): ____–____; m. 12, beat 1: ____ beat 3: ____; m. 13, beat 1: ____; m. 14, beat 1: ____

11c) What interval do you get from the lowest to the highest and down again? _____

What is the approximate shape of this structure? _____

How well prepared is this structure? _____ How does the balanced and controlled nature of this structure make you feel? _____
_____

How does the structure of this melody line express the meaning of the poem? _____
_____

12a) Note how m. 14 is identical to m. 1, allowing each strophe of the song to be introduced by the same two-bar phrase. At the end of the third strophe, mm. 14–15 sound like the opening two bars. What is the significance of Schubert using the same two bars (mm. 14–15) both to begin and end each strophe? Think about the general mood of the work and its goal; what does Ellen pray for, and how would repetition of a cadence progression over a tonic pedal contribute to this goal? _____
_____

12b) Schubert adds an additional two bars (mm. 16–17) to close the work. What is the direction of m. 16, and how does it make you feel? _____
_____

* * *

This song is all about **faith despite adversity**! How will you express this in your performance? Make sure that you understand the subtle differences in each stanza of the text so that you can shape this strophic song in a way that gradually builds in meaning and emotion. The audience should feel fear and discomfort along with the miraculous wonder that Maria's power can sweeten and soften the roughest abode and chase away any demon or human wishing to do them harm.

Finally, this song reveals Ellen's deep and abiding love for her father, which is suggested in earlier stanzas, but only named in the very end of the poem, just before her final exhortation to the Virgin. If your audience is not weeping at this point, you're doing it wrong.

13a) What have you learned about the meaning of the song from your analysis? _____
_____
_____
_____
_____

13b) How will you express it through your performance? _____
_____
_____
_____
_____

NOTES

1. Scott's original poem, Storck's German translation of it, and an English line-by-line translation of Stork's German version by Richard Wigmore are found in Graham Johnson, *Schubert: The Complete Songs* (New Haven: Yale University Press, 2014), 3:166–67.

2. Johnson, *Schubert: The Complete Songs*, 3:166–67.

12

"Du liebst mich nicht" (D 756b)

In addition to his beautiful melodies, Schubert is particularly well known for his harmonic progressions, and sometimes they tell the story even better than the melody. When studying a Schubert song, listen carefully for all the cadences and mark them in your score. (This may take a few times listening while studying the score.) In what key a phrase cadences and where it avoids cadencing are often significant markers and may tell a story which goes much deeper than the text or the melody!

"Du liebst mich nicht" is an example of a song in which the opening cadence may not correspond to the original key, and your job is to find out why. Even more distinctive is a set of cadences that tell us something profound about the character: what they want, how they feel, and what they are left with.

Not everything about a song is clear from just the text; sometimes knowing the context in which the poem was written and the song was composed can change its meaning in significant ways, as you will find.

In this song you will create a **cadence map** in order to understand how the ordering of cadences (and **missing cadences**) can tell the story. Other aspects you will investigate include the use of **monotone**, the **choice of key**, the **shape of the melody**, **circling**, and a very characteristic **Romantic motive**.

* * *

During the early Romantic period, a number of poets were influenced by Persian poetry, particularly that of the fourteenth-century poet Hafiz. After the first translations into German became available in the very late eighteenth century, poets such as Goethe, Rückert, Heine, and Platen were inspired to write in the new style.

"Du liebst mich nicht" is a *ghazal*, which is a Persian form in five couplets with an internal rhyme and a refrain. These poems were typically about loss in a love relationship, which makes it the perfect form for this poem.

TEXT

1a) Read through the English translation of the poem carefully. What has happened to the protagonist in the poem, and how does this person feel? _____

List several emotions and explain how they are suggested in the poem. _____

1b) The poem can be divided into two parts (Hint: look at the punctuation). If each line of the poem is numbered in order (10 lines total), which lines are in the first half and which in the second? _____ How does the mood shift between the two parts?

1c) Read lines 7–8 carefully: "vermissen" means to miss, give up. Why would the protagonist "give up" the sun, the moon, and the stars? What is being implied here? _____

How will this understanding affect the way you perform this song? _____

1d) Is there a text refrain? If so, write it here, in German and English:

How many times does the text refrain appear in the poem (as opposed to the song)? __

How many times does it appear in the song? _____ Does this seem excessive? _____

2a) Read the German text of the first line out loud, emphasizing the accents so you can discover the meter. What kind of meter is "Mein **Herz** ist zer**ris**sen"? Is it triple (like a horse galloping) or duple (like a march)? _____ What meter is "du **liebst** mich **nicht**"?

2b) Does this metrical pattern continue throughout the poem (i.e., all lines in the same meter except for the phrase "du liebst mich nicht")? _____ Why do you think the poet does this? (Hint: How does the obstinate nature of this clash express the meaning of the poem?)

How will you incorporate this clash into your performance? _____
_____
_____

2c) Read the first line out loud again in German. Which consonants sound like hissing? Circle them. Why would Platen begin a poem with so much hissing? _____
_____
_____

2d) The ghazal generally contains an internal rhyme. The first of these is "zerrissen." What does this mean? _____ Why is this a key word? _____

Are there any rhymes for "zerrissen"? Write them all here, circling the hissing: _____
_____
_____

Now write their translations here: _____
_____

Note how each of these rhymes tells the story and expresses the protagonist's mood through a hissing sound![1]

MUSIC

Rhythm

3a) Listen to the song in its entirety, paying particular attention to the piano part. What **rhythmic pattern** appears over and over? (Hint: you will find it in mm. 1–2 and 3–4—it's five notes long—circle it.) Count the number of measures which contain this rhythmic motive (or variations of it) and write it here: _____ There are only fifty-six bars in the piece; is this a high percentage, and if so, what Romantic attribute is being conveyed? (Hint: see question 1d above.) _____ Schubert takes the obsessive quality in Platen's poem (already inherent in the ghazal form) and magnifies it by constructing the entire song around this rhythmic motive. Pianists, you are the perpetuators of obsession!

3b) In which two measures does this obsessive rhythm completely break down? What are the words these two measures set? (Hint: they are found in the last two stanzas of the poem, and they rhyme.) _____

Why do you think Schubert emphasizes these two words by holding them longer and breaking the rhythmic motive? _____

Some context on "Narcissus":

In order to answer this question, one must know the context behind the poem and its poet. Kristina Muxfeldt has written extensively about Platen and this song, reminding us that in a ghazal, the poet self-identifies in the final two lines. The flowers called "Narzissen" evoke the story of Narcissus, the beautiful Greek mythological figure who cannot love anyone else and only falls in love when he sees his own reflection—to disastrous result. In the nineteenth century, the figure of Narcissus (along with Ganymede and certain other beautiful men) was a way of suggesting homoerotic love during a time when this was not able to be openly discussed. Platen, the poet, had just experienced a difficult love affair with a man he specifically equated with Narcissus in his diary, writing "Hate and love, united in my breast, tear apart my heart" and later "When I think back on those days . . . when my entire heart was torn, I went so far as to wish a voluntary death for myself!"[2]

Before examining the harmonies of the song, think about the choice of key. Although you may know this song in A minor, it was originally composed in G♯ minor, a key that would have been considered extreme at the time. If you check the key descriptions of the poet and theorist Christian Friedrich Daniel Schubart in chapter 3, G♯ minor is described as "heart squeezed until it suffocates, wailing lament . . . difficult struggle!"[3]

Piano Prelude

4) As usual, Schubert tells the entire story of this song in the piano prelude. What is the key of the song? _____ On what chord does it begin? _____ To what chord is the first cadence in m. 4? _____ What is the function of this chord in the key of the piece (use a Roman numeral)? _____ Does this sound more positive or negative than the opening two bars of the piece? _____

The singer has not yet sung a note, yet the harmonic movement in the piano part reveals something of her emotion or her wish. What do you think it might be? _____
_____

> Cadencing immediately to the submediant (VI) is a bit unusual. Later in this analysis, we'll figure out why Schubert welcomes us with this distinctive opening. Note that no words have been spoken, but it magically moves to F! **(Hint: when something unusual happens in the opening of a song, there is always an important reason behind it!)**

5a) What is the general shape of the vocal melody in mm. 4–6? _____

Is one note more common than others? If so, which one? _____ Look at the vocal melody in measures 4–12; how many times do you hear that note? _____ Schubert is famous for writing beautiful melodies. Why do you think he opens this piece with such a repetitive melody line? (Hint: What text does it set?) _____
_____

5b) Look at the bassline in the left hand of the piano in mm. 1–2: What do you notice?
_____

> Schubert uses this **monotone** technique in order to express a character's flat affect (emotion) or depressed state. Further examples of intentional monotony may be found in "Meeres Stille" (see chapter 18).

Motive and Cadence Map

6a) What typical Schubertian motive do you find in mm. 5–12 (an interval)? _____

Go through the song and circle all the semitone motives!

6b) Go through the piece and find *every cadence* in your score (including in the piano introduction and postlude). Above each cadence write the name of the chord to which it cadences (e.g., B♭ or e) and circle it. You must listen to the music many times; **do not analyze this piece with only the score and no music!**

6c) After the first cadence to F in m. 4, what two cadence levels (notes) do you find in mm. 8 and 12? ___ ___ How does this relate to the key of the piece? _____

6d) Now write down the cadence levels (note name) in order from mm. 11–12 through to m. 28: (e.g., B, e, a, etc.)

12: ___   20: ___   24: ___   28: ___

6e) What do you notice about the direction of these cadences? _____

Given the text of the poem, what do you think Schubert is expressing about the protagonist's feelings with this direction and ordering of cadences? _____
_____
_____

6f) Which cadence level is missing in this ordering of cadences? (Which cadence level would be next in the pattern?) _____ Do we get it ever in this song? _____

6g) Look again at the harmonic movement in the opening four bars—on what chord did we cadence in m. 4? ___ Look again at which note is missing in the sequence of cadences (question 5b). Now can you imagine what this sudden shift in the opening four bars could mean (the one not achieved in the body of the song)? _____

Second Half

7a) How many measures are in this song? _____ Which measure is the exact halfway point? _____ Notice that the bar after this point is where Schubert begins the second half of Platen's poem, at "So soll ich die Sterne" (see question 1b above), and everything changes here. How does the psychological state of the protagonist change at this point?
_____

7b) Notice that all the phrases in the first half of the song begin with an upbeat across the bar. How does this change in the second half and why (beginning in m. 29)? _____
_____

How will you incorporate this understanding into your performance? _____
_____

7c) What is the name of the chord in the piano part in mm. 29–31 (downbeats)? _____ Where does this dissonant chord want to resolve? _____ Notice that our protagonist is trying again to reach the beautifully positive chord that the piano prelude moved to in m. 4!

7d) Write the names of the two bass notes in each bar of mm. 29–31: ___ ___ Notice how the two bass notes **circle** around the note F.[4]

> **Melodic circling** is a way in which composers can emphasize a particular note without necessarily landing on it. Semitone circling creates an even stronger push. In this case the bassline circles around the note that the protagonist has been trying in vain to reach!

7e) Notice the falling thirds in the melody line at "Sterne" and "Mond" (mm. 30–31); Graham Johnson points out that they sound like sobs.[5] How will you perform this passage?

_____

_____

8a) Name the downbeat chord in mm. 32 and 33: ___, ___What key is implied here? ___

8b) Mm. 29–33 (downbeat) are sequenced up a semitone. What key is implied here? ____

> Note that the **semitone motive** now appears at the level of the phrase: instead of just a melodic semitone relationship between two notes (A-B♭, as in, for example, the melody of m. 6), Schubert elevates this relationship to that of tonal area: one phrase in A minor and the other in B♭ minor. The use of motive at different levels of scale, **motivic parallelism**, is very common in nineteenth-century music and can often be found in Schubert songs.

8c) But just as we expect to land on an F^7 chord on the downbeat of m. 37 (sequencing the downbeat of m. 33 up a semitone), we are suddenly wrenched out of our comfort zone. Name the chords on the downbeat of mm. 37 and 38: _____ _____ In what key have we cadenced on in m. 38? _____What relationship does the B♭ minor section now have to the key of A minor? (Hint: it's related to a city in Italy!) _____

This same wrenching motion is repeated in mm. 38–40. (Notice the piano doubling of the voice part in mm. 32–33 and 36–40.) How will you and your collaborative pianist express these painful moments? _____

_____

9a) What surprise harmonic shift happens on the downbeat of m. 40? _____

> When Schubert shifts suddenly to major in a minor-key work, it is not necessarily a happy transformation, but often a signal of a shift to fantasy according to Kristina Muxfeldt.[6]

Notice also that the falling minor third sobs have now been inflected upward and we temporarily stay in A major (mm. 40–42), but thoughts of suicide "die Sonne vermissen" jump out with help not only from the highest note in the voice part and the lowest in the bassline (m. 43), the fortissimo dynamic marking, but also the sudden break from the monotonous (or obsessive) five-note rhythmic pattern that has led us inexorably to this point. What is the bass note on the downbeat of m. 43? _____ On what notes are the **semitone motive** in the bassline of mm. 42–43? _____–_____ What is the chord on the downbeat of m. 43? _____ Schubert writes another **harmonic semitone motive** if you compare the downbeat of m. 43 and of m. 45; write the two chords next to each other:_____ _____

9b) Mm. 45–49 are a repeat of the bassline of mm. 40–45, but instead of the cadence (as in m. 45), we are jerked back and forth in syncopation, with the voice singing an accented semitone and the bassline pounding out low E to prepare for a terrific cadence in m. 52.

Postlude

10) Carefully compare the piano postlude (mm. 52–56) with the prelude (mm. 1–4). Does the postlude cadence on F like the prelude? _____ Do we get any F major at all, and if so, where? _____ What is the bass motion to the next chord? _____
_____

Recognize the interval? _____
_____
_____

* * *

In this piece the protagonist has been searching for the elusive F major, but can never reach it. The opening shift from the reality of A minor to a cadence in F major happens only in their mind; it is the hope for love (see "Gretchen am Spinnrade," chapter 16, in which F major again is the hoped-for key). The first half of the song gradually slides down chromatically from A minor trying to reach F, but stops just short. The second half begins with strong but incomplete motion to F (E diminished chords, with melodic circling of F in the bass notes E and G-flat) and then emphasizes the semitone motive with harmonic motion to B♭ minor (semitone above) and G♯[7] (semitone below) tonic A minor. The postlude is the clincher: it opens on A minor as in the prelude, and—after a tantalizing measure on F major—we move by Phrygian (semitone!) motion to E to close in the truth of A minor.

11a) What have you learned about the meaning of the song from your analysis? _____
_____
_____
_____
_____

11b) How will you express it through your performance? _____

_____
_____
_____
_____

NOTES

1. Schubert originally wrote this song in what was for him the unusual key of G♯ minor, which Graham Johnson suggests may be a way of expressing extreme emotions. Graham Johnson, *Schubert: The Complete Songs* (New Haven: Yale University Press, 2014), 1:451–53.

2. Kristina Muxfeldt, *Vanishing Sensibilities* (Oxford: Oxford University Press, 2011), 176–80, 199–200.

3. Christian Friedrich Daniel Schubart, *Ideen zu einer Ästhetik der Tonkunst* (Vienna: Degen, 1806), reprint, ed. P. A. Merbach (Leipzig: Wolkenwander-Verlag, 1924), quoted in Rita Steblin, *A History of Key Characteristics in the Eighteenth and Early Nineteenth Centuries* (Ann Arbor: UMI Research Press, 1983), 124–25.

4. David Gramit, "Orientalism and the Lied: Schubert's 'Du liebst mich nicht,'" *19th-Century Music* 27, no. 2 (2003): 104.

5. Johnson, *Schubert: The Complete Songs*, 1:452.

6. Muxfeldt, *Vanishing Sensibilities*, 173.

13

"Lied der Mignon" ("Nur wer die Sehnsucht kennt")

Composers like Bach and Handel were known to rework their music into new pieces, making adjustments as necessary. In "Lied der Mignon," Schubert reuses an earlier song and adds a passionate recitative to fit the final lines of the poem.

This chapter includes examples of many different melodic techniques including the **outlining of important intervals** ("connect the dots," usually referred to as linear motion), **motives at different levels of scale**, **melodic circling**, and **chromatic linear motion**. The question of **functional harmony vs. voice leading**—or both—is explored, as well as the emotional effects of **harmonic instability**, **harmonic oscillation**, **sudden harmonic shifts**, and **drone fifths**. As in most songs, there is **modulation** and the use of **pivot chords** and the recitative provides a clear instance of the rhythmic device of **removing downbeats** to create forward motion.

The poem, originally from Goethe's *Willhelm Meister*, was set by Beethoven, Schubert, Schumann, Wolff, and Tchaikowsky, among others. Schubert himself set it six times, including as a duet between Mignon and the Harper. This famous setting is the fourth song of Schubert's *Gesänge aus Wilhem Meister* (op. 62, D.877, nos. 1–4). In his final attempt at setting this text, he simply borrows a previously composed song, "Die stille Land," adding an introduction/postlude and a new dramatic middle section.

In Goethe's novel the poem appears as a duet sung by Mignon and the Harper in the background of Wilhelm Meister's reverie of longing. The irony in the book was that Mignon herself was not physically "far away" from Wilhelm Meister whom she secretly loved, but in addition to being far from her homeland (from which she'd been abducted as a child), she was separated widely from him by fate.

"Lied der Mignon" ("Nur wer die Sehnsucht kennt")

TEXT

1) What is the subject of the poem and its main point? _____
   _____
   _____

2) What images and concepts of Romanticism do you find in the poem? _____
   _____
   _____

3a) What do you notice about the rhyme scheme? Try writing the rhyme scheme in letters (e.g., a, b, c, etc.) and you will discover it. Why do you think Goethe does this? _____
   _____
   _____

3b) What is the poetic meter (poetic foot and number of feet per line, and type of ending (strong or weak)? _____
   _____

4) What do you think of when you read this poem? Write down any similar experiences you have had, or anything this poem brings to your mind: _____
   _____
   _____
   _____

MUSIC

Mood and Form

5a) Listen to the song while you follow the score. How does the mood of the music change as the song proceeds? _____
   _____
   _____

5b) What formal sections do you hear? List the measure numbers of each small section, its length (in brackets), the dynamic level (in parentheses), and a brief description (what changes). The first section has been done for you:

    mm. 1–6   [6] (pp) piano prelude
    mm. ___-___,   [ ] ( )
    mm. ___-___,   [ ] ( )
    mm. ___-___,   [ ] ( )
    mm. ___-___,   [ ] ( )
    mm. ___-___,   [ ] ( )
    mm. ___-___,   [ ] ( )

5c) What do you notice about the dynamic level of each section? _____
_____

What technique do you need to be able to sing almost the entire song pianissimo? ___
_____

5d) What is the lowest note in the voice part? ___ The highest note? ___ How would you characterize the vocal range? _____
_____

Why do you think Schubert sets this text with this particular vocal range? _____
_____

5e) How many measures in this song? _____ Which measure is midpoint? _____

Anything interesting happen at this place? _____
_____
_____

> Always look for the **midpoint** or middle phrase of a song—you may find something interesting!

5f) This song is Schubert's sixth setting of this text. After five tries he finally reached back to an earlier song, "Ins stille Land!" and used his second version of that piece to set this text, adding only twelve bars that were truly new. Can you guess which bars they might be? mm. ___-___

5g) If this were an opera, how would you characterize those bars? _____

5h) The character of Mignon originally came from Italy from which she was abducted as a child. Do you suppose Schubert might have been suggesting Italian bel canto opera here? He was suffering from the overpopularity of Italian opera in Vienna (the Rossini craze) and was having trouble getting his own operas performed, as the Hapsburgs favored Italian culture. What aspects of this song remind you of bel canto opera?[1] _____
_____
_____

Before delving into the harmonies, think about the key that was chosen. The poet and theorist C. F. D. Schubart describes the key of A minor as appropriate for "pious womanliness and tenderness of character.[2] Does this seem to express the personality of the protagonist of this song?

Piano Prelude

6a) The usual function of the piano prelude in a Schubert song (in addition to introducing the key, meter, and basic melody) is to tell you what the song is about. What does this prelude tell you about the piece? _____

6b) The prelude begins and ends on which note? _____ In what key is the piece? _____
What chords are i, iv, and V in this key? _____

6c) What note is featured in the bassline of the prelude, and why doesn't it move? _____
_____

What do you think it suggests about the protagonist? _____
_____

6d) Why do you suppose Schubert puts the right hand in octaves?[3] _____
_____

What is the marked dynamic and style marking? _____

How is the pianist going to do this? _____

7a) What direction do the first five notes in the right hand move and by what interval? __
_____

7b) If you were to substitute just one melody note for the first two bars, what would it be? (Hint: the phrase begins and ends on this note.) _____ What is the interval to move to B♭ in m. 3? _____ On what melody note does the phrase end in m. 6? _____ So if you took the long view, the prelude is basically a long note with an upper neighbor over it. But what a neighbor! What do you think m. 3 is trying to say?

How will you bring this out in performance? _____
_____

7c) Look at the melodic descent from the B♭ in m. 3 all the way down to the B♮ in m. 4. What is this interval? _____ How does this bode for Mignon? _____

> Schubert often **outlines** a dissonant interval as a way of prefiguring the fate of a protagonist (see "Meeres Stille," for example).

8a) Write in the chords and function for the prelude (two chords per bar except for mm. 5–6). Note that some of the chords are over a tonic pedal, where the note A does not form part of the chord.

_____–_____, _____–_____, _____–_____, _____–_____, _____, _____

_____–_____, _____–_____, _____–_____, _____–_____, _____, _____

8b) In which secondary area do you spend a bar and a half? _____

What do you think this means? _____
_____

> Notice that Schubert uses the technique of **melodic circling** to push to the area of D minor: the top line of the left hand in mm. 2 and 3 emphasizes D♯ and C♯, circling D, which arrives in m. 4. (See "Der Neugierige" for an introduction to this technique.

To sum up the prelude: You are listening to a lovely rising melody—suddenly you stub your toe (the D♯ in m. 2 left hand). Ouch! Then you see something that makes you suddenly panic—the B♭ in m. 3 (supported by a fully diminished 7th!) and you fall to the floor in a faint (melodic descent outlining a dissonance in mm. 3–4) in the wrong key (pointing to the subdominant area), and finally turn back to tonic in m. 5. So if you were wondering if this song might bode well or ill for Mignon, what would the introduction tell you and why?

_____
_____
_____

9) Read the English translation of the poem "Ins stille Land" (below) whose music Schubert eventually used to base his final attempt at setting "Nur wer die Sehnsucht kennt." What do the two poems have in common, both literally and metaphorically?

_____
_____

Ins stille Land![4]
By Johann Gaudenz von Salis-Seewis

To the land of rest!
Who will lead us there?
Already the evening sky grows darker with cloud,
And the shore is ever more strewn with flotsam.
Who will lead us gently by the hand
Across, ah, across
To the land of rest?

To the land of rest!
To the free, ennobling spaces!
Tender morning dreams
Of fine souls! Pledge of a future life!
He who faithfully won life's battle
Carries the seeds of his hopes
To the land of rest.

O land
For all those threatened by storms.
The gentlest harbinger of our fate
Beckons us, brandishing a torch,
And leads us gently by the hand
To the land of the great dead,
The land of rest.

"Lied der Mignon" ("Nur wer die Sehnsucht kennt")   163

The second version of "Ins stille Land," which Schubert used for this song, is in the form ABA'. The composer used the A section of the earlier song to set mm. 7–14, the B section to set mm. 16–21, and the A' section to set mm. 34–46. Schubert added an extra bar as m. 15 and added two completely new sections (mm. 22–26 and mm. 27–33) which first extend the B section and then insert a dramatic recitative into the song.

Section A (mm. 7–15)

10a) Tessitura: What is the range of the vocal part? _____ Is this narrow or wide? _____

Why do you think Schubert made this decision? (Hint: think of both the mood and the age of the person singing.) _____
_____

10b) How does Schubert set the left hand, and what might it evoke? _____
_____

Does any of this appear in the piano prelude? _____

What other part of mm. 7 ff. appears in the prelude? _____
_____

10c) Sing the vocal melody of mm. 7–8 and note that it begins and ends on the same note. Circle the note the first time it appears (downbeat of m. 7). It is as if these two bars were a variation of that one note. Now do the same with mm. 9–10. Measures 11–14 form one phrase: do the same with this phrase. What essential melody do you get from mm. 7–14? _____

> Composers often present their motives at different levels of scale, a technique called **motivic parallelism**. In this case we see the A-B-C motive now appears stretched out over eight measures (mm. 7–14). Motivic parallelism also appears in "Du liebst mich nicht" when the semitone motive is expanded to the level of the phrase, with one phrase a semitone higher than the previous phrase.

10d) Listen to mm. 7–14 and notice when you reach a cadence in m. 14. What key has been tonicized? _____ How does this relate functionally to the key of the piece? _____

Might this be an expected area to turn to? _____

10e) How do we get to the new key? Which chord is the pivot chord, and how does it function in the old key and in the new key? Note how the change from F♮ to F♯ in the bassline changes the function of the chord. Include both of these chords.

m. ___   chords ___ ___   functions (key of piece) ___ ___   function (new key) ___ ___

Section B (mm. 16–21)

11a) How does the rhythm of the piano part change in m. 16 and following? _____
_____

What emotional effect does this new rhythm create? _____

Note the accents which create a stinging effect here, often used by Schubert to express pain and sorrow.

11b) What is the harmonic surprise in m. 16? _____

To what key does it move in m. 18 (arriving on the second half of the bar)? _____

Go backward from m. 18 and figure out the chord names and functions going back to m. 16. Now write them forward in order from mm. 16–18, both names and functions according to the key to which it moves. (Note the double neighbor tone on the first half of m. 18 which resolves on the second half.)

_____-_____, _____-_____, _____-_____

_____-_____, _____-_____, _____-_____

11c) How can the first chord of m. 16 function as a pivot (on the way to the chord in m. 18)? Write the two possible keys and function of the chords for each.

___: _____

___: _____

11d) Is moving to G minor normal in the key of A minor? _____ Why do you think Schubert is going to faraway keys to set this text? _____
_____

> **Offbeat rhythms** create tension and push the music forward. A **sudden harmonic shift** changes the mood.

12a) What is the chord and function of m. 21 in the key of the piece? _____

What kind of cadence is this? _____

12b) How did we return to the key of the piece? Go backward from m. 21 to m. 19 and figure out the chords and possible function in both the key of the piece and the key of m. 18. (Hint: the chords in m. 19 are related to the first half of m. 20.) Now write them out in order from m. 18 to m. 21. Leave them blank if they are no longer in the key.

	m. 19	*m. 20*	*m. 21*
Chords:	_____-_____,	_____-_____,	_____
Function (in a):	_____-_____,	_____-_____,	_____
Function (in g):	_____-_____,	_____-_____,	_____

Which bar is the pivot between the two keys? _____

"Lied der Mignon" ("Nur wer die Sehnsucht kennt") 165

12c) Compare the two moods expressed in the first and second halves of this section: "Allein und abgetrennt von aller Freude" ("Alone and separated from all joy," mm. 16–19) vs. "seh ich ans Firmament nach jener Seite" ("I look to the heavens in that direction," mm. 19–21). Can you now explain why Schubert shifted to the parallel minor in m. 16 and returned to the home key in mm. 19–21, ending in a half cadence?

_____
_____
_____
_____
_____

Section C (newly composed for this song, mm. 22–26)

13a) Observe the bassline in mm. 22–26; describe what it's doing: _____
_____

Now figure out the chords and functions and write them out:

Chords: ___-___-___-___-___

Function: ___-___-___-___-___

13b) What is this compositional technique called when you go back and forth between two chords? _____ How does it make you feel? _____
_____

Why do you think Schubert includes the technique to set the text line "Ach, der mich liebt und kennt, ist in der Weite" (Ah, he who loves and knows me is far away)? _____
_____
_____
_____

13c) What is the dynamic level of this section? _____ Why do you think Schubert uses this extremely soft dynamic level only in this section of the song? _____
_____
_____

> **Harmonic oscillation** can be used to induce a feeling of stasis—we're lulled by it and may drift off into sleep. This passage sounds like a lullaby.

Section D (newly composed for this song, mm. 27–33)

14a) How do the rhythm and intervals in the piano part create the effect of dramatic recitative in mm. 27–33? _____
_____

Are the piano harmonies consonant or dissonant? _____

What makes the voice part a recitative? _____
_____

How is the phrase type (upbeat versus downbeat) different from the rest of the song?
_____
_____

14b) What's that note in the left hand in mm. 27–28? ____ Where have we heard that note sticking out before? (Hint: start at the beginning of the song.)

14c) Write down the bassline from mm. 27–33:

___-___-___-___-___-___

Notice that the intervals between the five notes are symmetrical: two semitones on either side of the central whole step. What is the interval created across this section (from the first to the last note)? _____ What message is it sending? _____
_____

14d) **This chromatic bassline structures the harmonies across this section.** Some of this section is **functional** at the same time as it is moves by voice leading, controlled by the chromatic bassline (mm. 31–33). Other sections are thrilling despite or perhaps because they **move primarily through voice leading** (mm. 27–30).

> **Strong bassline motion is often used to structure harmonies**, which may move through **functional harmony**, **voice leading**, or **both** at the same time! Using voice leading to guide the harmony can allow for rich and surprising sounds.

OPTIONAL SECTION (MORE ADVANCED HARMONIC WORK)

Mm. 31–33 (functional harmony and voice leading)

15) Going backward from m. 33, write in your score the names of the harmonies from mm. 31–33. Now write the chord names and functions (going forward) of mm. 31–33 below, according to the key of the piece:

_____-_____, _____-_____, _____-_____,

a: _____-_____, _____-_____, _____-_____,

As you will see, mm. 31–33 function in the key of the piece, beginning with a secondary dominant in m. 31 to the dominant in m. 32, and ending in a half cadence in m. 33, to prepare for the return of the opening melody.

"Lied der Mignon" ("Nur wer die Sehnsucht kennt")

Mm. 27–30 (voice leading more important than functional harmony)

16a) Moving back to the beginning of the recitative: What is the chord on m. 27, and where does it want to move to harmonically? _____

Melodically? _____

16b) Play the chord in m. 28; what does it sound like (what is its quality)? _____

How is it spelled, however? _____ What function is suggested by the B♭ and the G♯? (Hint: they both want to resolve to an A, so what kind of chord is this?) _____

_____ To what chord might this resolve? _____

16c) Does m. 28 move to where you want to go melodically (i.e., the top note)? _____
Does it resolve to where you want to go harmonically? _____ How does this make you feel? _____
_____

Exactly how does the chord shift between mm. 27–28? (What note stays the same, which notes move what interval in what direction?) _____
_____

Do you see how raising each note in the right hand by a semitone adds to the tension?

16d) To what chord does it actually resolve in m. 29 (name and function in the key of the piece)? _____ _____ Do you feel resolved in any way? _____ Why not? _____
_____

16e) Name the second chord in m. 29: _____ What does a $^6_4$ chord usually signal? _____

_____ So what are we expecting afterward and to what key? _____

Do we get one on the downbeat of m. 30? ___ What chord do we get instead? _____

Notice the enharmonic respelling in m. 30: the second chord sounds exactly the same, but is spelled differently. Name the newly spelled chord and its new function: _____
_____

17a) Summarize harmonic and linear (related to voice leading) techniques used by Schubert to created drama and tension in the entire recitative section (mm. 27–33).

_____
_____
_____
_____
_____

17b) How does it feel to be moving in a confusing, nonfunctional way, shifting primarily through voice leading? Do you see how **Schubert evokes Mignon's feelings of sadness and isolation through the instability in the harmonies**?

A' section (mm. 34–40)

18a) How does the return of the opening section differ this time and why (think about harmonic movement and also the highest note)? What does it tell you about the mood or state of the protagonist? _____

18b) Why do you think Schubert changes the accent from "Sehnsucht" in m. 12 to "kennt" in m. 39, adding a *fz* and crescendo in the piano? _____

What chord and function sets the word "kennt" here, and how does it make you feel? _____

CHAPTER SUMMARY

19a) What have you learned about the meaning of the song from your analysis? _____

19b) How will you express it through your performance? _____

NOTES

1. John H. Gingerich, *Schubert's Beethoven Project* (Cambridge: Cambridge University Press, 2014), 53; and Graham Johnson, *Schubert: The Complete Songs* (New Haven: Yale University Press, 2014), 1:697.
2. Christian Friedrich Daniel Schubart, *Ideen zu einer Ästhetik der Tonkunst* (Vienna: Degen, 1806), reprint, ed. P. A. Merbach (Leipzig: Wolkenwander-Verlag, 1924), quoted in Rita Steblin, *A History of Key Characteristics in the Eighteenth and Early Nineteenth Centuries* (Ann Arbor: UMI Research Press, 1983), 124–25.
3. There is no prelude in the original song ("Ins stille Land!").
4. Translation by Richard Wigmore in Johnson, *Schubert: The Complete Songs*, 2:209.

14

"Du bist die Ruh"

What can one say about this exquisite song? A perfect union of Persian-influence poetry (see "Dass sie hier gewesen" for more on this trend) and transcendent harmonies, "Du bist die Ruh," makes any lieder lover sigh. Like "An die Musik," it is what I call a warm bath song, staying primarily in one key and saturating the listener with a feeling of well-being. And when it does finally modulate, it takes us to unexpected heights through smooth voice leading and a chromatic mediant. In this song you will learn about the **Neapolitan relationship**, **"sweet keys"** (in the flat area), and **suspensions**, and in the holiness and beauty of the song you will find rest.

* * *

TEXT

1a) What is the mood of this poem? How do you feel when you read it and why?
_____

1b) Not all is rest in this poem. What opposites do you find? _____
_____

Which stanza contains no opposites at all? _____

What images appear there? _____
_____

Circle the word "you" or "I" (or "me"/"my") everywhere it appears in the poem. Is stanza 1 mostly about "you" or "I"? _____ Stanza 2? _____ How does this change in stanzas 3–5? _____
_____

1c) The title of the original poem was actually "Kehr' ein bei mir" (Come commune with me) and not "Du bist die Ruh" (You are rest). The latter title resulted from an editor's use of the first line for a title.[1] How does this change your original impression of the poem? _____

_____

How does what you discovered in question 1b support the title of the original poem?

_____

2) To whom or to what is the poet speaking? Open your mind up to as many possibilities as you can! List and support them using references to the text (use stanza number and line number; e.g., "in stanza 3, line 2"): _____

_____
_____
_____
_____
_____

3) What elements of Romanticism do you find in the poem? Underline all words in the text that show Romantic expression. _____

_____
_____
_____

4) How many stanzas are there? _____

5) What is the rhythmic meter of the poem? (What is the foot, and how many accents are there per line?) Why do you suspect the poet might have used such short lines in this poem? _____

_____

6) Does each stanza follow the same meter and rhyme scheme? Write in the rhyme scheme for each stanza (e.g., abab) using the same letter for each line that rhymes. What do you notice about the middle stanza? _____

What is the rhyme scheme and where does it come from? _____

_____

Underline all the verbs in the poem. How does the poem change from stanza 2 to the following stanzas? (Hint: think about the grammatical mood of the verbs.) _____

_____

What do you think the poet might have been suggesting by placing these rhymes in the central stanza? _____

_____
_____

7) What do you think of when you read this poem? Write down any ideas or emotions this poem brings to your mind: _____
_____
_____
_____

MUSIC

8) Listen to the song while following the score in which you have added your translation. How does this song (as opposed to just the poem) make you feel? Write down a few adjectives: _____
_____
_____
_____

9a) Which words in the poem do you think Schubert has brought out in general and why?
_____
_____

9b) What is your absolute favorite section of this piece and why? (Use measure numbers.)
_____
_____
_____

9c) What is the primary dynamic level? What mood does this create? Where does the dynamic level change? (Be aware that any marking in brackets means it was added by an editor and is not original.) What words does it set? What is the effect of the sudden reversion to *pp*? _____
_____
_____
_____

9d) In what key is this song? How does the key express the meaning of the poem? Look at chapter 3 under "Choice of Key" to find what the theorist Christian Friedrich Daniel Schubart said about this key, and write it here: _____
_____
_____

Do you think his choice of this key was accidental? _____

Rhythmic Motive

10a) Describe the register and the position of the hands (close together, far apart?): _____

_____

Why do you think the composer made this choice? _____

_____

10b) Clap out the rhythm of the left hand in mm. 1–2. Where is the next place you hear this rhythmic motive? _____ So, what words is the left hand "singing" in mm. 8–9?

_____

Now listen to the whole piece and clap this rhythm every time it appears.

10c) Write the measure numbers of each time this rhythmic motive appears in the piece. The first one has been done for you:

Piano Prelude (mm. 1–7): 1–2

Strophe 1 (mm. 8–30): _____

Strophe 2 (mm. 31–53): _____

Strophe 3 (mm. 54–82): _____

Wow, that's a lot! Why do you think Schubert suffuses the piece with it? _____

_____

Why did Schubert choose this particular motive to play almost continuously through this setting of the poem? (Hint: What do you think it sounds like?) _____

_____

10d) In which sections of the piece does this motive *not* appear? _____

Why do you think he omits it here? _____

_____

Musical Structure (large scale)

11a) Are there any repetitions in the music? Indicate them below:

musical section #1: mm. 8–20 and ____–____

musical section #2: mm. 54–67 and ____-____

11b) Which stanzas of the poem does Schubert set in musical section #1 and in its repetition?

_____

11c) Which stanza does Schubert set in musical section #2 and in its repetition? _____

Piano Prelude

12a) In what register of the piano are the opening seven bars? How close are the pianist's hands together and why? What is the dynamic marking and why? _____
_____
_____
_____

12b) In what direction does the bassline move in m. 5? What interval does it create?
_____

12c) What direction and interval (beginning on B♭) is created in the top line of the right hand between mm. 1–4? (Remember this interval!) Between mm. 1–7? What might this direction and interval suggest, based on the poem? _____
_____
_____

12d) What is the shape created by the outside voices (rising top line and descending bassline) in the piano prelude? What might this opening up represent? _____
_____

12e) How would you bring this out in performance? _____
_____
_____

12f) What mood is created by the oscillating sixteenth notes in the prelude (and throughout almost the entire piece)? _____
_____

What happens to the direction of the oscillating sixteenths on the downbeat of m. 3, and how does it make you feel? _____
_____

How might this relate to the poem? _____
_____

12g) Another way of expressing opposition is through the use of suspensions and resolutions; a suspension creates a dissonance on the downbeat which then resolves to a consonance, musically expressing both pain and joy, desire and its quenching. Circle the suspensions in mm. 3 and 4 and write each suspension and the note it resolves to (as "X to Y") here. Do you feel the movement from pain to joy? How will you (the pianist) bring this out in your performance? _____
_____
_____

Vocal Line Enters

13a) Listen to the voice part in mm. 8–11: What direction does it move, and what interval is created between m. 8 and m. 11? _____

13b) Compare this with mm. 12–15. Same question: _____

If something repeats, it may be a motive. This must be a melodic motive!

13c) Look at the bassline from mm. 8–15: What note is the most frequently sounded? ____

Why do you think Schubert does this? _____

_____

13d) Write down the chords first and then the function of the chords in mm. 8–15:

_____

_____

13e) Does this chord progression make you feel at peace or does it create confusion or tension? How clearly is the tonic introduced and confirmed? Why do you suppose Schubert opens the first strophe with this progression? _____

_____

_____

14a) Listen to mm. 16–19 and raise your hand when you hear a cadence. What note does it go to? What is its function in this key? Is this a typical tonal area to move to? _____

_____

_____

14b) How do we get to this new tonal area? Write in the chord names in mm. 16–19. Then go backward from the cadence in m. 19 and write the chord functions in the new key (the key of the cadence in m. 19): _____

_____

_____

15a) Compare the vocal line in mm. 20–23 with that in mm. 16–19 (first beat); what two notes are different? _____

_____

15b) What is the relationship between the first melody note in m. 18 and the note in m.19? How does it help to confirm the cadence in m. 19? _____

_____

15c) Write in the chords for mm. 20–25. Now write in the functions of the chords in relation to the key of the cadence in m. 25:

_____

_____

15d) How does the first changed note in m. 22 help lead to the cadence in m. 25? _____
_____
_____

Are you surprised that one tiny note can make such a difference?

15e) Why do you suppose Schubert includes both A♭ and A♮ in m. 24?
_____
_____

15f) What is the direction and interval created in the melody from the first beat of m. 24 to the first beat of m. 25? Have we seen this before? _____
_____
_____

16a) Compare the modulatory section of the first musical strophe (mm. 16–19 and 39–42). What German word in the text is the same in both these passages, and what does it mean?
_____

16b) How do the meanings of the texts in mm. 20–25 and 43–48 move away from the meanings in mm. 16–19 and 39–42? _____
_____

16c) How does the music in mm. 20–25 and 43–48 move away from the four bars previous to each phrase? _____
_____

16d) So how is Schubert correlating the affect (emotion) of each line pair with its musical setting in mm. 16–25 and 39–48? _____
_____

16e) How is peace communicated in this song through tonal structure? _____
_____
_____

Piano interlude (mm. 26–30)

17a) What happens in the bassline from mm. 25–29, and what is its significance?
_____
_____

17b) Why do you think Schubert put accents on the alternating C♭s and C♮s in both hands in mm. 26–29? Does it remind you of any alternating chromatic notes in mm. 16–25?
_____
_____

17c) Why do you suppose Schubert included it in the interlude? _____
_____

17d) How can the pianist make the connection in performance? _____
_____

17e) Where does the little ornament in m. 29 originate? (Hint: look at mm. 1–4.) _____
_____

Where does it appear again in the piece? _____

What do you think it may symbolize or express? _____
_____

How will you express this in performance? _____
_____
_____

17f) Where does the mini-motive in mm. 29–30, the B♭-A-B♭, originate? (Hint: again look at the beginning of the piece in mm. 8–11.) _____
_____

Where do we see it again in the piece? _____
_____

How will you make this mini-motive seem familiar and welcome each time it reappears?
_____
_____

Melody of the second section (mm. 54–67)

18a) What mood and associations does the text of mm. 54–60 express? _____
_____
_____

18b) Why do you think Schubert repeats this stanza and musical setting almost exactly in m. 68 to the end? _____
_____
_____

18c) What melody are we expecting in m. 54 and following? When does it diverge? How do you feel when you hear the change? _____
_____
_____

18d) What interval and direction did the original vocal melody in mm. 8–11 outline? _____
_____

Is this same interval outlined in mm. 54–57? _____

Does he stop there? _____ How does it make you feel that the line keeps continuing upward? _____
_____

Is this the highest note of the piece? _____ Now outline this same interval from mm. 57–60: _____

18e) Describe the vocal melody in mm. 54–60 (direction, two intervals it creates):
_____

18f) Why does Schubert use this important interval twice? (Look at the text.) _____
_____
_____
_____

19) What is the effect of the measure of rest? _____
_____
_____

20a) Where does the music (vocal and piano) in mm. 62–65 originate? List measure numbers where it first appears: mm. ___-___

20b) Circle the first note in the voice on m. 61 and write it in here: _____ Now follow the line down stepwise; you should find one note each in m. 63, m. 64, and m. 65. Write them all here in order: ___ ___ ___ ___ What interval does this create (from first to last note)? _____ Does this seem familiar? (Hint: look at the left hand in mm. 1–5 and the voice part in mm. 8–11.) _____

20c) This motive repeats in mm. 76–79, but without its final note on tonic. In what measure does that final tonic note appear? _____
_____

21) Express the motive in mm. 1–4 and in mm. 62–65 in terms of the tonic. (Hint: If mm. 1-4 outline a descending P4 from tonic down to the dominant, what do mm. 62–65 outline?) _____
_____

Do you see how the opening motive leads us away from tonic and the closing motives (62–65 and 76–82) lead us back? Nineteenth-century composers never do anything by accident. **If a motive is set up in the beginning, it's going to be important somehow!**

Suspensions in the second section (mm. 54–60)

22) Before moving to the harmony, let's look at and listen to the amazing suspensions in the piano part in mm. 54–60, which recall those in the piano prelude (mm. 3–4). When we are trying to figure out a chord's name and function, we often think we must include all the notes in a vertical space. Real music, however, often includes suspensions which create dissonance and resolution, just like spice and herbs in a delicious dish. Follow the right hand of the piano in this passage: the B♭ in m. 54 rises to a C♭ in m. 55, which is then suspended (now as a dissonant note to the D♭ into the first two beats of m. 55, resolving to B only on the third beat. The C♭ in bar 56 is not part of the chord in m. 56, but a dissonance which resolves on the third beat. (Remember this when you do the harmonic analysis below.) The D♭ added in m. 56 is suspended over into m. 57 for two beats (resolving to the C♭) and clashes with the E♭. Just so, the E♭ in m. 57 is suspended into m. 58 (resolving to D♮), clashing with the F. What is the effect of three full bars of rising suspensions in mm. 56–58? _____

_____
_____
_____

Compare these suspensions with those in mm. 3–4. What directions do they move? Which one creates a stronger emotional response and why? _____

_____
_____
_____
_____

Harmony of the second section

23a) As usual, we will begin with the cadence and work backward.

Where does the music (vocal and piano) in mm. 62–65 originate? List measure numbers where it first appears: mm. _____-_____

23b) Review the chords and functions of the passage where it first appears (you have already analyzed it above). List the key and functions: ___: _____

23c) So you know what key you end in. Now let's go backward. Write in the chord name and function of m. 60: _____ _____

23d) Now write in the chord and function of m. 59: _____ _____

23e) Now write in the chord and function of m. 58; watch out for the appoggiatura on the downbeat! _____ _____

23f) Now write in the chord of m. 58. (The downbeat is an appoggiatura.) _____

23g) What is the interval between the roots of mm. 57 and 58? _____

That is a clue to the relationship between the chord in m. 57 and that in m. 58: which harmonic relationship is based on a chord a semitone above the root of the next chord?
_____

24a) Now let's go back to m. 55. If m. 54 was tonic (as expected), what is the chord and function of m. 55? (Hint: think about m. 57.) _____ _____

24b) So what is the chord and function in m. 56? _____ _____

24c) How does it feel to suddenly shift into a different key for several bars? _____
_____

24d) Why do you suppose the phrase ends on the IV in m. 60? (Again, think of the text.)
_____

24e) Does the theorist Christian Friedrich Daniel Schubart say anything about the key of C♭? Look at the section "Choice of Key" in chapter 3 to find out. If not, find the key closest in number of flats. (He is discussing choice of key, and this section involves a brief tonicization of C♭, but it is informative to ask the question.) _____
_____
_____
_____
_____

25a) Now look at the bassline in mm. 54–60; in what direction is it moving? _____

What is the interval between the note in m. 54 and that in m. 60? _____

25b) What direction is the vocal line moving in mm. 54–60? _____ So what kind of motion does this create? _____

Do you see how Schubert has taken the same motion from the piano prelude mm. 1–5 and expanded it to make it much stronger in mm. 54–60? The perfect fourth motive (in both hands, in contrary motion), the rising top line, the descending bassline, and the suspensions are all there in the first five measures of the song. This is why you must **always pay attention to the piano preludes** in Schubert songs—**they tell you the entire point of the piece!**

26a) Summarize all the different musical elements that make mm. 54–60 the most exquisite phrase in this song: _____
_____
_____
_____
_____

26b) How could you make this passage special in your performance? _____

_____
_____
_____
_____

27a) What have you learned about the meaning of the song from your analysis? _____

_____
_____
_____
_____

27b) How will you express it through your performance? _____

_____
_____
_____
_____

NOTE

1. The poems in Rückert's original 1822 publication, *Oestiche Rosen*, did not bear titles, so Schubert used the first line of the poem as a title when he published the song in 1823. Rückert added the title "Kehr' ein bei mir!" when he published his collected edition in 1834. Richard Law, "Du bist die Ruh D776," *Figures of Speech* (blog), February 20, 2020, http://figures-of-speech.com/2020/02/du-bist-die-ruh_1.htm.

15

"Frühlingstraum" (from *Winterreise*)

How can we tell the difference between reality and dreams? In German Romanticism, dreams were an important way of escaping what could sometimes be a painful reality. This famous song from *Winterreise* finds the wanderer in the middle of a pleasant dream in which he imagines himself first enjoying the flowers and sounds of spring and later the love of his sweetheart. Unfortunately he wakes up with a shock to cold and dark reality. "Frühlingstraum," the eleventh song of the cycle, represents a stop on his journey of memory and alienation.

The poem contrasts different times, states of being, and emotions, and is embedded with Romantic images. These contrasts are expressed musically through the juxtaposition of different styles of music, and include **tonal fluidity**, **chromatic harmony**, and **linear motion**.

* * *

TEXT

1a) What does the title tell you about the poem? "Frühlingstraum" is the eleventh in the twenty-four-song cycle, and it is winter from beginning to end. What could this title suggest? _____
_____
_____

1b) What is happening in this poem? Who is speaking? Who are they speaking to? _____
_____
_____
_____
_____
_____

1c) Read the poem out loud. For each stanza, write the time (past, present, fantasy/future), state of being (reality, dream, or fantasy), and the emotion expressed.

Frühlingstraum

Time/state/emotion

Ich träumte von bunten Blumen	I dreamt of bright flowers	**past**
So wie sie wohl blühen im Mai;	that blossom in May;	**dream**
ich träumte von grünen Wiesen,	I dreamt of green meadows	**joy**
von lustigem Vogelgeschrei.	and merry birdcalls.	
Und als die Hähne krähten,	And when the cocks crowed	_____
da ward mein Auge wach;	my eyes awoke;	_____
da war es kalt und finster,	it was cold and dark,	_____
es schrieen die Raben vom Dach.	ravens cawed from the roof.	
Doch an den Fensterscheiben,	But there, on the window panes,	_____
wer malte die Blätter da?	who had painted the leaves?	_____
Ihr lacht wohl über den Träumer	Are you laughing at the dreamer	_____
der Blumen im Winter sah?	who saw flowers in winter?	
Ich träumte von Lieb' um Liebe,	I dreamt of mutual love,	_____
von einer schönen Maid,	of a lovely maiden,	_____
von Herzen und von Küssen,	of embracing and kissing,	_____
von Wonn' und Seligkeit.	of joy and rapture.	
Und als die Hähne krähten,	And when the cocks crowed	_____
da ward mein Herze wach;	my heart awoke;	_____
nun sitz ich hier alleine	now I sit here alone	_____
und denke dem Traume nach.	and reflect upon my dream.	
Die Augen schliess' ich wieder,	I close my eyes again,	_____
noch schlägt das Herz so warm.	My heart still beats so warmly.	_____
Wann grünt ihr Blätter am Fenster?	Leaves on my window, when will you turn green?	_____
Wann halt' ich mein Liebchen im Arm?	When shall I hold my love in my arms?	

1d) What do you notice about the patterns of the stanzas? Do you see how stanzas 1 and 4 are similar, as are 2 and 5, and 3 and 6? _____
_____

How would you characterize the three states (by time, state of being, and emotion)?
_____
_____

1e) What do the fluidity of time, states of being, and emotions, as well as the interiority of this poem, tell you about the protagonist of this poem (and of the cycle of poetry that became *Winterreise*)? _____
_____

2a) The ambiguity in this poem is characteristic of German Romanticism, as are the images within. For each stanza, list the images that appear and explain to what sense or emotion they appeal. Stanza 1 is done for you:

"Frühlingstraum" (from Winterreise*)*

Stanza 1: past: flowers blossoming (vision, scent), meadows (vision, scent) and birdcalls (sound)

Stanza 2: _____

Stanza 3: _____

Stanza 4: _____

Stanza 5: _____

Stanza 6: _____

2b) In stanzas 2 and 5, something awakes; compare what each suggests: _____

2c) In stanzas 1 and 2, bird sounds are heard; compare them in terms of the emotion they inspire: _____

2d) Leaves are mentioned in both stanzas 3 and 6; compare their meaning: _____

2e) Note that stanzas 1–3 refer to nature (longing for spring), while in stanzas 4–6 the same fluidity of states now all refer to yearning for his love. What do you think "my heart awoke" means in the context of this poem and the *Winterreise* cycle? _____

3a) Compare the use of alliteration in stanzas 1 and 4. Write the words that display alliteration, and circle the repeated consonants: _____

3b) Now look for harsh sounds (cacophony) in stanzas 2 and 5. Write the words that display cacophony, and circle the harsh sounds: _____

Note that the soft "B" sounds return in stanzas 3 and 6, as the wanderer reverts to fantasy.

The poet also softens the poetic meter of the dream stanzas by mixing triple and duple meters. If you scan the opening line, you hear a triple foot shifting to duple feet:

\- / - - / - / -
Ich träumte von bunten Blumen,

The next line is all triple:
\- / - - / - - /
So wie sie wohl <u>blühen</u> im Mai;

and lines 3 and 4 repeat this pattern. However, stanza 2 shifts primarily to a duple meter (iambic trimeter), with the exception of the last line about the cawing ravens ("es schrieen die Raben vom Dach") which hearkens back to the last line of stanza 1, "von lustigem Vogelgeschrei" (and merry birdcalls), suggesting that the birds he dreams about may in real life be the ravens on the roof!

A triple meter line at the end of stanza 3 links to the opening line of the poem, as it is set in the same alternating triple/duple meter and, like it, also involves flowers:

\- / - - / - /
der Blumen im Winter sah?

Other mixed meter lines in the poem include "und denke dem Traue nach" (and reflect upon my dream).

Stanza 4, so similar to stanza 1 in meaning, is written in duple meter (iambic trimeter again), except for the first line, "Ich träumte von Lieb' um Liebe" (I dreamt of mutual love), which is in the same triple-duple combination as the opening line of the poem. The most mellifluous triple meter ends the poem: "Wann halt' ich mein Liebchen im Arm?" (When shall I hold my love in my arms?)

Keep an eye out for ways in which Schubert sets lines containing poetic triple meter feet in the music.

MUSIC

Etwas bewegt means "somewhat moving," referring to the dotted quarter note.

4a) Does Schubert follow the structure of the poem (A, B, C; A, B, C) in his musical setting?
_____

4b) Describe the general mood of each of the three sections:

1) _____

2) _____

3) _____

"Frühlingstraum" (from Winterreise)

Piano Prelude

5a) Listen to just the piano prelude. If you didn't know this was by Schubert, who might you think the composer could be and why? _____
_____

5b) Describe the texture, melody, and meter; explain how they contribute to the mood:
_____
_____
_____

Performing the opening with clarity and delicacy is essential in setting this off from the other songs in the cycle. It is the most optimistic possible memory of an idealized time in the wanderer's life, and it is decidedly unreal. (But what is reality, anyway?)

5c) Why do you think Schubert opens this song in the Classical style? What could it have meant to him? How does this equate with the protagonist's emotions? _____
_____
_____
_____
_____

5d) The key of A major is described by the poet and theorist C. F. D. Schubart as "declarations of innocent love, satisfaction with one's state of affairs, hope of seeing one's beloved again when parting; youthful cheerfulness and trust in God."[1] Which part of the song does this match? Is it reality, dream, or fantasy? _____
_____
_____
_____

The prelude of Frühlingstraum is only four bars long, but immediately conveys the sense of lighthearted antiquity (notice the lovely appoggiatura in m. 2 and the ornaments in m. 3, in addition to the light texture and clear harmonies throughout). Schubert always tells the story in the prelude and this song is no different; we are clearly in a dreamlike state far removed from the tramping of "Gute nacht" and the other songs that led to this moment.

The first full measure contains two motives, an upper neighbor and a rising sixth. Mark them in your score; you will be on the lookout for them throughout the song.

Stanza 1 (mm. 5–14)

6a) Does the musical setting of the first stanza remain in this Classical style? _____

6b) What words are set by the two trills in m. 11? _____

Do you now understand the meaning of these trills in m. 3? _____

6c) Which words are emphasized in the setting of the first stanza, and how is this done?

Notice how the "B" alliterations are brought out in the melody.

Stanza 2 (mm. 15–26)

Schnell means "fast," referring to the dotted quarter note.

7a) How is the rooster sound evoked?

7b) How does the mood change in section B?

What creates the change? (Hint: look at tempo, mode, rhythm, texture, articulation, dynamics, dissonance, and tonality.)

7c) Note how the harmonic landscape has moved from a very clear and diatonic A major to set the first stanza, to a fluid tonal area, shifting through several tonal areas before arriving at a cadence to A minor in m. 22. What areas do we pass through in mm. 15–16, 17–18, and 19–20?

Note that, due to the mode change, the neighbor tone motive from m. 1 is now a semitone (mm. 15, 19, and 21). Semitone motion creates melodic dissonance which, combined with the repeated note figures, increases the tension of this section.

7d) Schubert intensifies the tension by adding sudden and unusual dissonances (in mm. 16, 18, 20, 22, and 24), amplified by extreme dynamic contrasts. What do you think these dissonances represent in the poem?

Can you figure out what the chords are? (Hint: play each chord and listen to its quality, but ignore how it resolves: this chord does not resolve the way you'd expect!)

7e) What interesting chord do you find in m. 23? (Hint: the left hand is a pedal A, which is not part of the chord.)

What is the relationship of this chord to the key of the song (i.e., what interval from tonic is its root?)? _____

Do you see how the melodic semitone motive is now expressed at the harmonic level?

7f) What animal do you think is being represented by the octave sixteenth notes in the left hand in mm. 22–25? _____

Note that the noisy raven octaves derive from the rooster motive of mm. 16ff.; they are louder, lower, more insistent, and apparently more numerous! What do you imagine they are doing in the rising octaves m. 26, and why do you think Schubert marks it *ff*? _____

_____

What emotion could the ravens represent? _____

_____

7g) The text is repeated here, but now with the addition of this noisy left hand. What do you think the character is thinking the second time he repeats these words? _____

_____

_____

_____

_____

How will you perform it so that the audience can hear the difference? _____

_____

_____

Stanza 3 (mm. 27–43)

Langsam means "slow."

8a) What is the mood of this section and how is it conveyed musically? What elements of music change? _____

_____

_____

_____

8b) In the top line in the left hand you will find a rhythmically augmented (slowed-down) version of the "tramping motive" (four even staccato notes) that we first heard in "Gute Nacht," the first song of the cycle. Schubert specifically notates it with staccato markings, but requires the pianist to play the other notes legato (spelled "ligato" in the score), so clearly it needs to be heard, as it was distinguished in this way. What do you think the triple-octave A's represent in this passage? _____

_____

_____

_____

8c) Compare the general tessitura (vocal range) of mm. 29–36 with that of mm. 15–26. Which section has the higher tessitura with more leaps? _____

If you "connect the dots" (look at the linear motion) in the melody, you will see that the essential melody moves from D (mm. 29–31) to C♯ (m. 32) to B-A (mm. 33–34 and 35–36), in a simple, folklike motion.

9a) How does the mood change in mm. 37–42? _____
_____

How is this created musically? _____

What harmonies do you find in mm. 37–42 (write names and functions)?

chords: _____

functions: _____

Do you see how the plagal sound, combined with the shift to the parallel minor adds to the feeling of wistfulness in this passage? But notice that the cadence in m. 42 is neither to A major nor A minor, but to bare octaves. What might Schubert be suggesting? ___
_____
_____

This section ends as it began, with the "tramping" motive suggesting the frost on the windows, but now an octave lower, as though it is passing into a new state of consciousness, only to rise up into a new dream state in m. 44.[2]

9b) The semitone motive appears in this passage; can you find it? (Hint: "connect the dots"—look for linear motion from one measure to another.) _____
_____

9c) Compare and describe the two musical settings of "der Blumen im Winter sah" (who saw flowers in winter): _____
_____
_____
_____

How will you express the two feelings in your performance?

Stanzas 4–6 (repeat of music from first half, mm. 44–88)

10a) The three-part musical setting repeats, now setting stanzas 4–6. Due to the parallel structure of the poem, the repetition of the music fits perfectly. But of course, you will not perform it exactly the same. How will you shape your performance of the second half of the song so that it deepens from merely looking forward to spring to fully longing for love? _____
_____
_____
_____

10b) Silence plays an important part in this song. Notice that between parts 1 and 2 (mm. 14 and 58) and 2 and 3 (mm. 26 and 70), there is a pause, a short rest that is, however, notated with a fermata. How long will you take, and what will your character be thinking at that moment? _____

_____

_____

Each repetition of part 3 concludes with a four-octave A (mm. 41 and 46), with the question left hanging: major or minor? The answer is not revealed until the final bar of the song (m. 88), and only in the piano part: A minor. Here the piano and vocal parts have distinct roles: the piano, unlike the wanderer, signifies reality and foreshadows his future fate by closing in the key of A minor. The singer does not complete a song in this key until the bitter end of the cycle, in "Der Leiermann." It is only then that we realize the answer he could not see was there all along.

11a) What have you learned about the meaning of the song from your analysis? _____

_____

_____

_____

_____

11b) How will you express it through your performance? _____

_____

_____

_____

_____

NOTES

1. Christian Friedrich Daniel Schubart, *Ideen zu einer Ästhetik der Tonkunst* (Vienna: Degen, 1806), reprint, ed. P. A. Merbach (Leipzig: Wolkenwander-Verlag, 1924), quoted in Rita Steblin, *A History of Key Characteristics in the Eighteenth and Early Nineteenth Centuries* (Ann Arbor: UMI Research Press, 1983), 124–25.

2. Graham Johnson reminds us that Schubert often uses the subdominant as a "magical realm," also noting how instead of descending into a dream "in the topsy-Turvy world of inverted values, the traveler rises to his." Graham Johnson, *Schubert: The Complete Songs* (New Haven: Yale University Press, 2014), 3:673–74.

16

"Gretchen am Spinnrade"

To be able to create a convincing performance of this song, Schubert's very first Goethe setting, you must understand the work from which the poem is taken. The poet's monumental play *Faust* (published 1808) begins with a wager between God and the Devil over the nature of humans—whether they are good or evil. God picks as his test subject his favorite human, Dr. Faust, and the Devil attempts to tempt him.

Faust is bored to death with his life as a scholar and eventually sells his soul to the Devil (Mephistopheles) in order to be able to have all the experiences life has to offer. Among other things, he wishes to feel love, and through the magical help of Mephistopheles, he first meets and woos the simple girl Margaret (Gretchen), who still lives at home with her mother. Mephistopheles has transformed Faust into a handsome young man and provided him with jewels to turn her head. Unfortunately for Gretchen, the magical attraction she has for Faust was created by the Devil, and will in the end cause ruin and death for her and her family.

The spinning wheel scene is a turning point in the play. After this point, Faust impregnates Gretchen and then leaves her, along the way causing the deaths of both her mother and brother. Faust later finds out that Gretchen is in prison for killing her baby. When he tries to save her from execution with the help of Mephistopheles, she refuses to go with him, praying to heaven instead, and her soul is redeemed by the angels.

As you can see, although we typically hear this song as an expression of the blossoming of desire in a young girl, the added context of supernatural forces of destruction make this a fundamental contest between good and evil, which can be heard throughout the song. Which do you think is winning at this point in the story?

You will find many different expressive techniques in this song, including a **semitone motive**, a **German augmented sixth chord**, a I_4^6 **chord used to modulate**, **withholding of cadences** to a certain key, **third relationship**, **sudden shift to a new key**, **motivic parallelism**, **pedal points**, and **melodic circling**.

TEXT

1) Describe the general emotions of the poem. How does Gretchen feel and why?

_____
_____
_____
_____

2) In your text of the poem (not the score), circle words with Romantic resonance, and explain which aspect of Romanticism is represented: _____

_____
_____
_____
_____

3) In the play, Gretchen is clearly a simple and religious young girl who still lives with her mother. What hints do you find in the text that what Gretchen is experiencing goes beyond typical romantic longing and has been affected by supernatural forces?

_____
_____
_____

The repetition of the first stanza as a refrain originates with Goethe, who uses it as an organizing device (stanzas 1, 4, and 8).

4a) What is the focus of the first section, stanzas 1–3? _____

_____
_____
_____

4b) What is the focus of the second section, stanzas 5–7? _____

_____
_____
_____

4c) What is the focus of the third section, stanzas 9–10? _____

_____
_____
_____

Schubert made several alterations to the poem in his setting. For each alteration below, explain why you think he made each change:

5a) In the refrain, the words "ich finde" are repeated (see mm. 7–8). Why, do you think?
_____
_____
_____

5b) Stanza 10 is repeated, but Schubert changes the first line from "Und küssen ihn" to "O könnt ich ihn küssen." He also repeats the last two lines of this stanza again: "an seine Küssen vergehen sollt!" Why do you think he did this? What does it add to your understanding of Gretchen's character and emotion at this point? _____
_____
_____
_____

5c) Schubert added a **repetition of the first half of the refrain** at the end of the poem. How does this change the placement of Gretchen's emotional state at the end (from the poem to the song)? _____
_____
_____
_____
_____

6a) What is the rhyme scheme in general? _____
_____

6b) What happens to it in stanza 2? _____
_____

6c) Why do you suppose Goethe changed the rhyme scheme in this stanza? _____
_____
_____
_____

7a) Are the text lines generally short or long? _____
_____

7b) What does this suggest about the person singing? _____
_____
_____
_____

7c) Why do you think Goethe wrote them this way? (Think both of who is singing and what she is doing.) _____
_____
_____
_____

7d) Why else might the text lines be this way (think about her mood)? _____
_____
_____
_____

8) Say the word "nimmer" (never) over and over again. Does it start to sound like Gretchen's spinning wheel? Why do you think Goethe write "nimmer und nimmermehr" instead of just "nimmer"? _____
_____
_____

Alliteration is where a particular initial consonant is repeated, and consonance is where the same consonant appears within a word; cacophony is when the words sound noisy.

9a) Which hard consonant is repeated three times in stanza 2? _____
_____

9b) How does it make you feel when you say it? _____
_____
_____

9c) How does this express the meaning of the words? _____
_____
_____

9d) How will you bring this out in your performance? _____
_____
_____

10a) What hard consonant appears three times in stanza 3? _____
_____

10b) In what words does it appear? _____
_____
_____

(Note that this consonant is the unvoiced version of the same repeated consonant in m. 2.)

11a) How does the poem change in stanza 5? _____
_____
_____

11b) How is this expressed by the opening word of each line? _____
_____
_____

11c) What hard consonant returns three times in stanza 6? _____
_____

What words contain this sound? _____
_____

Notice how the same hard consonant that formerly emphasized the bitterness of her life is now transformed, expressing positive emotions when she describes Faust. It's almost as if the same sounds are magically transformed.

11d) Why do you suppose Gretchen describes Faust's speech as having "magic flow"? _____
_____
_____

12a) What is the hard consonant in stanza 7 (end of one word, beginning of another)? ____
_____

12b) List the words in which it appears: _____
_____

12c) Are they important words? _____
_____

In his song, Schubert changes the first line of stanza 10 from "Und küssen ihn" (and kiss him) to "O könnt ich ihn küssen" (if I could only kiss him).

13) Why do you think he makes this change? (Think about the hard consonants we've seen earlier in the poem.) _____
_____
_____

14) Gretchen's song expresses not only a young girl's first experience of passion, but one clearly aided by the Devil. In what letter sounds which Goethe (and Schubert) put in the poem might the voice of the Devil be speaking through her? _____
_____
_____
_____
_____

15) What Romantic concept does Goethe place in the last two lines of the poem? _____
_____
_____

MUSIC

The Spinning Wheel

16a) Schubert is famous for his illustrative preludes, and in this song he sets the whirring of the spinning wheel and the clacking of the bobbin. Explain how each is portrayed musically: _____
_____
_____
_____
_____

16b) What else might the rhythmic eighth notes in the left hand represent? _____
_____
_____

16c) At what points do they stop? Why? _____
_____
_____
_____

The Semitone Motive

The **semitone motive** in m. 3 (A-B♭-A) plays an essential role in this song.

17a) Why do you think Schubert chose this motive? (What does it suggest?) _____
_____
_____
_____

17b) Note the inverted semitone motive on the C-B-C in m. 8 (including pickup). Why do you think it occurs on the words "ich finde"? _____
_____
_____
_____

17c) Go through and circle this motive wherever you find it in the piece (including transpositions and inversions); look for any strong neighbor tone or m. 2 motion. Approximately how many times does it appear? _____
_____

17d) What Romantic emotion might the composer be expressing by repeating this motive so often through the song? _____
_____
_____

The Key and Meter

18a) This piece is in D minor, the same key as Schubert's later masterpiece "Death and the Maiden." Christian Schubart (also the poet of "Die Forelle") describes this key in his treatise on musical aesthetics as expressing "melancholy womanliness; the spleen and humours brood."[1] Can you see how Schubert would have thought to choose this key again for "Death and the Maiden"? What famous works does Mozart set in this key?
_____
_____

18b) How does the $\frac{6}{8}$ meter evoke the idea of spinning? _____
_____
_____
_____

Almost all of the phrases begin with an upbeat. How do these upbeat phrases help to express the anxiety of the protagonist? _____
_____
_____
_____

There is only one single phrase that begins on a downbeat (emphasizing the second big beat in the compound duple meter, the fourth beat in $\frac{6}{8}$). Where does it occur, what words does it set, and what does the shift to a downbeat phrase tell you about Gretchen's mood at this point? _____
_____
_____
_____

The Refrain

19a) How does the musical refrain give structure to the song? _____
_____
_____
_____

19b) What is unusual about its last appearance (mm. 112–20), and why do you think Schubert does this? _____
_____
_____
_____

"Gretchen am Spinnrade"

19c) Why will Gretchen never find rest/peace? _____
_____
_____
_____
_____

The first part of the vocal refrain (mm. 3–6 with pickup) is made up of ten individual notes.

20a) Which note is the most repeated? _____
_____

20b) How many times is it sung in these four bars? _____
_____

20c) Which note predominates in the bassline? _____
_____

20d) What might we call this type of bassline, one that doesn't really move? _____
_____

20e) How many times does the right-hand sixteenth-note figure repeat exactly in mm. 1–6?
_____

20f) What impression does this lack of change in all three lines (vocal, right hand, and left hand) create? _____
_____
_____

21a) In what key does the refrain begin? _____
_____

21b) How long does this chord continue? _____
_____

21c) What happens in the bassline in m. 7? _____
_____

21d) For how long does it continue? _____
_____

21e) What chords do you hear in mm. 7–11? _____
_____
_____

21f) A pedal may be used to set up the dominant chord. If this is the case, toward what key might this passage be pointing? _____
_____

21g) Do we get a cadence in this key? _____
_____

21h) What happens instead (in the second half of m. 12 and following)? _____
_____
_____

21i) Why is it so easy to move from C to this chord? (Which note stays the same? Which note moves? Which note doesn't appear?) _____
_____
_____

21j) Why do you suppose Schubert doesn't cadence to the desired key, but instead returns to the tonic? _____
_____
_____
_____

22) How is the listener made to feel when the desired cadence at the end of each refrain is avoided and this manipulation occurs **three times** in the song? _____
_____
_____

23a) Stanza 2 (pickup to m. 14) begins the same as the refrain but is set differently. To what two cadence areas does it move in mm. 17 and 21? _____
_____

23b) Going backward from each of the cadences, write in the chords and functions and then write them in here (forward). You can think of mm. 14–21 in A minor with a brief tonicization in E minor.

    Chords: 14___ 15___16___ 17___   18___ 19___ 20___ 21___
    Function: a: 14___ 15___16___ 17___ e: 18___ 19___ 20___ 21___

23c) How is tonic reinterpreted in m. 14? _____
_____

23d) How might the A minor chord of m. 17 be interpreted in the key of mm. 18–21?
_____
_____

23e) Do you see how the note A predominates in the melody in mm. 14–18? Follow the melody down the scale to m. 20. The first one is done for you. m. 18: A, m. 19: ___, m. 20: ___, m. 21: ___

23f) So the "monotone" A now descends. Why do you suppose Schubert does this? _____
_____
_____
_____

24a) Why does Schubert suddenly move up an octave in mm. 22ff.? _____
_____
_____
_____

24b) What else suggests Gretchen's emotional state? _____
_____
_____

24c) If you were going to write one melodic note to stand in for mm. 22–25, what would it be? _____

24d) For mm. 26–29? _____

24e) What important motivic figure is thus created across these eight bars? _____
_____
_____

Recall how Schubert creates desire at the end of each refrain by writing a half cadence to the dominant of the longed-for key, F (cf. mm. 10–11). Can you see that he does something similar in mm. 28–29?

25a) Name the chord in m. 29: _____

25b) If this is a half cadence, to what key does it want to go? _____

25c) Going backward, write in the chord names and functions in relation to the key the passage is trying to reach. Now write them in (forward) below:

    Chord: m. 26_____   m. 27_____   m. 28_____   m. 29____
    Function: _____ m. 26_____   m. 27_____   m. 28_____   m. 29____

25d) Measure 26 is the pivot chord between the two passages. What is its function in the key of mm. 22–25? _____

25e) What is its function in the key of mm. 26–29? _____

26a) To summarize Schubert's harmonic expression of desire, to what key does the refrain try to go in m. 11? _____

26b) To what key does the refrain try to go in m. 29? _____

27a) The refrain returns in mm. 32–42. In what key does it begin in m. 32? _____

27b) What key is it pointing to in m. 40? _____

So far we have been denied arrival to a desired key area three times: mm. 11, 29, and 40. Keep your eyes open for this technique of expressing thwarted desire!

Stanzas 5–7 (mm. 43–73)

Stanzas 5, 6, and 7 deal directly with Gretchen's lover (beginning at "Nach ihm . . ."). Read these three stanzas of the poem (not from your score) closely.

28a) In what direction does she seem to be moving (in her imagination)? _____

28b) Measures 43–46 begin like mm. 14–17, with the same chord progression and cadence area. How do mm. 47–50 differ from mm. 18–21? _____

28c) List the keys of the two cadences in mm. 46 and 50: ___ ___

29) Earlier we noted the sudden change in the poetry of stanza 5 of the original poem, in which every line begins with the same word. What is this word, and what is this stanza all about? _____

30a) What chord suddenly appears at this point (m. 51)? _____

30b) How many times have we been "longing" for this key so far, indicated by half cadence to its dominant? _____

30c) What do you think this key represents? _____

"Gretchen am Spinnrade"

30d) How does the rhythm in the left hand change at this point, and what does it imply?

_____
_____
_____
_____

30e) Why do you suppose Schubert now sits in this key for four bars (51–54) and cadences in it? _____
_____
_____
_____
_____

30f) How does the stability and mode and tonal level of the harmony make you feel? ____
_____
_____
_____

> You may already know that the third relationship was very popular in the nineteenth century, giving a sense of freshness and novelty to the harmony. By moving directly from the key of A minor at the end of stanza 4 (m. 50) to F major beginning stanza 5 (mm. 51–54), Schubert allows Gretchen to reach her favored key—showing us what she's been longing for!—and at the same time offers a third relationship to create a freshness that shows her sudden change of mood as she thinks about her lover.

31a) Write the chord names from mm. 55–62: ____ ____ ____ ____ ____ ____ ____ ____

31b) What is the pattern to this passage in terms of chord function? _____
_____
_____

31c) Now write the bass notes of mm. 54, 56, 58, and 60: ____ ____ ____ ____

31d) What interval and direction does this form? _____
_____

31e) Returning to the opening of the piece, name the interval and direction formed by the first four notes in the vocal melody in mm. 2–3: _____
_____

> This is an example of a **motivic parallelism**, where a melodic motive is expanded to a larger level of structure, from four notes to four chords. This technique plays a particularly important role in "Erlkönig." **Always remember to pay close attention to the beginning of a work, for important motives will be introduced at the beginning that will usually be developed in the song.**

202   Chapter 16

31f) How does the succession of rising sequences with strong bass motion make you feel?
_____
_____
_____

31g) What words do they set? _____
_____
_____

31h) What words set her reaching her desired key in mm. 59–61? _____
_____
_____

Note that in the rising sequence of V^7-I chords from mm. 55–62, the B♭ chord in m. 62 gets the strongest articulation; we are in this tonal area for a full four bars, making it equal to the length in F major. F and B♭ are the two flattest cadential areas of the song (in circle of fifths ordering) and it is no accident that Schubert uses the "sweetest" keys here to set Gretchen's magical fantasy of her lover. Chapter 3 discusses the historical distinction between flat and sharp keys and the associations of flat keys with love. The theorist C. F. D. Schubart describes F major as "Complaisance and calm" and B-flat major as "Cheerful love" and "hope," which accords with the traditional views, and Schubert seems to view F major, in particular, as the key of hope, as can be seen in his significant use of it in sections of "Der Tod und das Mädchen" (also in D minor), "Du liebst mich nicht" (in A minor), "Die junge Nonne" (in F minor), and "Ganymed" (ends in F major).[2]

Vocal melody

Recall the semi-monotone emphasis on the note A that features in the refrain. Note that this monotone continues in stanza 4 (mm. 43–50) and somewhat in the first part of stanza 5 (mm. 51–54), until the vocal line starts rising.

32a) Fill in the main notes of the vocal line from the A in m. 54. The first one is done for you.

   m. 54: A, m. 56: ____, m. 58: ____, m. 60: ____

32b) What is the interval created? _____ Look familiar?

32c) See how this last note continues to predominate from m. 60 through to m. 67, when it suddenly rises what interval? _____

33a) Schubert writes *cres. poco a poco* beginning in m. 55. What was the dynamic from m. 42?
_____

33b) Why does Schubert do this? _____
_____
_____

34a) What is she remembering in mm. 63–64? (What word is particularly important?) In what three ways does Schubert signal this? _____
_____
_____

34b) By the way, "drück" of "händedrück" is really more like a squeeze; what tells you that Schubert thought so too? _____
_____
_____

34c) Write the chord in your score as best you can for mm. 63–68. It's okay if you don't answer m. 63 and the first half of m. 65 at this point; we will go over that in a minute.

34d) Play the chord in m. 63; what quality does it have? _____

34e) Is it spelled correctly for this quality? _____

34f) Remember how this quality may resolve in a different direction (outward to an octave). What type of chord is this? _____

34g) To what chord and function would this resolve in the tonic key of d minor? _____
_____

_____ Does it go to this chord in m. 64? _____

34h) Now write in the chord names and the functions of mm. 63–68. There may be a pedal point in this section.

Name:	m. 63:	m. 64:	m. 65:	m. 66:	m. 67:	m. 68:
	___ ___	___ ___	___ ___	___	___	___ ___
Function:	m. 63:	m. 64:	m. 65:	m. 66:	m. 67:	m. 68:
	___ ___	___ ___	___ ___	___	___	___ ___

34i) In m. 68, which chord is the more dissonant: the one on the first half or the second half of the bar? _____

34j) Are you surprised that Schubert ends stanza 5 with a strong unresolved dissonance? Why do you suppose he does this? _____
_____

> A funny but true joke about nineteenth-century music: Q: How do nineteenth-century composers resolve a dissonance? A: With an even stronger dissonance!

Semitone motive hidden in the spinning wheel pattern

35a) Look closely in the right hand of mm. 42–54; you hear the spinning wheel pattern from the refrain. Now follow the first note of every bar, and what do you notice? What two notes oscillate, and what is the interval created? _____–_____

35b) What is the melody created by the first notes in the right hand of mm. 54–60 (without repeating any note)? ____–____–____–____–____–____

35c) What interval is created? _____

35d) What is the melody created in the right hand by the first and third beat of every bar from mm. 62–68? Write the notes:

___ ___	___ ___	___ ___	___ ___	B♭	___	___ ___
m. 62	m. 63	m. 64	m. 65	m. 66	m. 67	m. 68

35e) What is the function of this oscillation, and what might it suggest about the meaning of the semitone motive? _____
_____
_____
_____
_____
_____

36a) The original semitone motive from m. 3 is A-B♭-A. Look at the top line of measure 68: Is the semitone motive complete here? _____

36b) Another way of leaving us feeling unfulfilled, like Gretchen! In what measure is the A returned to us in the piano? _____

36c) In the voice? _____

37a) How does it feel to sing the high G in m. 68 and then to quickly go back to a lower register when the refrain returns in m. 73? _____
_____
_____

37b) Why does the composer do this? _____
_____
_____

How could Schubert just leave that high G sitting there? It isn't an important note in the key (i.e., not 1 or 5). Typically, a composer will pick up that high note, returning and resolving it later in the piece, so keep your eyes open for it to resolve!

Stanzas 9–10

If after this climax the listener is not yet clear about Goethe's representation of Gretchen, formerly a simple and obedient girl, now expressing an extreme state of lust, they have only to read the original line that Goethe wrote in stanza 9. Instead of "Mein busen drängt sich nach ihm hin" (My bosom longs for him), he wrote "Mein Schoss! Gott! Drängt Sich nach ihm him" (My womb—God!—longs for him!). It is clear that after this key monologue in which Gretchen reveals her transformation, nothing can be the same.[3]

Review each refrain (mm. 3–12 and 32–41) and notice what happens immediately after: the new melody begins with the F-G-A opening (mm. 13–15, 42–44).

38a) Why do you think Schubert neglects to do this in mm. 85–86? _____
_____
_____
_____
_____

38b) What is the melody created in the voice part by the downbeat of every other bar from mm. 85–91? Write the notes:

____   ____   ____   ____

m. 85   m. 87   m. 89   m. 91

38c) What is the interval here? _____

38d) How well do things bode for Gretchen at this point? _____
_____

38e) How does this compare to the rising line setting stanza 5 (mm. 55–62)? Write down the notes, the interval created, and the affect expressed as a result:

____ ____ ____ ____ ____ , _____
_____

Now look at and listen to the bass line and harmony in mm. 85–92.

39a) Write the chord names from mm. 85–92:

__ __ __ __ __ __ __ __

39b) What is the pattern to this passage in terms of chord function? _____
_____
_____

39c) Now write the bass notes of mm. 86, 88, 90, and 92: ____ ____ ____ ____

39d) What direction does it move, and what interval does it form? _____
_____
_____

39e) How does this compare with the bassline outlined in mm. 54–62, and what might this suggest about Gretchen's emotional state? _____
_____
_____

39f) How does the succession of rising sequences with strong bass motion combined with the rising melody line in mm. 85–92 make you feel? _____
_____
_____

39g) What words do they set? _____
_____
_____

40a) The bassline reaches E♮ in m. 91; this E continues as a pedal tone until m. 96. What text does it set, and why does Schubert do this? _____
_____
_____
_____

Notice that the resolution in m. 92 is not to a root position chord, but to a I$_4^6$ chord. After a modulatory section, the appearance of a I$_4^6$ acts as a sort of floor, setting us up for the confirmation of a new key through a cadential progression. (This is very common in the nineteenth century and is one way in which late nineteenth-century composers such as Wagner and especially Strauss suggest a temporary tonic feeling, though we are often quickly torn away from it.) So, we feel we are preparing to establish the key of A minor.

40b) In this light, write both the chords and the functions of mm. 93–96 relating them to the key of A minor. (Remember that you are over a pedal E; not all chords will include that note as part of the chord; if necessary write "X over E ped.")
_____
_____

40c) What is the relationship between mm. 93–94 and mm. 95–96? _____
_____

41a) What happens to the tonal level in mm. 97–100? (What is the main melody note? Hint: it ends the phrase on m. 100.) _____

41b) Compare this with the main melody note in mm. 91–96; in which direction have we moved? _____
_____

41c) What is the text of this phrase? _____

_____

_____

_____

_____

41d) Why does Schubert move in this direction? _____

_____

_____

42a) To what key is the cadence in m. 100? _____

42b) What is the significance of this key? _____

_____

42c) Where is the next cadence, and what key does it confirm? _____, _____

43a) By measure 100 Schubert has gone through all his text and cadenced on tonic. Why isn't the song over at this point? (Think about the implied key of mm. 91–96.) _____

_____

_____

_____

43b) Now why do you think Schubert repeats stanza 10, and with an altered first line? ____

_____

_____

_____

44a) Listen to mm. 101–4 ("O könnt ich ihn küssen so wie ich wollt'") and write down the notes of the bassline: ____ ____ ____ ____ Do you recognize the semitone motive? Note that two notes are **circling** around Gretchen's monotone A. It's yet another musical representation of the spinning wheel as metaphor for Gretchen's heightened emotions, which are spinning out of control. Compare this with the (completely chromatic) circling in the right hand of mm. 62–68.

44b) Now listen to mm. 105–8 ("an seinen küssen vergehen sollt'") and write down the notes of the bassline: ____ ____ ____ ____

44c) What has changed between the two basslines? _____

_____

_____

44d) To what key is the cadence on the downbeat of m. 108? _____

44e) What type of cadence is it? (On what note of the scale does the vocal part end?) _____

44f) Why do you think Schubert repeats these four bars with a slightly altered vocal part?

Remember the high G on "Kuss" in m. 68 that was just left hanging with no resolution? We finally get the resolution of that note in its correct register in mm. 107 and 111. Hooray! We now break the P4 motive (from D to high G in 68) when it becomes a P5 (D up to the high A in 108 and 111).

In *Faust*, Gretchen's Devil-assisted transformation from simple and obedient to helplessly passionate is what sets her on a downhill path to ruin. Ending on this moment of extreme emotion perfectly registers this shift, indicating that nothing will ever be the same.

45) Why do you think that Schubert does not also end his song on the second climax like Goethe, but instead adds a repeat of the first two lines of the refrain? _____

> Nineteenth-century composers strongly believed in the affective association of keys, and Schubert was famous for his harmonic expressiveness. He used all the tools at his disposal—melodic, motivic, harmonic, voice-leading, rhythm, and texture—to pack even more meaning and expression into this famous poem—and he did it all when he was only seventeen years old!

46a) What have you learned about the meaning of the song from your analysis? _____

46b) How will you express it through your performance? _____

NOTES

1. Christian F. D. Schubart wrote the treatise around 1784, while he was still in prison; it was published in two journal articles (including sixteen keys in 1787 and all twenty-four in 1789). The treatise in which it also appears wasn't published until seventeen years after his death. Christian Schubart, *Ideen zu einer Aesthetik der Tonkunst* (Vienna: Degen, 1806. Reprint, ed. P. A. Merbach. Leipzig: Wolkenwander-Verlag, 1924). In Rita Steblin, *A History of Key Characteristics in the Eighteenth and Early Nineteenth Centuries* (Ann Arbor: UMI Research Press, 1983), 121, 242.

2. C. F. D. Schubart, *Ideen zu einer Ästhetik der Tonkunst*, quoted in Steblin, *A History of Key Characteristics*, 124–25.

3. Graham Johnson, *Schubert: The Complete Songs* (New Haven: Yale University Press, 2014), 1:797.

Part 4
MORE COMPLEX SONGS
TO ANALYZE

17

"Erster Verlust"

Do you ever think about that first great love? The protagonist of Schubert's "Erster Verlust" (First Loss) plunges into the painful world of obsessive memory, expressed through **key ambiguity**, **motivic parallelism**, **modulation**, **avoidance**, and **denied cadences**. Set to a masterfully succinct poem by Goethe, the song squeezes a thousand sighs from a scant nine lines of text. In this song you will explore the use of the I_4^6 and pivot chords to aid tonicization, recognize an augmented sixth chord, and find the semitone motive everywhere.

It is hard to believe that Schubert was only eighteen years old when he wrote this song. "Erster Verlust" was included in the works he sent to Goethe in 1816. For a poet who only wanted his songs set to simple folklike melody and accompaniment, one can only imagine how Goethe might have reacted to this highly expressive song!

POEM

Meaning

1a)   What is the subject of Goethe's poem? _____
_____
_____
_____
_____

1b)   Which line most clearly states what the protagonist is longing for; write it in German and English: _____
_____
_____

1c) How is this lost time to be brought back according to lines 1, 3, and 8?[1] _____

1d) Who could this person be, do you think? _____

1e) What opposite emotions are contrasted in line 7 of the poem? (Write it in German and English.) _____

Strong oppositions of emotion will certainly be expressed in any musical setting, so keep your ears open for this!

1f) Note that the first and last stanzas end with an exclamation point. Why does Goethe use this punctuation, when lines 1–4 appear to be questions ("Wer bringt . . ."/Who brings . . .)? _____

What does the exclamation point tell you about the protagonist's strength of emotion, and how will this affect your performance? _____

Rhythm, Meter, and Sound

2a) Speak the poem out loud in German to find the pattern of accented and unaccented syllables and mark them into the text.

2b) What is the basic foot? _____

2c) How many feet are in each line? _____ Is it the same in each line, throughout the poem? _____

2d) Are there any short feet (where the unaccented syllable is missing)? If so, where? _____

How does it affect the poem? _____

2e) Which harsh consonant might wake the daydreaming protagonist? (Hint: they are at the end of several lines.) _____ In which lines do these appear? _____

Rhyme Scheme

3a) Write the rhyme scheme into the poem by adding a letter at the end of each line. The first stanza is done for you:

a, b, c, d

___, ___, ___

___ ___

3b) Notice that none of the first four lines rhyme. However, the other lines either rhyme with or repeat previous lines, except for one. Which line never gets a rhyme, and what is the word (German/English)? _____

> **ALWAYS PAY ATTENTION TO RHYMES, ESPECIALLY IF ONE IS MISSING!**

The missing rhyme here is exactly what is missed by the speaker—first love!

MUSIC

As usual, Schubert deepens the meaning of the poem and adds considerably to it in his musical setting. Look closely at the musical setting to see what the composer is trying to say about how the protagonist feels at every moment.

4a) Before we look at every line in detail, take a look at the **dynamic level** through the piece.

The majority of the song is at what dynamic level? ____ Now go through the song measure by measure and indicate which measures change from pianissimo, along with the text line (in German and English) for that measure or measures; the first two are done for you:

mm. #:	*dynamic:*	*text:*
mm. 2–6:	*fp*	"schöne" (beautiful)
m. 7:	*cresc.*	"eine Stunde" (one hour)
_____	_____	_____
_____	_____	_____

4b) Which sections get louder? _____

Line 1: "Ach, wer bringt die schönen Tage"

Melody

5a) What do you notice about the shape of melody in m. 1? _____

Schubert often uses a monotone (flat vocal line) to express depression. What mood does the flat melody and the word "ach" convey? How does it feel to sing a guttural (the "ch" in "ach")? _____
_____

5b) If you connect the first and last note of the setting of line 1 ("Ach" to "Tage"), what do you get? _____ How far have you moved from the first note to the last? _____ The vocal range of the first line is narrow—only a fourth. Only one word is set to more than a semitone interval; what's the interval and the word (German/English)? _____
_____

Why does Schubert emphasize this word with an expressive interval? _____
_____

What does the flat melody of the rest of the line suggest about the singer's present feelings?
_____
_____

5c) How does the semitone up and down on "-nen Tage" make you feel in mm. 2–3? ____
_____

> **An appoggiatura is like a musical sigh.** The first note is usually a dissonance, resolving to a consonance in the second note. To make an appoggiatura expressive, give a little more to the dissonant note and then decrescendo a bit after you arrive on the resolution. The first note of an appoggiatura may not match the chord it is over; the beautiful sensation of a sigh is often created by the resolution of a dissonance. A semitone appoggiatura is particularly expressive, and Schubert often uses it to express grief or pain. You will often find a semitone motive in music by Schubert and other nineteenth-century composers, and in this case the semitone motive structures the entire song, in a technique called **motivic parallelism**, in which a motive appears at different levels of scale.

5d) Look at the semitone appoggiatura in m. 3 (D♭-C). Now write in the downbeat note or notes in the following measures:

m. 1: ____   m. 6: ____   m. 9: ____ ____   m. 15 (with pickup): ____ ____   m. 17: ____

Do you see how the D♭-C semitone motive governs the structure of the song (motivic parallelism), beginning at text lines 1, 3, 5, 7, and 8 (and 9 also, if you include the C at the pickup to m. 20). Notice too that the text lines that set the sad present time (lines 5 and 7 in stanza 2) begin with the sighing semitone motive D♭-C, while those setting the pleasant past begin with a single note, either C or D♭.

Harmony

The poet and theorist C. F. D. Schubart describes the key of F minor as "deep depression, funereal lament, groans of misery and longing for the grave," and A♭ major as "the key of the grave. Death, grave, putrefaction, judgement, eternity . . ."[2] How well do you think this choice of key expresses the meaning and emotion of the poem? _____
_____
_____

> Telltale signs of tonicization or modulation include **the appearance of a I_4^6 chord**, which generally serves to prepare for cadences. Another hint is the **presence of several secondary chords** in a row; if you find yourself writing this, it is likely that there is a temporary shift in key.

6a) Based on the first and last measures, in what key is this piece? _____

6b) What is the chord on the downbeat of m. 2? _____ What is its function in F minor? _____

6c) What is the chord on the third beat of m. 2? (Note that it contains a passing 7th in the voice part!) _____ What is its function in F minor? _____

6d) Red flag—you should have noticed that in m. 2 you have both a $_4^6$ chord and a seventh chord. In what key would this be a cadence preparation (e.g., I_4^6–V^7)? _____

6e) How is this key related to the key of the piece? _____

6f) Why do you suppose Schubert immediately leaves the minor tonic to set up a cadence to the relative major? (Hint: What is the song about, and what word does m. 2 set?) __
_____
_____

6g) Where (past or present) is the speaker in m. 1, and how can you tell? _____
_____

6h) Where (past or present) is the speaker in m. 2, and how can you tell? _____
_____

7a) What chord are we expecting on the downbeat of m. 3? (What would we like to have there, considering we've had I_4^6–V^7 chords?) _____ What function would that be in the new key? _____

7b) Do we get it? _____ How does that make you feel? _____
_____

7c) What chord do we get instead? _____ Is this a consonance or a dissonance? _____
How does that make you feel? _____
_____

7d) What are the chords on beats 2 and 3 of m. 3? _____

7e) What key might this suggest? _____ In this key, write the function of the first three beats of m. 3: _____

7f) Listen to mm. 1–3 again. In m. 3, do you feel as if we've cadenced in F minor again, or does it feel more like temporary motion to vi in A♭ major? _____
_____

How would you write the functions for m. 3 if it were still feeling like A♭ major? _____
_____

7g) Why do you suppose Schubert begins in one key in m. 1, prepares for a joyous ("beautiful") cadence in the relative major in m. 2, spoils it with a dissonance on the downbeat of m. 3, and (sort of) cadences in the original key? (Think of the meaning of the poem—what does each key represent?) _____
_____
_____
_____

7h) Are you amazed that Schubert expresses the entire idea of the poem harmonically in the first three bars?! _____

Line 2: "Jene Tage der ersten Liebe" (mm. 3–5)

Melody

8a) Listen to the first five bars. What is the vocal range of line 2 (mm. 3–5), and how does it compare with the vocal range of line 1 (mm. 1–3)? _____
_____

8b) Compare the first and last notes of line 2: Do we end up in a different place than we began? _____ What does this tell us about the emotion of the character at this point? Has it changed from the first line, according to Schubert? _____

How will you express this change in your performance? _____
_____

What words do you think inspire Schubert's melodic expansion (German/English) and why? _____
_____

Harmony

Can you hear what kind of cadence is in m. 5? If not, do the following:

9a) Write the names of the chords on the first and third beats of m. 5 (the end of the phrase): _____ What is their function and in what key? _____

How does this measure compare with the harmonies of m. 2? What do they both do?
_____

When a phrase ends with motion to the dominant, as this one does, it's called a **half cadence**. **The preparation** I_4^6–V is characteristic of a half cadence. The feeling of a half cadence is that of a temporary rest; **we expect to soon have a cadence to tonic in this key**.

9b) Measures 4 and 5 feature spectacular contrary motion, first diatonic (m. 4) and then chromatic (m. 5). Why do you think Schubert changes the texture so dramatically to set this line? _____
_____
_____

9c) What chord is created on beat 2? _____

What is its function and in what key? _____

Now write the functions (Roman numerals) of the chords in m. 5; don't forget to include the key first: _____

In addition to helping to prepare for a cadence, the chromatic motion in m. 5 also has an expressive purpose. What word does m. 5 set (German/English), and why does the chromaticism add to the expression? _____
_____
_____

Lines 3–4: "Ach, wer bringt nur eine Stunde / Jener holden Zeit zurück!" (mm. 6–9)

> **If the text repeats in a song, look to see how the musical settings are similar and how they differ.**

Melody

10a) Goethe repeats the phrase "Ach, wer bringt" (Ah, who will bring) in line 3. Compare Schubert's setting of the two phrases (m. 1 vs. m. 6): What is similar and what is different?
_____
_____

10b) Why do you think Schubert now sets the opening phrase higher? What does this say about the emotional level of the character? _____
_____
_____

10c) Describe the melodic shape of the vocal part in the setting of line 3 (mm. 6–7) and compare it with that of line 4 (mm. 8–9); make sure to include the beginning and ending note of each, the interval, and the general direction of each phrase:

1st note-last note   interval   direction of phrase
_____
_____

10d) Compare the emotion of each phrase: How does the character feel when the melody is slowly rising chromatically vs. when the melody descends diatonically, landing on a local tonic? _____
_____
_____

For each phrase of this section, where do you think the character is mentally—in the present (longing for the past) or in the past (happy)?

Phrase 1 (mm. 6–7): _____

Phrase 2 (mm. 8–9): _____

Rhythm

11a) Compare the accompaniment rhythm in m. 1 with that of mm. 6–7. How is it different, and what does it add to the mood of this phrase? _____
_____
_____

11b) How does the accompaniment rhythm change again in mm. 8–9, and what effect does it create? _____
_____

11c) Based on the rhythm in the right hand, how does the character feel in mm. 8 and 9?
_____
_____

11d) How does the left-hand rhythm change from mm. 6–7 to mm. 8–9? _____
_____

When the left hand is moving quickly, that often means the harmonies are changing more quickly, which also creates excitement! The harmony in mm. 6–7 changes every two beats, but in mm. 8–9, it changes every beat until we arrive (feeling excited and happy!) at a cadence on A♭ in m. 9.

11e) How will you express these rhythmic transitions in your performance? _____
_____
_____

Harmony

12a) As usual, to figure out the harmony it is helpful to **go to the cadence and work backward**. Play mm. 6–9 again and listen for the cadence in m. 9. To what chord is the cadence? _____

What is its function related to the key of the piece? _____

What have the first several bars taught us about the relationship of these two keys (tonic and relative major) to the present and the past and the emotion associated with each?
_____
_____

12b) Twice already in the piece Schubert has set up a cadence on the relative major, A♭, but wrenched us away at the last moment (see mm. 2–3 and 5–6). This technique of preparation followed by painful avoidance is a very typical way for composers (particularly Schubert) to express longing. How does it feel now to finally cadence on A♭ in m. 9? What emotion is the character feeling at this point? _____
_____

Do they feel they are in the unhappy present or the happy past? _____

> **Do you see how Schubert tells you very clearly through the music the exact emotional state of the protagonist? Always thoroughly examine the piano part as well as the vocal part.**

12c) Now that you know the key of the cadence in m. 9, *work backward* and write in the names of the chords in mm. 8–9, and only then, write in the functions in the key of the cadence, with four chords/Roman numerals in the first bar and three in the second. Be sure to write in the key!

        Key:
Chords: ___ ___ ___ ___ | ___ ___ _____ |
Functions: ___: ___ ___ ___ ___ | ___ ___ _____ |

12d) After you have written in the functions, notice that all the chords function clearly in A♭ except for the first one, because a half-diminished chord is usually a ii$^{\varnothing 7}$ chord and not vii$^{\varnothing 7}$. But if this chord were still in F minor, it would be a ii$^{\varnothing 7}$. Hmmm—maybe we enter m. 8 in F minor and **pivot** to A♭ major on the second chord, A♭^{6}, which could function both as III^6 in F minor and I^6 in A♭ major? To see if this makes sense, let's now look at the chords in mm. 6–7.

12e) What is the first chord in m. 6? _____ A fully diminished seventh chord suggests a function of vii$^{\varnothing 7}$, which points to (wants to move to) i.

If so, what key is this suggesting and to what chord do we want to go? _____ What is the chord on the third beat of m. 6? _____ Did we get the chord we wanted? _____ What is it called when we want a chord and instead get a different one? _____ What is the function of this chord in F minor? _____ Is this typical of a deceptive motion? _____ **(Deceptive motion is very easy to create because the difference from tonic and the submediant [VI] is only a semitone!)**

12f) Go ahead and write in the chords for mm. 6–7 below. Work forward, two chords per bar this time. When you are done, add the functions of the chords in the key of F minor and circle the deceptive chord. Only then, write in the function of the same chords, but in the key of A♭:

Key:
Chords: ___ ___ | ___ ___ | ___
Functions: f: ___ ___ | ___ ___ | ___
Functions: A♭: ___ ___ | ___ ___ | ___

Can you see how it mostly makes sense in both keys? The tipoff that suggests *the phrase is more in F minor* is the fully diminished seventh moving to a deceptive D♭^{6} in m. 6. So perhaps the protagonist is mostly in the present in mm. 6–7, wishing for a mere hour of the happy past, while in mm. 8–9 they are almost thoroughly in the past, happily cadencing on A♭!

Compare your analysis of mm. 8–9 with that of mm. 6–7 (above); do you see how the key of F minor continues to govern the tonality until the pivot chord of A♭ on beat 2 of m. 8?

Despite the fact that we see a shift from F minor to A♭ in this phrase, this analysis should show you that **Schubert is intentionally being ambiguous about whether some sections are in f or A♭, in the present or the past!**

TO FIGURE OUT THE FUNCTION OF A PHRASE:
Work backward from the cadence and forward from the beginning of the phrase. Where they overlap is the pivot chord or chords.

The next cadence does not occur until the end of line 7, so lines 5–7 form part of a larger musical grouping with three subsections.

Line 5: "Einsam nähr' ich meine Wunde" (mm. 10–12)

Text

13a) Let's review the meaning of line 5. Write it in English here: _____
_____

"Erster Verlust"

13b) How is the character feeling here? _____
_____

13c) Do you think the character is feeling in the present or in the past and why? _____
_____
_____

Melody

14a) Go through the vocal line and mark a circumflex (^) over every semitone in mm. 10–12. List them in order (the first one is done for you): D♭-C ____ ____ ____

14b) What do you notice about the direction of each one? _____

Wow, four descending semitones in only two and a half bars; why do you think Schubert sets line 5 this way? _____
_____

Remember from the discussion on semitones above (line 1) that appoggiaturas are expressive devices and sound like a musical sigh, creating a wonderfully mournful quality to the vocal line. How will you express this in your performance? _____
_____
_____

14c) Write down the first and last notes of this phrase: ____ ____ What direction does it move over the course of the phrase, and what is the interval created? (Please write it exactly as written—it's not a 3rd.) _____ How does this direction and interval express the text line? _____

What dissonant interval do you find in m. 11? _____ What effect is created? _____
_____

Texture and harmony

15a) What happens to the texture in the left hand in this phrase? _____

This text line deals with nurturing wounds, and later lamenting; can you think of a mythological character famous for his laments? (Hint: he was Greek, and could make the rocks cry with his sad songs!) _____ Schubert may be referring to the laments of Orpheus to his lyre through the sudden introduction of harplike arpeggiations in the right hand.

15b) What do you notice about the texture of the right hand of the piano (compared with the voice part)? _____

What is the first word of this text line (German/English)? _____

224   *Chapter 17*

Now why do you think Schubert doubles the voice part here? _____
_____

Notice how the sudden introduction of an additional voice in the piano in m. 12 (on a long appoggiatura, no less!) re-creates the suffering caused by the wound ("Wunde"). Schubert marks it with an accent—for good reason: the pianist needs to cause some pain in the listener at this point!

15c) Go ahead and write out the chords to mm. 10–12 on the first line and the function on the second; the first bar is done for you:

$$D\flat^6 \text{——} C^6\ f^6\ |\ \_\_\ \_\_\_\_\_\ \_\_\ |\ \_\_\ \_\_\ \_\_\_\_$$
$$\text{key: \_\_\_ f} \quad VI^6 \text{——} V\ i^6\ |\ \_\_\ \_\_\_\_\_\ \_\_\ |\ \_\_\ \_\_\ \_\_\_\_$$

Our last phrase ended in a cadence to A♭ (finally!) in m. 9. The first chord of m. 10 (D♭^{6}) could function as IV^6 in the key of A♭. What would its function be in the key of f? _____

So the key of the first chord is not clear, as it works fine in both keys. The next two chords in that bar are C^6 and f^6; do they function more clearly in A♭ or f, and if so, what is their function? _____

15d) This suggests that we may be back in F minor again. In terms of what we know about the association of keys with the present or past, would F minor make sense to set "Einsam nähr' ich meine Wunde," and if so, why? _____
_____

15e) Go ahead and write in the functions of mm. 10 and 11 below your chords (above, in question 15c). Don't forget to write in the key!

15f) Yes, it works very well in F minor, with the D♭^{6} chord acting as a pivot from A♭ major. Notice that m. 11 ends with a V$^6_5$ chord, setting up for a cadence to F minor. Do we get our tonic chord in m. 12? _____ What chord do we get instead? _____ Oh no—not another wrenching shift instead of a cadence! Why do you think Schubert chooses to pull the rug out from under our feet at this point? (Hint: look at the text.) .
_____

So, in addition to Schubert setting an appoggiatura in the voice and a really long appoggiatura in the top line of the right hand, he wallops us with an evaded cadence on the downbeat.

15g) Are we still in F minor in m. 12? Remember that **whenever you are confused, look ahead to see where the harmony leads!** What is the chord in m. 13? _____ And the chord immediately preceding it (m. 12, beat 3)? _____ So, what is the functional relationship between this chord and the following chord? ____–____ It looks like we might have a temporary tonicization of B♭ minor (iv in F minor); let's see if this is the case. Work backward in m. 12, writing in the functions in the key of B♭ minor above. Do you see how the protagonist is not able to cadence in the key of the present (i.e., F minor)?

Line 6: "und mit stets erneuter Klage" (mm. 12–14)

Text

16a) Let's review the meaning of line 6. Write it in English here: _____
_____

16b) What is the key word in this line that tells us how the character is feeling? _____

16c) Do you think the character is feeling in the present or in the past and why? _____
_____

Melody

17a) How does Schubert set the word "Klage" (lament)? _____

Why does he do this?_____
_____

Name the last two notes of this phrase: ____ ____ Now name the first two notes of the phrase: ____ ____ What is the interval of each? _____ Why do you suppose Schubert continues to emphasize this interval? _____
_____

How does the composer set "erneuter" (renewed) and why? _____
_____

17b) Connect the dots from the first note (A) to the last two notes (A♭-G). Do you see the short chromatic descent here? Later we will be connecting the dots from mm. 10–16 and, eventually, across the entire song.

17c) Find the lowest note in the song. Write it here, along with the line it is setting: _____
_____

Does it help to explain why the reprise from m. 17 to the end has a more subtle meaning, now that we have experienced the depth of grieving? How will you express a slight change in the last section? _____
_____
_____

Harmony

18a) We left off the previous phrase with a V²-i⁶ motion in B♭ minor (from the end of m. 12 to m. 13). The b♭⁶ could be i⁶ in B♭ minor or iv⁶ in the tonic F minor. It could even be ii⁶ in A♭ major. So how do we figure this out? Look at the chords in mm. 13–14; write them on the first line and their function on the second line:

    ____ | ____ ____
Key: ___ ____ | ____ ____

18b) Since a fully diminished chord usually functions as vii°, what key do these two chords (inversions of the same chord) suggest? _____ Now go back and write in the key for mm. 13–14 and their function. So mm. 12–13 shift temporarily to b-flat minor (iv), followed by diminished chords that clearly point to F minor.

18c) Line 6 is the loudest line in the song (though still only *mf*), and it speaks of "ever renewed lament." How will you convey this sense of lamentation in your performance?
_____
_____

Line 7: "traur' ich ums verlorne Glück" (mm. 14–16)

Text

19a) Let's review the meaning of line 6. Write it in English here: _____
_____

19b) What are the key words in this line that tell us how the character is feeling (in German/English)? _____

19c) Do you think the character is feeling in the present or in the past and why? _____
_____

19d) Notice that this is the only line in the poem that is set with phrase beginning with an upbeat. Why do you think Schubert did this, and how can you use it to deepen your performance? _____
_____

Melody

20a) What interval are the words "traur' ich" (I grieve) set to? _____

20b) What direction is the melody moving, and what is the interval outlined in mm. 15–16? _____ So the vocal line setting "I grieve for the lost happiness" plummets down an octave from C to C, the lowest note in the piece! So if you're ever not sure what a song is about, Schubert will helpfully underline it for you with his music, as he does here!

Harmony

21) Before we move to the harmony, note that Orpheus's lyre is now silent, replaced with slow-moving chords which get down to the business of telling us what the problem is.

Write down the chords in m. 15 and the first chord of m. 16. (It's okay if you don't know how to name the second chord in m. 15.)

```
              ___  ___ | ___ |
Key: f        ___  ___ | ___ |
```

Now work backward to determine their function. (Hint: we are still in F minor.) Notice that the phrase ends on a half cadence (motion to V that prepares for tonic in the next phrase). But how do we get to this dominant? Look at the second chord in m. 15. Notice that the top note (B) moves up to C in the next chord, and the lowest note (D♭) moves down to C. **When you hear or see a sixth moving to an octave, chances are it's an augmented sixth chord. Augmented sixths allow for a strong move to the dominant with their two semitones in contrary motion going to the octave.** There are three types of augmented sixth chords. This one is a German augmented sixth chord, because it sounds like a dominant seventh chord (as D♭7), but resolves by sixths opening up to the octave. The first chord of m. 15, of course is f^6, which is i^6 in F minor.

Summary of Lines 5–7 (mm. 10–16)

Melody

If you were to "connect the dots" between key notes in mm. 10–16, you would find the following basic melodies:

mm. 10–12: (D♭) **C** (B♭ A) **C**
mm. 13–14: (A-B♭) A♭- G
mm. 15–16: (D♭) **C** (B♭-A♭-G) **F – C**

Or you could think of it as **a descent from C ($\hat{5}$) down to F ($\hat{1}$)**, with a leap back to C. Keep your ears and eyes open for emphasis on important structural tones—all eighteenth- and nineteenth-century composers do this. More about connecting the dots later in this discussion!

22) One more thing: Look through the voice part from beginning to end. **There is only one measure that actually contains the tonic low F**; which is it? _____

What is the significance of the F suddenly appearing for the first time? _____
_____

Composers sometimes intentionally avoid a note or a chord in order to emphasize that something is missing (**withholding**). Examples of this technique abound in Schubert's songs and provide important clues to their essential meaning.

> **Always notice if something typical is missing—it's usually intentional avoidance.**

Here the composer cadences on every level of the scale except for $\hat{1}$. In other songs we may see cadences on every level except the dominant, or **avoidance of cadences to the tonic**.

Line 8: "Ach, wer bringt die schönen Tage" (mm. 17–19) (reprise of line 1)

> **Whenever you hear a text reprise, look to see how the music compares to its earlier setting.**

23) Does Schubert repeat the same melody and harmony from mm. 1–3? _____ As a reminder, this phrase opens in F minor and then suddenly shifts to A♭ major (with a I_4^6-V^7) on "schönen" (beautiful) to set up a cadence on A♭, but we are suddenly wrenched back to F minor (vii°^{7}–V$^6_5$–i) in m. 3, creating a shifting pull between the painful present (F minor) and the happy past (A♭ major).

Line 9: "Wer jene holde Zeit zurück" (mm. 19–21) (slightly altered reprise of line 4)

24a) Compare the musical setting of "Wer jene holde Zeit zurück" (who [will bring] that lovely time back?) in mm. 19–21 with its first appearance in mm. 8–19. Is it exactly the same? What three things are different? (Hint: look at the last beat of m. 19—two are present here; also look at the right hand.) _____

Steady rhythm: The right-hand rhythm is now steady, moving along with the vocal part, as opposed to being on the offbeat as earlier (mm. 8–9).

Added chord: The last line of Goethe's original poem did not begin with "Wer"; Schubert actually added it, as composers sometimes did. Can you see how it helped him to connect the two musical phrases setting the original lines 1 and 4? The f^6 chord makes motion to the g$^{ø6}_5$ on the downbeat of m. 20 more fluid; Schubert is gluing the two phrases together with the inversion on "wer." Again, as a reminder, the key shifts back to A♭ major via a pivot chord on beat 2 of m. 20 (III^6 in F minor = I^6 in A♭ major).

24b) *Change of dynamic*: What is the effect of raising the dynamic level of the last phrase (from *pp* in mm. 8–9 to piano)? In what way does this suggest a slight change the protagonist's emotion, and how will you perform it? _____

24c) Listen to the song again up to the end of m. 21. What perfect authentic cadences do you find? (Note: we are not talking about half cadences or incomplete or deceptive cadences.) _____ What important cadence level is missing? _____ Is this an example of **avoidance** (also called **withholding**)? _____ Why do you think that during the entire vocal part of the song, there is not even a single cadence to the tonic? _____

Piano Postlude (m. 22)

25a) If the piece ended in m. 21, it would have a different meaning. Immediately after the vocal part ends with a happy cadence to A♭ major, the piano part repeats the exact same melodic figure with the identical harmonic function to cadence in F minor. What do you think this means? _____
_____
_____

What a powerful and ironic ending to this song—it goes to show that the singer may not always be aware of what key they're in, but the pianist always knows![3]

25b) Why do you think Schubert selected this key (these keys) for this text? The theorist C. F. D. Schubart describes F minor as "deep depression, funeral lament, groans of misery and longing for the grave." Does this accord with the external key represented by the piano? Clearly Schubert is using the A♭ major to represent a happier time. Although usually the flat major keys have positive associations and both B♭ and E♭ major express love, according to the theorist, A♭ major is described as "the key of the grave."[4] See chapter 3 under "Choice of Key" for more on these associations.

Connecting the Dots

One last thing: if you were to assign one (or a few) primary notes to each text line setting ("connecting the dots"), you might find the following:

1–2)	**C** (D♭) **C**	mm. 1–5
3–4)	D♭	mm. 6–9
5–7)	(D♭) **C**	mm. 10–16
8)	**C** (D♭) **C**	mm. 17–19
9)	**C** (B♭-A♭)	mm. 19–21
Postlude:	(G)-**F**	m. 22

The whole song essentially wavers between C and D♭, grieving semitones that toggle between the past and the present. Note that the descent which sets line 9 (mm. 19–21) stops at A♭; the pianist needs to complete the descent in the postlude!

26a) What have you learned about the meaning of the song from your analysis? _____
_____
_____
_____
_____

26b) How will you express it through your performance? _____
_____
_____
_____
_____

NOTES

1. Schubert added the word "Wer" to the beginning of line 9. Graham Johnson, *Schubert: The Complete Songs* (New Haven: Yale University Press, 2014), 1:534.

2. Christian Friedrich Daniel Schubart, *Ideen zu einer Ästhetik der Tonkunst* (Vienna: Degen, 1806), reprint, ed. P. A. Merbach (Leipzig: Wolkenwander-Verlag, 1924), quoted in Rita Steblin, *A History of Key Characteristics in the Eighteenth and Early Nineteenth Centuries* (Ann Arbor: UMI Research Press, 1983), 124–25.

3. Deborah Stein and Robert Spillman write that "the vocal line could be considered essentially in A♭ and the accompaniment essentially in the relative minor." Deborah Stein and Robert Spillman, *Poetry into Song: Performance and Analysis of Lieder* (New York: Oxford University Press, 1996), 123.

4. Schubert, *Ideen zu einer Ästhetik der Tonkunst*, quoted in Rita Steblin, *A History of Key Characteristics in the Eighteenth and Early Nineteenth Centuries*, 124–25.

18

"Meeres Stille"

Only eight lines of poetry was enough for Goethe to create this masterpiece pitting a becalmed sailor against the much more powerful ocean. Schubert is justly famous for his beautiful melodies, but he will do anything to tell this tale, including hypnotize the listener with repetitive rhythms and a **monotone** melody. The composer gives many hints as to the possible fate of his protagonist, through the falling cadence levels, obsessively motivic rhythm, **withholding** of an important note and chord, and a **frame structure** which imprisons the sailor on his ship.

* * *

TEXT

This text is by Goethe, the most famous German Romantic poet. Read it slowly out loud in German and English.

1a) What is the subject of the poem and its main point? _____
_____
_____
_____

1b) Who are the two main protagonists? (Remember that a protagonist can be a form of nature.) _____

1c) Why is the sailor troubled? _____
_____

1d) What elements of Romanticism do you find in the poem? Underline all words in the poem that show Romantic expression. _____
_____
_____

1e) Compare the first two and last two lines of the poem. What do they have in common?
_____
_____

1f) Compare the middle four lines of the poem. What do they have in common? _____
_____

1g) Why do you think Goethe structured the poem this way? _____
_____

Who is stronger and more powerful? _____

Who is anxious, fearful? _____

What words show this for the ocean in lines 1 and 7? _____
_____

What words show this for the sailor in lines 3 and 6? _____
_____

1h) What is the rhythmic meter of the poem? _____

There are weak beats and strong beats; how many strong beats do you find per line?
_____

1i) What is the rhyme scheme? _____

Which two words do not rhyme and why not? _____
_____

1j) What do you think of when you read this poem? Write down anything this poem brings to your mind: _____
_____
_____

Figure 18.1. "Meeres Stille": first edition, published by Diabelli in 1821.

MUSIC

2a) Look at the facsimile of the early nineteenth-century publication by Diabelli (figure 18.1). Look at it the normal way, and then also turn it 90 degrees to the right and observe the patterns. Just by looking at it, in what ways does the visual image of the score express the text and meaning of the poem? _____
_____
_____
_____

2b) Note the overtone series in the piano part: what impression do you think this creates?
_____
_____

2c) Would you consider the piano part to be low, medium, or high? _____
_____

Why do you think Schubert writes it this way? _____
_____
_____

2d) What is the meter sign and tempo marking? _____
_____

What kind of music does this suggest? (Hint: this combination is discussed in chapter 2 of this book.) _____

Do you see how Schubert conveys the danger of the situation simply by marking the tempo and meter?

Listen to the song while following the score in which you have added your translation.

3a) How does this song (as opposed to just the poem) make you feel? Write down a few adjectives: _____
_____

3b) What is the tempo? _____

3c) What else might this music be appropriate for? _____

3d) Which words in the poem do you think Schubert has brought out in general? _____
_____
_____

3e) What do the rolled chords remind you of? _____

Motive

4a) Clap the two-bar rhythmic motive in the voice part in mm. 1–2 and describe it: _____
_____
_____

4b) Where else do you see this motive? Clap the rhythm through the entire piece. Circle any two-bar phrase where it is missing. (Note: a half note slurred to a quarter note will count as a dotted half for this exercise.)

4c) Why do you think Schubert sets most of the poem this way? _____
_____

4d) Where does it change and why? _____
_____
_____
_____

4e) In which section of the poem do these changes occur and why? _____
_____

4f) Note the repetition of the dotted figure and falling third interval in mm. 13 and 14. How does it make you feel, and how does it express the feelings of the sailor? _____
_____

4g) What words does it set? _____

Melody

5a) What and where are the highest and lowest notes in the song, and with what word are they associated? _____
_____

Why the extremes on those words? _____
_____

5b) What do you notice about the melody in mm. 1–8? _____
_____

5c) Which note appears most often? _____ How many times? _____

5d) Schubert is famous for the beauty of his melodies. Why do you suppose he wrote a melody like this? _____
_____

5e) Where else do you see this melodic technique? On what notes? _____
_____

5f) What earlier section is recalled at m. 25? _____

5g) Why do you suppose it is set differently? _____
_____

5h) In which measure and on what note is the highest point in the voice part? _____
_____

5i) Why do you think this word was set high? _____
_____

5j) What technique is used to give it extra emotional weight? _____
_____

5k)   Do you see any waves in the melody? _____
      _____

5l)   What are the melodic intervals created in mm. 6–7 and 17–18, and what words do
      they set? _____
      _____

Dissonant melodic intervals do not bode well for the protagonists in Schubert songs!

Text Setting

6)   Does Schubert set the text equally to music? (That is, does each line of text get the same
      number of measures?) _____ Why do you think he does this? _____

The trick for Schubert is how to suggest monotony on a becalmed ship without having the actual song be monotonous. He does it through harmony!

Bassline

7a)   But before we get to harmony, let's look at the bassline: What basically happens in the
      bassline from mm. 1–5 and why? _____
      _____

7b)   What happens in the bassline from mm. 13–17 and why? _____
      _____

7c)   What happens in the bassline from mm. 17–22 and why? _____
      _____

7d)   What interval is created? _____

7e)   What does this say about the emotional state of the sailor? _____
      _____

7f)   At the same time that the bassline is descending in mm. 17–22, the right hand of the
      piano is also rising chromatically, from D♯ up to F♯. Why do you think Schubert set this
      strong contrary motion here? _____
      _____

The right hand tries to rise against the pull of the bassline (ocean), but fails, getting stuck on F♯ and sliding back down to D♯ again in m. 24. Notice that from mm. 16–22 the note A stands unmoving like the surface of the ocean (no wind), while the harmony moves around it.

Cadence and Harmony Journey

8a) What key is this piece in? (Look at the final chord.) _____ (Did you say "Sea" major?) The poet and theorist C. F. D. Schubart described this key as "completely pure. Its character is innocence, simplicity, naivety, children's talk."[1] However, this song is in no way a traditional C major song, as you will see.

8b) Write the chords for I, IV, and V in this key. These are typically important chords.

  I: _____   IV: _____   V: _____

8c) What is the first chord? _____

8d) Do you feel pretty comfortable in this key? Why? _____
_____

Why do you think we get so much of the first chord in the beginning? _____
_____

9a) In what measure does it go out of this key? (Hint: look for accidentals.) _____
Name this chord: _____

9b) Now write its function (related to the key of this piece): _____

9c) What word does this chord set? _____

9d) Why is this word important? _____
_____

9e) To what chord does it want to go? _____
What would its function be? _____ Does this seem a pretty normal place to go? _____
Do we get the chord we want to go to? _____
Why do you think we don't get this chord? _____
_____
_____

9f) Now write the names of the chords in mm. 7–8: ___ ___

9g) What is surprising about the quality of the chord in m. 8 (consider the key signature)?
_____

What is its relationship with tonic? _____

9h) What is the relationship between the two chords in mm. 7–8? _____
_____

We'll write in the functions of these chords in a minute. **Often analyzing backward is the easiest because we can see where we get to!**

10a) First write in the chord names for mm. 9–12: ___ ___ ___ ___

10b) What is the relationship between these two chords, if the second chord is i? ___ ___

10c) If we assume that the chords in mm. 10 and 12 are implying the tonic of our temporary key, then how would you write the function for mm. 7–8? ___ ___

10d) Thus what type of cadence could we consider mm. 7–8 to be? _____

10e) What key and function (related to the key of the piece) does it imply? _____

11a) How do we move from the chord in m. 12 to that in m. 13? _____
_____

Notice how deep the "ocean" becomes in m. 13!

11b) To what note do we cadence in m. 16? _____ What is its function (Roman numeral) in the key of the piece? _____ What is its function (Roman numeral) in relation to the key that Schubert has been implying from mm. 9–12? _____ Why is Schubert emphasizing this functional area so much? _____
_____

11c) How do the chords move primarily in mm. 17–22: functionally or by voice leading?
_____

What happens in the bassline? _____
_____

What happens in the upper voice of the right hand? _____
_____

12a) What is the name of the chord in m. 20? _____ Where does it want to go? _____
_____

12b) What function is this (the place it wants to go) in the key of the piece? _____ Does it go there in the next bar (or ever)? _____ With what word or idea is this key associated? (Hint: see m. 6.) _____ So why doesn't Schubert go there? _____
_____

12c) What is the name of the chord in m. 21? _____ What is its intervallic relationship to the key of this piece? _____ What melodic interval occurs in the voice part between m. 17 and m. 18? _____ How do things look for that sailor according to the musical setting? _____

12d) What is the name of the chord in m. 26? _____ What is its function related to the key of the piece? _____ What functional level are we still trying to reach and why?
_____
_____

12e) What cadence level have we been lacking this whole song (see mm. 6–8 and 20)? ____
_____

12f) What note is emphasized in mm. 29–31? _____ Did we ever get that chord? _____
_____

What is the significance of this withholding? _____
_____
_____

Can you see how Schubert expresses the lack of motion in the poem through his use of harmony? Sometimes places that are avoided are even more important than places that are arrived at!

Large-*scale harmonic structure*

13a) Is this piece stable harmonically (lots of cadences on the same level) or unstable (goes through many keys)? _____

13b) Why do you think Schubert set it this way? _____
_____

13c) Listen to the piece again and circle each cadence. For each text line, write the name of the chord on the last measure of each four-bar phrase; the first two are done for you:

1) C   2) E   3) ___   4) ___   5) ___   6) ___   7) ___   8) ___

13d) What do you notice about the chords ending lines 1–2 and 7–8? _____
_____

Do you remember that lines 1–2 and 7–8 represented the ocean? What do you think Schubert is doing here? _____
_____

Make a box around lines 1–2 and 7–8 in the chart above (question 13c).

13e) Which notes of the C major scale do you see in your chart above? _____

Which cadence level do we *never* get? _____ With what is this level associated? (Hint: look at measure 6.)

13f) Look at the chords in your chart above from lines 3–6. What is the interval between each one? _____ In what direction are they moving? _____

What is the significance of the tonal ordering in this song? _____

Performance Considerations

14a) What have you learned about the meaning of the song from your analysis? _____

14b) How will you express it through your performance? _____

NOTE

1. Christian Friedrich Daniel Schubart, *Ideen zu einer Ästhetik der Tonkunst* (Vienna: Degen, 1806), reprint, ed. P. A. Merbach (Leipzig: Wolkenwander-Verlag, 1924), quoted in Rita Steblin, *A History of Key Characteristics in the Eighteenth and Early Nineteenth Centuries* (Ann Arbor: UMI Research Press, 1983), 124–25.

19

"Die junge Nonne"

"Die junge Nonne" shows Schubert at the height of his musical and artistic abilities. Jacob Nicolaus Craigher's powerfully constructed poem bursts with techniques of prosody including **cacophony**, **consonance**, **assonance**, **alliteration**, **onomatopoeia**, and **opposition of vowel sounds** to portray the storms without and within, and the steadfastness of the young nun as she awaits heaven. As in many Schubert songs, motives in the piano prelude tell the story and represent both the physical and the emotional worlds. The motives are expanded to a higher level of structure, creating **motivic parallelism**. You will find a **semitone motive**, **an enharmonic shift**, **augmented sixth chords**, and **plagal tonal areas**. The tonal and linear structures intensify the meaning in miraculous ways and you, like the young nun, will also be transported to a higher realm!

* * *

TEXT

(Before you begin, make sure to number the lines in the poem just to the left of the German text.)

General Meaning

1a) What do you think this poem is about? _____
_____
_____
_____

1b) Who is speaking? _____
_____

1c) What is happening? _____
_____

1d) How does the young nun regard the storm? Why? _____
_____
_____

Stanzas

2a) How many stanzas are in this poem? _____

2b) Compare lines 1–4 and lines 7–10. What is the same? _____
_____

2c) What is different? _____
_____

2d) What is the object of the action in stanza 1? _____

2e) What is the object of the action in stanza 2? _____

2f) What is doing the action in stanza 1 and 2? _____

2g) What does line 6 tell us about the relationship between stanza 1 and 2? _____
_____

2h) To whom does she speak in stanza 3? _____
_____

2i) What characteristically Romantic poetic concept is expressed in stanza 4? _____
_____

Poetic Meter

- Read through the poem out loud in German, listening for and feeling the meter.
- Go through the poem and mark a slash (/) over the accents in each line.
- Review the section on poetic meter in chapter 1.

3a) What is the general poetic meter? _____

3b) What is the physical and emotional effect of this particular meter? _____
_____
_____

"Die junge Nonne"

3c) Do you recognize this from any other Schubert settings? If so, from what song? _____
_____

3d) Does the poetic **meter** (i.e., trochees, iambs, etc., not the number of feet per line) stay mostly the same throughout? _____

Poetic Feet

To the left of the German text (and to the left of your line numbers), write in the number of poetic feet for each line of the poem.

4a) Divide the poem into the following groupings by line: 1–6, 7–10, 11–15, 16–21, 22.

4b) What patterns in the number of feet per line do you notice within these groupings?
_____
_____

4c) What pattern is broken in the final strophe, at line 19? _____
_____

4d) What happens to the poetic meter in line 22? _____
_____

4e) How does this express the entire meaning of the poem? _____
_____
_____
_____

Rhyme Scheme

5a) Does this poem have a regular rhyme scheme? _____

5b) If not, are there any rhymes at all? If so, write them here with the line numbers:
_____

5c) How do any rhymed words express the meaning of the poem? _____
_____
_____
_____

5d) Why do you think the poet adds these in the second half? _____
_____
_____
_____

Alliteration and Consonance

6a) Find and underline alliteration and consonance in the poem. (Note: consonance is the repetition of consonants in a line of poetry; alliteration is a subset of consonance in which the repeating consonants begin the word. Review chapter 1 for some examples of these techniques.) Now write the letters that are emphasized through alliteration/consonance in each stanza and put the line in which it appears in parentheses. Some stanzas will have up to four examples. Stanza 1 is done for you:

stanza 1: W = v sound (line 1)

stanza 2: _____

stanza 3: _____

_____

stanza 4: _____

_____

6b) Compare the amount of alliteration between stanzas 1–2 and 3–4. What do you notice?
_____
_____

6c) Why do you think the poet does this? _____
_____
_____

6d) What might the poet be conveying through this? _____
_____
_____

Cacophony

7a) What harsh sounds appear in the storm stanzas (1 and 2)? _____
_____

7b) How can you use these to create a more compelling performance? _____
_____
_____

MUSIC

Cadence Map and Phrasing

Listen to the song with the score and write down each cadence level (note name) above the bar of the cadence. Now go to your text and translation and write the note name of each cadence at the end of each text line in which it occurs.

8a) What do you notice about the first half of the song (to m. 51)? _____
_____

8b) On what notes (tonal levels) do you find cadences in the second half (from m. 52 to the end)? _____
_____

8c) What is the general difference in key between the two halves of the song and why?
_____
_____

8d) Is this mostly a modulating piece or one that stays primarily in a single key? Why? ___
_____
_____
_____

8e) The piano prelude contains strong downbeat phrases all through it, yet once the voice enters, the phrases all begin with upbeats, except for a few distinctive sections. List the measure numbers of these exceptions, and write in the words they set: _____
_____
_____

Why do you think Schubert distinguishes these sections with a change in phrase type?
_____
_____
_____

8f) The poet and theorist C. F. D. Schubart describes the key of F minor as "deep depression, funeral lament, groans of misery and longing for the grave," while F major is described as "complaisance and calm."[1] How well do you think Schubert's choice of key expresses the meaning and emotion of the poem? _____
_____
_____
_____

Piano Prelude

9a) What is the mood of the piano prelude? _____
_____

9b) How is this mood created by the key? _____
_____

The meter? _____
_____

The general range of the piano? _____
_____

The technique in the right hand? _____
_____

9c) Describe the galloping motive in the left hand of the piano (first four notes). What direction is it moving and to what interval? _____

Is it on a downbeat (strong) or an upbeat (weak)? _____

How does its direction and placement in the bar affect its emotional impact? _____
_____

Describe the rhythm (which notes are long and which short?): _____
_____

9d) What happens to the register in the left hand beginning in m. 2? _____
_____

Describe this motive, and remember it: _____
_____

9e) What might the two motives (very low and then high) represent in a storm? _____
_____

9f) What is the dynamic level at the beginning? _____ What effect does this create? _____
_____
_____

Graham Johnson describes the prelude as presenting "both the diabolical and the divine in the human condition.[2]

"Die junge Nonne"

Strophe 1 (mm. 10–35)

10a) The voice takes up the rising galloping motive from the left hand of the piano, but adds to it. How is it altered and why? _____
_____
_____
_____

10b) Accents in Schubert's music serve to emphasize the damage being done to the house (and the person); notice how Schubert puts these words of destruction right on the downbeats of mm. 11, 15, and 19: "heulen," "zittert," and "leuchtet." How will you bring them out? _____
_____
_____
_____

Linear motion

11a) Look at and write down the highest notes of the melody line in mm. 10 through 28:

    10   11   14   15   18   19   22   23   24   25   27   28

    ___ ___ ___ ___ ___ ___ ___ ___ ___ ___ ___ ___

11b) Now circle the highest note in the series (the first one).

11c) Count the number of measures from mm. 10 to 19 (including m. 10) = _____ mm.

11d) Count from 19 to 28 (including m. 19) = _____ mm.

11e) What do you notice? _____

11f) How has Schubert structured his voice leading in the passage from mm. 10–28? _____
_____

11g) Why do you suppose the top note of the voice part moves so little? _____
_____
_____

12a) Schubert uses linear motion to create his harmonic movement. For each pair of measures, write the names of the two chords and indicate the note or notes that changes in parentheses. The first one is done for you:

                chords   *linear motion*

    mm. 10–11: f^6-$D\flat^6_4$ (C-D♭)

    mm. 14–15:   ___ ___   (   )   (   )

    mm. 18–19:   ___ ___   (   )

What is the term for a shift in spelling from flats and sharps? (See chapter 3 for discussion of this technique.) _____

12b) What is the interval and direction in the left hand between mm. 21–22? _____

What text line begins with this interval? _____

Do you see the association? Schubert often uses dissonant melodic intervals to set a mood.

13a) Schubert toggles between two chords in mm. 22–23 and in mm. 23–24, using a semitone to move between each. Write in the name of each chord on the lines, and then put the two notes that are different in each one. The first one is done for you:

mm. 22–23: g♯^{ø7}-g♯^{ø7} (F♯-F)
mm. 24–25: ___ ___   ( )

13b) Notice that in m. 25 the chord changes on the fourth beat. What is that chord? (To figure it out quickly, look at the chord in m. 26.) _____

13c) How does the bass move to the low C? Write the two notes, including 2 ____–____

13d) How does the right hand move to middle C? ____–____ You have contrary motion to the octave (C), so what kind of chord are we dealing with? _____

13e) Figure out which type it is where it resolves, and what it prepares for: _____

14a) How does tonic shift at "Immerhin" (nevertheless, still) in mm. 31–32? _____

Why do you think Schubert includes a pedal tone on F from mm. 28–32? _____

14b) With what chords (by function) does Schubert set "Immerhin" in mm. 31–32 and why?

14c) Why do you think Schubert shifts the tonic and uses this particular harmonic motion in mm. 31–32? _____

14d) Why do you suppose the highest note so far appears on "immerhin" (in m. 32)? _____

14e) Why does Schubert shift back to F minor in the middle of m. 33? _____

Strophe 2 (mm. 36–51)

15a) How is strophe 2 (mm. 36–51) similar to strophe 1 (mm. 10–30)? _____

15b) How is it different and why? _____

15c) What is the emotional effect of the second strophe being presented in a more condensed way? _____

Strophe 3 (mm. 52–61)

16a) Compare the opening of the third strophe in m. 52 with the openings of the first and second strophes of the song in mm. 10 and 36. What important shift has occurred and why?

16b) Compare the second measure of strophe 3 (m. 53) with mm. 11 and 37. How is it different melodically and rhythmically? _____

16c) Why do you think the melody is now different melodically and rhythmically? _____

16d) The short-short-long motive in m. 53 derives from a simplification of the vocal melody originally found in m. 11, which itself comes in m. 2. Beginning in the vocal part in m. 53 and then continuing in the bass part until the end of m. 60, how many times altogether is this rhythmic motive sounded? _____ Why do you think Schubert is emphasizing this motive so thoroughly in the third strophe? _____
_____

16e) Compare this rhythmic rhythm with the poetic meter of the piece, and what do you discover? _____
_____

16f) How do the quasi-cadences to C (over a G pedal) in mm. 54 and 56 make you feel?
_____

17a) How does it feel to move from C major to an A major chord in mm. 55–56? _____
_____

Why might Schubert have moved to this chord? (Hint: think of the verb.) _____
_____

What is the term for moving to a chord a third away (with a chromatic shift)? (See chapter 3 for discussion of this technique.) _____
_____

17b) What tonal area might Schubert be preparing us for with the A major chords and the melodic B♭ (especially the augmented second C♯-B♭)? _____

17c) Do we go there in m. 58? _____ If not, where do we go (chord and function in A major), and why? _____
_____

17d) What are the relationships between the tonal areas in the second half of mm. 54 and 55 (C), 56–57 (A), and 58 (F), and what effect does it have? _____
_____
_____

18a) Look at the cadence in m. 61 to find the key, then name the chords and functions in mm. 58–61:

	58	59	60	61
Chord:	__	__ __	__ __	__
Function:	__	__ __	__ __	__

18b) What makes the cadence in m. 60 so thrilling? _____
_____
_____

18c) Why do you suppose Schubert lavished such attention on this third strophe? _____

19) How many high Fs appear in strophes 1 and 2? _____ How many are in strophe 3 (not counting repeated notes) and why? _____

Strophe 4 (mm. 62–83)

20) Where is the highest note in the song, and why? _____

21a) What is the chord that begins the strophe in m. 62? _____

21b) To what chord does it move in m. 63? _____ What would its function be in F major? _____ Have we seen emphasis on $\hat{6}$ before? If so, where? _____

What text was it set to? _____

Is the subject related? _____

David Kopp writes about the importance of the mediant relationships in this song and the textual link between these two passages, and notes how the "direct, functional mediant shift" creates a sense of disjunction appropriate for conveying a shift in awareness or a transcendent state.[3]

21c) How do we get from the first chord to the second (name the technique and which notes change)? _____

21d) What is the relationship between these two chords? _____

21e) To what note is the cadence to measure 65 and how does it make you feel? _____

Note that Schubert's contemporary, Christian Schubart, author of a book which includes characteristics of each key, describes this key as "A leering key, degenerating into grief and rapture."[4] Both composer and theorist clearly understood D♭ major as an extreme key in the flat area (traditionally associated with love, beauty, and sweetness), and "rapture" certainly describes this passage.

21f) Observe the bassline in mm. 62–65: what is it doing, and how does this contribute to this fantastic feeling in this passage? _____
_____

What can the pianist do here to increase it? _____
_____

Does this remind you of the bassline's rising chromatic lines earlier in the song? Look at mm. 12–22; perhaps the tension of the world has been transformed into excitement at her imminent union with her bridegroom. (Do mm. 67–68 remind you of "Gretchen am Spinnrade," mm. 22–25, with its two bars of semitone motive? Does it sound like the soul is trying to free itself?)

22a) What happens harmonically between mm. 66 and 67, and why do you think Schubert writes it this way? (Hint: look at the text.) _____
_____

22b) What chords evoke a religious feeling in mm. 67–68? _____
_____

23a) What rhythmic motive repeats incessantly in the left hand (treble clef) from mm. 69–80, and what does it represent? _____
_____

How many times does it ring? _____ So what time is it? _____

Does this fit with the rest of the poem? How do you know? _____
_____

23b) As you may have guessed by now, **the sound of the bell ringing**, which first appears in m. 2, is key to the expression of meaning in the song. The motive consists of two strikes (ding-dong) and this binary oscillation structures mm. 65–81, as you will see shortly. What do you think the two parts of the bell ringing could represent? _____
_____
_____
_____

23c) For each measure grouping, write in the harmony that oscillates (local function and key).

The first has been done for you:

65–66: V^7-I ($A\flat^7 \rightarrow D\flat$)

67–68 (two possible keys and functions): _____
_____

69–72: _____

73–74: _____

75–77: _____

78–79: _____

80–81: _____

In mm. 67–68 the key and function can be ambiguous. You have just cadenced to D♭, so it sounds like m. 67 is iv-I in C♯ (an enharmonic shift). Of course, it also could be i-V in f♯, and in m. 69 another enharmonic shift sounds like a C♯⁷ chord, which would support this. However, it turns out to function as a German sixth and instead of moving to F♯ minor, it moves to F major! Why do you think Schubert is surprising us at this point in the song? What could this mean? _____
_____
_____

24a) How does Schubert create excitement in mm. 75–77? _____
_____

24b) Why are mm. 80–81 a surprise, as compared to mm. 75–77 and 78–79? _____
_____

25c) On what chord do we cadence in m. 83? _____ On what functional level does the group of sequences end (in the second half of m. 81)? _____ How has this functional level been important in this piece? _____
_____

26a) From what earlier section are mm. 80–83 derived (list measure numbers)? _____

26b) In terms of the structure of the poem, how are they similar? _____
_____

26c) How are they related in terms of meaning? _____
_____
_____

26d) What makes the melodic setting so perfect for expressing this? _____
_____

27a) What is the dynamic in mm. 83–86, and why? _____
_____

27b) How does the melodic style change completely here, and why? _____
_____

27c) Go back to the mention of the little bells in the tower in mm. 72–74; which notes oscillate in the melody? ____-____-____-____-____ Do you see how the bell becomes her simple "Alleluia"?

27d) Now go back to the question about linear motion in mm. 10–28 with the melodic line of C D♭-D-D♭-C. Now why do you think Schubert limited the melodic line to one whole step in that passage and in mm. 36–49? _____
_____
_____

27e) Go back to mm. 76–81 and notice that the nun is singing the same notes as the bell.[5] What might this suggest? _____
_____
_____
_____
_____

28a) The bell is mentioned only in the last stanza of the poem—why do you think Schubert incorporates it into the entire song? _____
_____
_____
_____
_____
_____

The ringing bell is likely the Angelus bell, which reminded people to recite the prayer, which is devoted to Mary.[6]

28b) What do you think the bell represents, and why? _____
_____
_____
_____
_____

> In the beginning the left hand sounds more important and takes all our attention with its dramatic rising motion and distinctive rhythm; we hardly notice the bell motive, which at first seems bland with its even notes. It isn't until the fourth strophe that we truly notice it. This song is a reminder to us all, that through the storm of life, the bell is always there; we just have to listen for it!

29a) Listen one more time to mm. 1–2. Now what do you think is represented by the first two bars of this song? _____
_____

How can the pianist express this essential duality? _____
_____
_____

29b) Review your **cadence map** from the beginning of the analysis. How is the duality seen in the ringing bell expressed across the song, and what could it represent? _____
_____
_____

What cadence level stands out and why? _____
_____
_____

30) Describe the emotional voyage throughout the song: _____
_____
_____
_____

This song contains multitudes! Schubert contrasts the dark uncertainty of human emotions with the ecstatic glory of transcendence. How will you present this powerful contrast?

31a) What have you learned about the meaning of the song from your analysis? _____
_____
_____
_____
_____

31b) How will you express it through your performance? _____
_____
_____
_____
_____

NOTES

1. Christian Friedrich Daniel Schubart, *Ideen zu einer Ästhetik der Tonkunst* (Vienna: Degen, 1806), reprint, ed. P. A. Merbach (Leipzig: Wolkenwander-Verlag, 1924), quoted in Rita Steblin, *A History of Key Characteristics in the Eighteenth and Early Nineteenth Centuries* (Ann Arbor: UMI Research Press, 1983), 124–25.
2. Graham Johnson, *Schubert: The Complete Songs* (New Haven: Yale University Press, 2014), 2:34.
3. David Kopp, *Chromatic Transformations in Nineteenth-Century Music* (Cambridge: Cambridge University Press, 2002), 258–59.
4. Christian Friedrich Daniel Schubart, *Ideen zu einer Ästhetik der Tonkunst*, quoted in Rita Steblin, *A History of Key Characteristics in the Eighteenth and Early Nineteenth Centuries*, 121–24.
5. Kopp, *Chromatic Transformations*, 261.
6. Johnson, *Schubert: The Complete Songs*, 2:34.

20

"Die Liebe hat gelogen"

Everything about this song is fake—except for the pain, which is absolutely real and drenches every measure. In this song about betrayal, the harmonies are ambiguous and often deceptive. Elements of surprise burst out in the form of unexpected chords, sudden dynamic shifts and accents, **enharmonic reinterpretation**, and **astonishing tonal shifts**. In analyzing this song you will find numerous delicious chords, including **augmented sixths** and a **Neapolitan**, **chromatic third relationships**, **modal mixture**, and (of course), **a semitone motive**.

* * *

TEXT

The poem was written by Karl August Graf von Platen-Hallermünde, a nobleman from Vienna with a terrible (for the time) secret—he was attracted to men.[1] He expressed the bitterness of his situation in a number of his poems; the only other Platen poem set by Schubert is the equally devastating "Du liebst mich nicht."

In 1821 a friend brought manuscripts of Platen's poetry to Schubert and his circle and the song was composed the next year. The subject of betrayal must have resonated strongly with Schubert. Austria was under a repressive government, a virtual police state trying to stamp out liberal thought which was considered dangerous after the experience of the French Revolution and Napolean. Censorship was rife and in 1820 Schubert and his friends were raided by the police. Schubert's friend, the poet Johann Senn, had his papers seized and was imprisoned for over a year for his "moral and political beliefs and actions" and then permanently exiled from Vienna; this apparently made a big impression on Schubert.[2] "Die Liebe hat gelogen" was published in a collection that also included two songs with texts by Senn, suggesting that Schubert was thinking about his friend's fate when the songs were published.[3]

1a) Read the poem out loud in German and English. What is the poem about? _____
_____
_____

1b) How do the two stanzas differ? What happens in the first? In the second? _____
_____
_____
_____

1c) What is the poetic meter? _____

1d) Speak the first line; what do you notice about "Liebe" and "gelogen"? Why do you think the poet did this, and how will you bring it out in your performance? _____
_____
_____

1e) Schubert's song shows changes to Platen's published poem. The composer may have been using an earlier version of the poem, or he may have made the changes himself. Originally, line 5 read "Es rinnen heiße Tropfen" (hot tears run down). Schubert, however, replaced "rinnen" with "fließen."[4] Say this line out loud: "Es fließen heiße Tropfen." What do you notice? Why do you think it was changed? (As a reminder, the eszet [ß] is pronounced like "ss.") _____
_____
_____

1f) Lines 7–8 were originally "Laß ab, laß ab, zu klopfen, / Laß ab, mein Herz, laß ab" (Let up, let up, from pounding / let up, my heart, let up).[5] Why do you think Platen repeats "Laß ab" so many times? Try saying it many times: What rhythm does it sound like?
_____
_____

1g) Schubert's version of the final two lines removes two of the repetitions of "Laß ab"—"Laß ab, mein Herz, zu klopfen, / Du armes Herz, laß ab" (Heart, beat no more; Poor heart, beat no more!)—and then repeats the opening stanza.[6] Why might the text have been changed in this way? _____
_____
_____

Schubert received the Platen poems in manuscript form in 1821, composed the song in 1822, and published it in 1823. We do not know whether Schubert altered the last two lines for his song (composed in 1821 and published 1823) or whether the poet changed them prior to publication. Based on Schubert's setting of that line (discussed later), it is likely that the composer made the change. This removal of obsessive repetition is an interesting contrast with Schubert's intensification of the obsession in "Du liebst mich nicht"—the other Platen song about rejection and betrayal—by increasing the total number of refrains in the poem from six to ten.

MUSIC

Rhythmic Motive, Form, Upbeat Phrasing, and Key

2a) Clap the rhythm of the bassline in first four bars. What do you notice? _____
_____

Describe the rhythm: _____
_____

2b) Where is the accent in the first bar and how is it expressed? _____
_____

Is this where you would expect an accent? _____ Why do you think Schubert put the accent here? _____
_____

2c) How is the mood set by the rhythmic motive in the piano? What kind of music does it sound like? _____
_____

Now listen to the entire song. Where do you find this motive? _____
_____

Where is it missing? _____

Why did Schubert set it this way? _____
_____
_____
_____

2d) What is the large-scale form of this musical setting? _____

The first stanza of the poem is set with phrases beginning with an upbeat, but then Schubert switches to phrases beginning with offbeats in the middle section of the song. Write the text set in mm. 8–11: _____
_____

Now why do you think Schubert makes this shift? _____
_____

How will you incorporate this into your performance? _____
_____

3a) How many measures in each section?

   _____   _____   _____   _____

   Prelude   Stanza 1 (A)   Stanza 2 (B)   Stanza 1 (A')

3b) What do you notice about the structure? _____
    _____

3c) Schubert clearly selected the key of this song carefully. The poet and theorist C. F. D. Schubart described this key as "Declaration of love and at the same time the lament of unhappy love. All languishing, longing, sighing of the love-sick soul."[7] How well do you think this key expresses the emotion of the poem? _____
    _____
    _____

Piano Prelude

4a) Listen to the piano prelude. Does anything about it surprise you? What and why? ____
    _____
    _____
    _____

4b) What key is this piece in? _____ List tonic and dominant in this key: _____

4c) On what chord and function does the prelude begin and end? (i.e., m.1, beat 1 and m. 2, beats 3–4). _____ _____ What kind of cadence is this and why? _____
    _____

4d) Name the chord on m. 1, beat 3: _____ Is this chord natural to the key of the piece? _____ What is the interval between the root of this chord and tonic in this key? _____ So what is the function of this chord? _____

   What function does this chord often lead to? _____ Does this chord lead to that function in m. 2, beat 3? _____

4e) Name the chord and function on beat 1 of m. 2. Note that the C at the end of m. 1 is suspended over the barline and so is dissonant to the chord: _____

   Name the function of the chord in bar 2, beat 2 (note that the A♭ moves down to G and the F♯ moves up to G): _____

   What note does this chord share with the special chord in m. 1, beat 3? _____

   This chord moves strongly to the dominant by contrary motion of what interval?
   _____ Tasty!

4f) Why do you suppose Schubert didn't end the prelude on the original tonic chord?
_____
_____
_____

Section A (first vocal section, mm. 3–7)

5a) What is the vocal range of this section? Highest note: _____ Lowest note: _____

Would you consider this a wide or a narrow range? _____

Why do you suppose Schubert set the poem with this type of range? _____
_____
_____
_____

5b) At what dynamic level does the voice enter? _____ Why do you think it is even softer than the opening piano prelude? _____
_____

5c) What is the effect of beginning the vocal part with an eighth-note upbeat? _____
_____

5d) Sing just the vocal line of mm. 3–4 alone without the piano. How would you describe the melodic shape in general? _____
_____

Why do you suppose Schubert included the two large intervals at the beginning and the end? _____
_____
_____

5e) Now listen to the recording of mm. 3–4, paying particular attention to the piano part. Are there any surprises in m. 3? (Hint: listen to beat 3.) _____
_____

On what word is this surprise, and what does it mean? _____

How did Schubert get from the chords in beats 1–2 to the chord on beat 3? (What technique is used; what interval does a note move between the chords?) _____
_____

What note does this chord have in common with the surprise chord in m. 1, beat 3? __

What important interval is emphasized in both chords? _____

5f) Name the chord and function which sets the word "Sorge": _____

Why did Schubert use a dissonant chord on this word? _____
_____

Oh my goodness—what is that colorful chord on the second beat of bar 4 (name and function)? Again, notice the A♭ in the bass moving by semitone to the G and the F♯ in the right hand moving by semitone to the G; does this seem familiar? _____
_____

What note does this share with the previous chords on beat 3 of each bar? _____

What interval is important in the motion from the chord on beat 2 to the chord on beats 3–4? _____ What, again?! That's the fourth one—could this be a motive?

5g) What does the expression "lastet schwer" mean? _____

Why do you think Schubert repeatedly uses this particular interval? _____
_____

6a) Sing the melody in mm. 5–6 alone. Besides now being in C major, does it sound like a typical melody? _____ What word is set on the first C major chord (m. 5, beat 1), and what does it mean? _____

How real and appropriate does the C major feel? _____
_____

6b) The C major chord repeats on beat 2, but B♭ is added on the second half of beat 2. Now what do you call the chord? _____ Where does this chord want to resolve? _____ What is its function now in the key of the piece? _____ So much for tonic major! How does the switch to C major make you feel in mm. 5–6? _____
_____

6c) What is the name of the chord on beats 3–4? _____ Say what?! Did the chord just before (2nd half of beat 2) resolve the way we wanted? _____ Why not? _____
_____

How does the chord on beats 3–4 make you feel? _____
_____

By what interval does the bassline move to the chord on beats 3–4? _____

This is starting to sound repetitive! What note finally *isn't* the same as the previous beat 3 chords? _____ Why, do you suppose? _____
_____

How do the other voices move (the technique and notes)? _____
_____

To what word does Schubert set this chord? _____

How does Schubert emphasize this with dynamics? _____
_____

6d) Schubert may have chosen the chord in m. 5, beat 3 because it is so far away from the true tonic. How many sharps or flats are in the key signature? _____

How many sharps or flats are in the key of the chord in m. 5, beat 3? _____

What word does it set again, and why this chord? _____
_____
_____
_____

6e) Name the chord on the downbeat of m. 6: _____ Isn't this the chord we were looking for before we were so rudely interrupted? _____ Is this chord major or minor? _____ Wait, what was that passing tone again? _____

That note sounds awfully familiar—where have we heard it before (list measures)?
_____

Notice that the "surprise chords" on beat 3 or mm. 1, 3, and 5 of section A are all major, "betraying" the minor mode (and mood) of the song. But it finally changes in m. 16—reality has set in!

6f) Sing the melody of measure 6 (with the pickup). Does it seem like a nice C major cadence? _____ Now name the chords and functions of the progression in m. 6:

chords: _____

functions: _____

Why do you think Schubert keeps turning I into V^7/IV? _____
_____

7a) Name the chords and functions in m. 7:

chords: _____

functions: _____

7b) What do you make of the ambiguity between the F major and F minor in m. 7? _____
_____
_____

What note keeps returning? _____

7c) Follow the melodic line beginning with the top voice in the piano on the chord on beat 3 of m. 5 and moving to the lowest voice of the right hand in m. 7. Write down the notes; there is one upper neighbor (in parentheses):

___ (___) ___ ___ ___ ___ ___ ___ ___ ___ ___

Describe the direction and interval created by this line: _____
_____

How does this line support or contradict the bright C major mode of this cadence?
_____
_____

7d) Which is more important in mm. 3–6: the voice or the piano part, and why? _____
_____

Why do you suppose Schubert made them so different? _____
_____
_____

How will this affect your performance? _____
_____
_____
_____

7e) Why do you think Schubert made the piano part so soft in m. 7 and put in a < > in the bar? _____
_____

Section B (second vocal section, mm. 8–13)

8a) How and why does the rhythm change in mm. 8–11? _____
_____
_____

How does this compare with the setting of section A, and why? _____
_____
_____

What is the purpose of the grace notes? _____
_____

8b) How does the rhythm change in mm. 12–13? _____
_____

What is the subject of these two bars? _____

Now the dotted rhythm in the vocal melody (repeated from the opening) is revealed to represent what? _____ Now do you understand why this rhythmic motive pervades the A and A' sections of the song?

8c) Circle the first sung note of each bar in the vocal melody in mm. 8–11 and write them here: ___ ___ ___ ___

Now write the note on the downbeat of m. 12 and its resolution on beat 3 of m. 13 here: ___ ___

This simple line will serve as your safety rope during the chromatic shifts in mm. 8–11. Hang on—here we go!

Harmonic analysis of mm. 8–11

9a) Listen to mm. 8–11 and raise your hand each time you hear a cadence. Now go through and circle the cadence levels in your score and write them down here:

___ ___ ___ ___

Compare the melody of mm. 8–9 with mm. 10–11; what do you notice? _____
_____

What is the interval difference between them? _____ Does that sound familiar? Oh, yes—it's motivic!

9b) Once you know in which key each bar cadences, the functional analysis is easy. Begin each measure of 8–11 by writing in the key (in which the bar finishes), and then figure out the names of the chords and their functions. Remember to put in the key before the functions.

	key				
m. 8 chord names:		___	___	___	___
m. 8 functions:	___:	___	___	___	___
m. 9 chord names:		___	___	___	___
m. 9 functions:	___:	___	___	___	___
m. 10 chord names:		___	___	___	___
m. 10 functions:	___:	___	___	___	___
m. 11 chord names:		___	___	___	___
m. 11 functions:	___:	___	___	___	___

9c) Now compare mm. 8–9 with mm. 10–11 in terms of their functions. How do they compare? _____

What text do they set and what does it mean? _____
_____

In what tonal direction does each pair of phrases move (i.e., compare the keys of each phrase; do they go up or down)? from mm. 8–9: _____ from mm. 10–11: _____

Why does Schubert set the line this way? _____
_____

In what key would the beginning of the next phrase be if there were a third sequence?

_____ We will see hints of what could be in this sequence in section A' (mm. 14–18).

9d) Step back for a moment and compare the first chord of the piece with the chord on beat 3 of m. 5: ____ ____ What is their relationship? _____

Now compare the chord on the first beat of m. 8 with that on the last beat of m. 11:

____ ____ Why do you think that Schubert makes a big deal out of these two chords? (How does it express the meaning of the song?) _____
_____
_____

Voice leading mm. 8–11

10) Explain how Schubert uses voice leading to move from the last chord in each bar to the first of the next. Name the two chords and explain which note stays the same (common tone), which moves up, and which goes down (and by what interval)? The first one is done for you:

7–8: C major to C minor (<u>C and G stay the same, E♮ to E♭</u>)

8–9: _____

9–10: _____

10–11: _____

11–12: _____

12–13: _____

How does all this tonal sliding around make you feel? _____
_____

Do you see how Schubert's harmonies express so much emotion?

Mm. 12–13 (end of B section)

11a) Compare the melody of mm. 12–13 with that in mm. 3–4. What is the same and what has been changed? _____
_____
_____

11b) When you hear the return of the opening melody in m. 12, what do you think might be happening in the song? _____

In what mode (minor or major) are mm. 3–4? _____ In what mode (minor or major) are mm. 12–13? _____ Is the harmony in mm. 12 similar to the harmony in m. 3? _____ What key is m. 3 in? _____ What key is m. 12 in? _____ So is this a real refrain? _____
_____

Now compare the key of m. 4 with the key of m. 13: _____
_____

What function do they both end on? _____

Bassline motion in mm. 12–13

12a) Write down the note names of the quarter notes in the bassline of mm. 12–13: _____

What note does Schubert use to get from A to G in the bassline (we've seen this note somewhere before . . .)? _____

12b) Look through the entire piece for A♭ or G♯: Are there any measures it's not in? Write down the measure and reason:

m. ___: _____
m. ___: _____
m. ___: _____
m. ___: _____

Compare m. 17 with m. 6: Where's the A♭/G♯? Why do you think Schubert removed it here? _____
_____

Does it appear in the final bar? _____ Why? _____
_____

Section A' (third vocal section, mm. 14–18)

13a) The opening refrain returns beginning in m. 14 (with pickup). It starts off the same, but what happens in m. 15 (melodically and harmonically)? _____
_____
_____

13b) Name the chord on the first two beats of m. 16: _____ To what chord do we expect this chord to resolve? _____ Where in the song have we seen the key of this chord we are expecting, and with what image is it associated? _____
_____

What chord do we actually get in the second half of m. 16? _____ Is this a surprise? _____ If so, why? _____
_____

In what inversion is the "betrogen" half-note chord in m. 16? _____ What does this suggest about the key? _____
_____

13c) Name the chord on the downbeat of m. 17? _____ Would this chord have a function in the key that Schubert was setting up a cadence for in the second half of m. 16? If so, what would it be? _____

What is its function with respect to the actual cadence in m. 18? _____ Typically, the chord has enough ambiguity, which allows the composer to suggest two keys at the same time. Why do you suppose Schubert would do that? _____
_____
_____

13d) Returning to the downbeat of m. 16, notice that the F in the bass moves down a semitone to E♮, and the E♭ in the top voice moves up a semitone to E♮, thus creating contrary motion to an octave. Can you now figure out the function of the first chord in m. 16 in relation to that of the second? _____ Write the name of the surprise "betrogen" chords in the second half of mm. 5 and 16: _____ _____ By what interval is the bassline of each approached? _____ Can you see that this interval is motivic?

13e) Compare m. 17 with m. 6: What note is missing in the right hand? _____ Why do you think Schubert added the dotted note rising figure in the bassline? (Think of one practical reason and one expressive reason.) _____
_____
_____

(Notice that Schubert changed the dynamic marking from *fp* to *ff* here.)

13f) Circle and write in here the first vocal note of each bar in mm. 14–16: ____ ____ ____

Now compare this descent with that of the right hand at the moment of the surprise chord on "betrogen" in mm. 16–17 (beginning beats 3–4 in m. 16); write the top line notes:

____ ____ ____ ____ ____ Notice how the descent has changed. Is either one of them "real" (following the key indicated by the key signature)? _____

SUMMARY QUESTIONS FOR "DIE LIEBE HAT GELOGEN"

14) Why do you think Schubert added the repeat of the first stanza of poetry, and why do you think he changed the musical setting? _____

What do you think is the function of the major mode in this song?[8] _____
_____
_____
_____

Does the ending of the piece feel conclusive or satisfying? Why or why not? _____
_____
_____
_____
_____

15a) What have you learned about the meaning of the song from your analysis? _____
_____
_____
_____
_____
_____

15b) How will you express it through your performance? _____
_____
_____
_____
_____
_____

NOTES

1. Kristina Muxfeldt, "Schubert, Platen, and the Myth of Narcissus," *Journal of the American Musicological Society* 49, no. 3 (Autumn, 1996): 500.
2. Raymond Erickson, *Schubert's Vienna* (New Haven: Yale University Press, 1997), 22–23; Muxfelt, "Schubert, Platen, and the Myth of Narcissus," 504.

3. Walter Dürr, "Lieder für den verbannten Freund: Franz Schubert und sein Freundeskreis in Opposition zum Metternich-Regime," *Zeichen Setzung: Aufsätze zur musikalischen Poetik* (Kassel: Bärenreiter, 1992), 135–40, in Muxfeldt, "Schubert, Platen, and the Myth of Narcissus," 505.

4. Walther Dürr, ed., *Franz Schubert: Neue Ausgabe sämtlicher Werke*, ser. 4, vol. 2a (Kassel: Bärenreiter, 1075, xvii, and Muxfeldt, "Schubert, Platen, and the Myth of Narcissus," 481.

5. Translation by Kristina Muxfeldt, "Schubert, Platen, and the Myth of Narcissus," 481.

6. Translation by Richard Wigmore in Graham Johnson, *Schubert: The Complete Songs* (New Haven: Yale University Press, 2014), 2:182–83.

7. Christian Friedrich Daniel Schubart, *Ideen zu einer Ästhetik der Tonkunst* (Vienna: Degen, 1806), reprint, ed. P. A. Merbach (Leipzig: Wolkenwander-Verlag, 1924), quoted in Rita Steblin, *A History of Key Characteristics in the Eighteenth and Early Nineteenth Centuries* (Ann Arbor: UMI Research Press, 1983), 124–25.

8. Kristina Muxfeldt suggests that the major mode in Schubert often represents a shift to fantasy. Kristina Muxfeldt, *Vanishing Sensibilities: Schubert, Beethoven, Schumann* (Oxford: Oxford University Press, 2011), 173.

21

"Ganymed"

"Ganymed" is a song about transformation and transcendence. In Greek mythology, Ganymede was said to be so beautiful that he was taken up to heaven by Zeus himself to serve as cupbearer to the gods. Goethe's poem is one of a contrasting pair he wrote about two possible relationships with the divine: Prometheus, who rebelled against the gods and stole fire, is set in opposition to Ganymede, who adulates first nature and then Zeus; both poems were set by Schubert.[1]

Ganymede is one of several beautiful young men in Greek mythology whose appearance in literature and art has homoerotic associations (see chapter 12, "Du liebst mich nicht," for a discussion of Narcissus).[2] Lawrence Kramer associates the first part of the poem with feminine nature (spring's regenerative powers and "endless beauty") and the second, with the masculine divinity of an all-loving Father. Expression of an ecstatic state appears throughout, but the rapture originally found in nature ("Liebeswonne") is transformed through his heavenly flight to a divine unity with the god.[3]

Schubert set Goethe's poem using **progressive tonality**, when a song closes in a different key than it began. "Ganymed" is an extreme (and wonderful) example, moving through many different keys in order to express the multitude of different emotions on the journey to transcendence. You will also find an example of an **enharmonic shift** (using enharmonic notation to shift from flats to sharps or vice versa) and the use of distinct **key characteristics** (the use of specific keys to express associated emotions).

* * *

TEXT

1a) Number the lines in your copy of the poem and its translation.

1b) Who is speaking? _____ To whom is he speaking? _____

_____

1c) What are their relationships, and how can you tell? _____
_____
_____

1d) In what ways are Ganymed's feelings about spring expressed as that of a lover? List words and phrases that reveal these feelings: _____
_____
_____
_____
_____
_____

1e) Which lines contain these yearning and loving expressions? (List them by number.)
_____

1f) Do you see how the overall emotion of the entire first section is yearning and sensual love, as if for a person? "Yearning love" ("sehnenden Liebe") will, in fact, appear in the second half of the song.

2a) What event changes this expression of nature adoration and sets things in motion?
_____

What do you think is the meaning of the nightingale's call in this poem? _____
_____
_____
_____

2b) In what way do lines 18–19 and 20–21 change the nature of the poem? _____
_____
_____

2c) Lines 22–25 continue the narration, describing Ganymed's journey up through the clouds. What does it mean that the clouds "bow down to yearning love"? _____
_____
_____
_____

2d) What emotions do you think Ganymed expresses in line 20 ("I come, I come"), line 21 ("Ah, whither? whither"), and lines 22–25 ("Upward I soar, upward! The clouds float downward; the clouds bow down to yearning love—")? (List each line's answer separately.)

Line 20: _____

Line 21: _____

Lines 22–25: _____

2e) How does this emotion change in lines 26–31 ("to me! To me! Into your lap, upwards! Embracing, embraced! Upwards to your bosom, all-loving Father!")? _____
_____
_____

3a) Is Goethe's poem in a regular meter and rhyme scheme or is it in free verse? _____
_____

3b) Are there any rhymes? If so, list them here: _____
_____

MUSIC

4a) Is this a strophic song or a through-composed one? _____

4b) Is there one general mood in the music or several? _____

4c) How would you divide the song into sections and why? Mark your text and translation with lines dividing the sections, and list the measure numbers here: _____
_____

4d) Do most phrases in this song begin on upbeats or downbeats. Why? _____
_____
_____

Which phrases stand out and why? Include the measure numbers. _____
_____
_____
_____
_____

5a) Compare the general rhythm of each section; look at the subdivisions of the beat as the song progresses. Do you find a steady subdivision of the beat or does it change (and if so, how)? _____

If it changes, does it make the song sound slower or faster as it goes along? _____

5b) Does this song stay generally in one key or does it modulate? Listen to the song while following the score and circle every cadence you hear. You may need to listen several times. **Make a cadence map** by writing in the cadence levels (e.g., B♭) next to your text and translation. Write the cadence levels in here: _____

5c) Does the song end in the same key as the beginning? _____ Why do you think Schubert does this? _____
_____

5d) Write the key in which the song begins, and the key in which it ends: ____ ____ In the circle of fifths, which key is higher (more in the sharp direction)? _____ Based on the poem, does it make sense for the tonality to move in this direction and why? ____
_____
_____

5e) Reread the discussion of "Choice of Key" in chapter 3. For each cadence area, write in the key and its description as noted by poet and theorist C. F. D. Schubart. Do the key areas accord with Schubart's descriptions? _____
_____
_____
_____
_____
_____
_____
_____

Piano Prelude (mm. 1–7)

The tempo marking in Diabelli's 1825 publication is *Etwas langsam* (somewhat slow) in common time, but Graham Johnson notes that two copies of the original manuscript bear the marking *Etwas geschwind* (somewhat fast) in cut time.[4] The opening prelude does give the impression of *alla breve* time, with its emphasis on the half note pulse, and one would not want to begin too slowly, in deference to the long lines. However, the entire song moves forward, with the rhythms becoming quicker through the song, so a moderate tempo that allows for increasing subdivision of the beat is suggested.

6a) Schubert's piano preludes always tell the story of the song. How does the direction of the melody in m. 1 express the story of Ganymede? _____
_____
_____

Notice the same holds true for mm. 1–6 in both the top line of the melody as well as the bassline, which moves from low A♭, arriving to the A♭ an octave above in m. 7.

6b) What is the interval outlined in the top line of m. 1? _____ Keep an eye out for this interval!

6c) Notice the appoggiatura on the downbeat of m. 2. Appoggiaturas represent a musical sigh; they usually emphasize a dissonant note and then resolve down a step. (The story of Ganymede requires many sighs, so you will need to bring them out!) To what chord is the A♭ dissonant? _____ What is the interval of A♭-G? _____ If you have done some of the analyses in this book, you may immediately recognize this as a semitone motive, which is very common in nineteenth-century music. Note that each appoggiatura in the right hand is accented, so bring them out. (Note that some are semitones and some are whole steps.)

Keep an eye out for both the sighing and the sixth motives.

6d) Why do you think Schubert marks the left hand as staccato and the right as legato? __
_____
_____
_____

6e) How clear is the tonality in mm. 1–7? _____ How is this done? _____
_____

How clear is the phrasing? _____ How long is each phrase? _____

Are you surprised by the break in this pattern in m. 7? _____ How does it make you feel? _____
_____

6f) What is the direction and interval outlined in the top voice of m. 7? _____

Does this look familiar? Keep your eyes open for the semitone and sixth motives.

Part 1 (mm. 9–18)

7a) Are you surprised that the voice begins with such slow-moving notes? What does this suggest about Ganymed's mood in the beginning of the song? What might he have been doing before this? _____
_____
_____

7b) What direction and interval does the voice sing in m. 9? _____ Notice how mm. 9–15 contain both the sighing and the sixth motives.

7c) The two phrases in mm. 9–15 begin on downbeats. What happens in mm. 16–18, and what does this tell you about how he is feeling? _____
_____
_____

Compare the first note on "Frühling" with that in m. 9; what do you notice? _____
_____
_____
_____

7d) What motives do you find in the melodic setting of "Frühling, Geliebter!" (spring, beloved!)? _____

Why do you think Schubert does this? _____
_____

7e) Mm. 1–6 end with half cadences. How does the cadence in m. 18 setting "Geliebter" (lover) make you feel? _____

Notice how we finally get a downbeat?

Part 2 (mm. 19–31)

8a) How does the rhythm change in this section? _____
_____

Do phrases in this section begin primarily with downbeats or upbeats? _____

How does this change the mood, and why does Schubert do this? _____
_____

How else is "thousandfold rapture" expressed musically? _____
_____

8b) What key are we in now, beginning in m. 19?_____In the circle of fifths, is this higher or lower? _____

8c) What borrowed chord (name and function) do we hear in mm. 25–26? _____ _____

How does it make you feel? _____
_____

What words does it set? _____

8d) In what key does "unendliche Schöne!" (endless beauty) cadence? _____ Is this a "normal" or an extreme key? _____ Do you see how Schubert uses an extreme key to set the idea of infinite love? And it's a very warm key, being the farthest down in the flat direction. C-flat major doesn't even appear in Schubart's chart of key characteristics (see discussion in chapter 3), but B major is described as "Strongly colored, announcing wild passions."[5]

8e) How does Schubert arrive at C♭ major from E♭? To figure this out, go backward from the cadence in m. 31. Write the names and functions of the downbeat chords in mm. 30 and 31:

___, ___ (___, ___)

Now write down the names and functions of the downbeat chords in mm. 28–29:

___, ___ (___), (___/___)

"Ganymed"

8f) What is the name and function of the chord on beat 4 of m. 29? ___ (___)

8g) Do you feel thoroughly in the new key now? ____

8h) How did we get from E♭ major in m. 27 to C♭ major in m. 28? Describe the voice leading: What notes move to what? _____

8i) What is the relationship between E♭ major (in mm. 20–27) and C♭ major (in mm. 28–40)? (Hint: it's related to the dominant of E♭ major and it is motivic.) _____
_____

How do you usually write the Roman numeral of this chord? (Hint: What is its melodic interval from tonic?) _____ Do you see how this chord is a harmonic expression of the semitone motive?

Part 3 (mm. 31–46)

9a) Again the texture shifts in the piano. Describe the new melody in the right hand of m. 31: _____

Which beats are emphasized in the piano part? _____ What effect does this syncopation have? _____

9b) What length are the short phrases in the vocal line in mm. 32–39? _____

9c) What is the effect of the empty downbeats in the voice part and right hand? _____
_____

9d) Do you see how these also add to the forward push in each short phrase? Notice all the appoggiaturas in this passage. Which words are emphasized through the forward push and the appoggiatura? _____
_____
_____

9e) To what key do we cadence on the downbeat of m. 46? _____ How did we get there? Go backward from the cadence and find the pivot chord that will work in both keys. Write the measure number, chord, and function in each key:

m. ____, ____, C♭: ____ G♭: ____

Part 4 (mm. 46–56)

10a) What happens in the middle of m. 46? _____

From what key to what key does it shift? _____

Why does Schubert do this? (Hint: see what happens in m. 56.) _____
_____

10b) In what key are mm. 50–56? (Hint: look again at what happens in m. 56.) _____

10c) In terms of the circle of fifths key characteristics, is this a warm (flat area) or cool (sharp area) key? _____ What text does it set? _____
_____

The music theorist Schubart describes this key as "laughing pleasure and not yet complete, full delight."[6] Does that seem about right? _____

10d) Since you know what key you're in, beginning in m. 50, now go backward to figure out how you got there. Write the name and functions of the chord in m. 46; show the function in both the key you cadenced in (in the new key signature), in m. 46, and also in the context of the cadence level in m. 56:

name: _____, function in m. 46 key:___:_____, function in m. 56 key: ___:_____

Notice the pedal point on F♯ in mm. 46–49; it remains through this passage even as we are moving into a new key.

10e) What kind of cadence do you hear in m. 53? (Hint: What chord are you expecting and what do you actually get?) _____ How does that kind of cadence make you feel? _____
_____

10f) Look for the two main motives (6th and semitone) in mm. 49–53. Where do you find them? _____

Part 5 (mm. 56–74)

11a) What do you think the trills in mm. 56–59 represent? _____

11b) How do the left-hand repeated eighth notes affect the mood? _____
_____

What happens to the mood when the downbeats (1 and 3) disappear beginning in m. 60?
_____

11c) What compositional technique is used in mm. 61–64? (Hint: it is used in all parts and they add to the excitement.) _____

11d) On what tonal level do we stay in mm. 64–67? _____

11e) What is the meaning of the Nightingale in this poem, in the context of the Ganymede myth? _____
_____
_____

11f) How does Schubert set the only rhymed couplet in the poem ("Ruft drein die Nachtigall / Liebend nach mir aus dem Nebeltal") in mm. 61–64 (name the technique)?
_____

"Ganymed"   279

12a) How do the texture, tempo, and dynamic level change in m. 68? _____
_____
_____

How does it feel? _____
_____

Notice how the tone clusters occur on the offbeats, making you wonder where you are in the bar, while the singer is singing "wohin?" (where).

12b) We will be modulating from "cool" E major to the often-desired key of F major (a goal in many Schubert songs, as in "Gretchen am Spinnrade," "Du liebst mich nicht," and "Die junge Nonne," among others). How does Schubert accomplish this? To answer this, name the chords in mm. 70 and 71: _____ _____ How is this accomplished? (What note moves to what?) _____
_____

How amazing is it that Schubert achieves this modulation by simply using the semitone motive!

12c) Now write their functions in the keys of E major (for the first) and F major (for the second): _____

Part 6 (mm. 75–121)

13a) Name the downbeat chords in mm. 75–78: ____, ____, ____, ____

13b) Now look to see what kind of chords occur right before each of these chords. What is their function? _____

What feeling does this create? _____
_____

13c) What do you notice about the direction of these chords? _____

13d) Why do you think Schubert sets these bars this way? (Hint: look at the words.) _____
_____

13e) Look at the left hand of the piano in mm. 79–80. What motive do you see? _____
_____

13f) Write the name and function of the chords in m. 80: ___ ___ (___ ___). What is this kind of cadence called? _____ Does the phrase feel complete? _____
_____

13g) What words are set in mm. 79–80? _____

Do you see a descending line in the top of the right hand of the piano? (D-C-B♯-A-G)? How would you describe the articulation in the right hand of the piano? _____
_____

13h) How many times do we hear this two-bar phrase ending in a half-cadence (including mm. 79–80)? _____ How does it feel to hear this three times in a row? _____
_____

14a) What chord is on the downbeat of m. 85? _____ Do we get our resolution on the downbeat of m. 85? _____ How does this make you feel? _____

Why? _____
_____

14b) How does the rhythm, texture, and articulation change at this point, and how does it add to the feeling? _____
_____
_____

Does this passage begin with upbeats or downbeats? How does this change express the new emotion we hear? _____
_____
_____

14c) What happens harmonically in mm. 85–88? (Compare with mm. 75–78.) _____
_____

How does this express the text and emotion? _____
_____

14d) What does "Mir! Mir!" refer to? _____
_____

What does Ganymed represent or embody in this passage? _____
_____

14e) Write the translation of the text in mm. 85–91: _____
_____

How has the emotion changed from lines 22–25? _____
_____

14f) What happens harmonically in mm. 88–91 (what two tonal levels are emphasized in mm. 88–89 and 89–90)? _____

14g) What type of instrument would typically play the melodic line setting "Umfangend umfangen!" (Embracing, embraced!)? _____ Why do you think Schubert sets it this way? How does it express the emotion of Ganymed at this point? _____
_____
_____
_____

14h) How and why does the rhythm, melodic shape, and articulation change in mm. 92–94?
_____
_____
_____

14i) In F major, what is the function of the two chords in m. 94? ___ ___

14j) What kind of cadence is this, and how does it leave you feeling? _____
_____
_____

Do we get a resolution in m. 95? _____ What do we get instead? _____
_____

15a) Compare mm. 96–99 with mm. 81–84; what do you notice? _____

15b) Now compare mm. 100–103 to mm. 85–89; what is different? (Make sure to look at both the melody and the harmony.) _____
_____
_____
_____

15c) Describe how the emotion has developed in the second setting of this text. _____
_____
_____
_____
_____

Note that Schubert only uses a strophic structure (repetition of a section) in the F major section, but not in any other part of the song. Lawrence Kramer notes that "the strophes stand as the fruits of a long, deeply pleasurable process of discovery."[7]

15d) Compare mm. 104–07 to mm. 90–93. Notice that instead of I_4^6– V chords as in m. 94 (and 95), the passage is extended with a secondary dominant (m. 108) to cadence in m. 110. Does this cadence feel complete? Why or why not? _____
_____

15e) Look at the melody line in mm. 108–09. Can you find both the sixth and the semitone motives? Write the notes in which these motives appear: _____

15f) Why is the high F in mm. 110–12 so long? _____
_____

15g) Notice the F-F melodic descent in mm. 110–16. Does this help you feel like we have truly arrived at a strong cadence on F major? _____ Why else might Schubert have written that long descent? What has happened at this point in the poem? _____
_____
_____

Notice the double semitone motive (lower neighbor) in m. 111. The sixth motive and semitone motive appear again in the melody of "Vater" in mm. 114–15, this time as D-F and B♮-C. Schubert is clearly intentional in his use of motive!

Piano Postlude (mm. 116–21)

16a) Compare the piano postlude to the prelude. How are they similar and how are they different? _____
_____
_____
_____

16b) Do you find any motives? Name the measure number and notes for each motive:
_____
_____
_____

16c) Compare how Schubert expresses the rapture Ganymed experiences through nature with the transcendent state he experiences when he realizes the true meaning of his ascent: _____
_____
_____
_____
_____
_____

16d) How will you express Ganymed's different states of emotion and understanding?
_____
_____
_____
_____

17a) What have you learned about the meaning of the song from your analysis? _____

_____
_____
_____
_____

17b) How will you express it through your performance? _____

_____
_____
_____
_____

NOTES

1. "Meeres Stille" (Calm Sea) and "Glückliche Fahrt" (Prosperous Voyage") is another oppositional pair of poems Goethe wrote, but Schubert did not set the latter. "Ganymed" is the German spelling; I use "Ganymede" when speaking of the mythological figure and "Ganymed" for the character in Schubert's song.

2. Kristina Muxfeldt, "Schubert, Platen and the Myth of Narcissus, *Journal of the American Musicological Society* 49, no. 3 (1996), 500–501.

3. Lawrence Kramer, *Franz Schubert: Sexuality, Subjectivity, Song* (Cambridge: Cambridge University Press, 1998), 119–21.

4. Graham Johnson, *Schubert: The Complete Songs* (New Haven: Yale University Press, 2014), 1:638.

5. Christian Friedrich Daniel Schubart, *Ideen zu einer Ästhetik der Tonkunst* (Vienna: Degen, 1806), reprint, ed. P. A. Merbach (Leipzig: Wolkenwander-Verlag, 1924), quoted in Rita Steblin, *A History of Key Characteristics in the Eighteenth and Early Nineteenth Centuries* (Ann Arbor: UMI Research Press, 1983), 124–25.

6. Schubart, *Ideen zu einer Ästhetik der Tonkunst*, in Steblin, *A History of Key Characteristics*, 124–25.

7. Kramer, *Franz Schubert*, 125.

22

"Dass sie hier gewesen!"

In order to enjoy the subtle meanings in this song, one needs to understand its Persian influence. A number of early nineteenth-century German poets became enraptured by Persian poetry, particularly by the ghazals of the medieval poets Rumi and Hafez. In 1812–1813 Josef von Hammer-Purgstall published his famous Hafez translation *Diwan des Hafis*; his work inspired Rückert (author of this poem, published 1822), Platen (who wrote "Du liebst mich nicht," also a ghazal), and Goethe (who published a collection of ghazals in 1819).[1]

The Persian ghazal was a poetic form based on couplets and repeated words or refrains, often hinting at sensual subjects. In the original form the couplets did not necessarily relate to one another in a clear way; the non-logical placement of the couplets could suggest meaning rather than represent clear directional thought and also create beauty out of seeming chaos, both of which may have appealed to those with anti-Enlightenment aesthetics.

Another advantage to the ghazal for German Romantics was that it allowed for some freedom of expression in an authoritarian society; in both traditional Islamic culture and the oppressive atmosphere of the Metternich state, the ghazal offered a way to escape reality for a moment as well as to sneak some material past the censor.[2]

The ghazal frequently addressed topics such as love (often disappointed love or sadness of separation), beauty, intoxication, and mysticism, and common tropes were the rose, nightingale, perfumed air, and wine (and the person who poured it). Charlotte El-Shabrway writes that in the ghazal "the only reality is a dream, or drunken state; and the desire to do without the world altogether is a common motif. Indeed, in the love poems, there is frequently a surrender and sacrifice of personality, a blissful longing for extinction of the self for the sake of the beloved." One can well imagine how the ghazal appealed to German Romantic poets![3]

"Dass sie hier Gewesen!" comes from Rückert's collection of poems, *Östlichen Rosen* (Oriental Roses, 1822–1823). Other poems Schubert set from this collection include "Du bist die Ruh" (discussed in chapter 14), as well as "Sei mir gegrüsst," "Lachen und Weinen," "Greisengesang," and "Die Wallfahrt."

This song is about things seen and unseen, and ways of knowing. The musical setting answers the question of how one represents things that can and cannot be seen. You will find advanced chromatic and dissonant harmony, as well as lyrical and diatonic harmony. This exquisite and blissfully confusing song is Schubert's contribution to the German Romantics' love for Persian poetry and aesthetics.

TEXT

The poem is difficult to translate, as much of its meaning relies on words that merely suggest and evoke rather than state directly. Many translations are possible, but unfortunately the final line, and thus the title, is usually mistranslated as "that she has been here." Although neither Rückert nor Schubert titled the song, it has been called "Dass sie hier gewesen!" since Diabelli's 1830 publication. As you will see, a more correct translation changes the meaning of the song significantly.[4]

1) What do you think this poem is about? _____
_____
_____

Structure of the Poem

2a) How many strophes do you see? _____

2b) Read the English translation out loud. Is there a refrain? _____ If so, write it here in German and English: _____
_____
_____

Is it always exactly the same? If not, how does it change? _____
_____

The meaning of "sie" in stanza 3 will be discussed below.

2c) Who do you think is speaking in each stanza? _____

To whom is this person speaking? _____

Notice that the poet speaks intimately (uses "du") to this person in stanzas 1 and 2. Be aware, too, that this other person may not actually be present.

3a) What word ends the penultimate (second to last) line in each strophe? _____

The German verb "kunden" (in this case, as "kundtun") means "to announce" or "to make known." Why do you think the poet repeats this word in each strophe? _____
_____
_____

3b) What do you notice about the rhyme scheme of the first two lines? _____

What is this called? _____ Are there opening rhymed couplets in the next two stanzas? _____

3c) What do you notice about the last two lines of every stanza? _____
_____
_____

The presence of couplets and repeated words plus refrain is intentionally evoking the form of the Persian ghazal.

Stanza 1

4a) What is unusual about the sentence structure of the first two lines? Is it a complete sentence? Where does it seem like it begins? _____
_____

Why do you think Rückert writes it this way? _____
_____
_____

4b) What is the subject of the first two lines? _____

To whom do you think it belongs? _____

What sense is invoked? _____ Is this subject generally positive or negative? Could anyone notice this subject if they were there; that is, is it external or internal? _____
_____

4c) Notice the word "hauchet" (breathes, used as a metaphor to describe how the gentle east wind blows). Is this sense strong or delicate? _____

How can you tell? _____

4d) What is announced in the first strophe? _____

How is it announced (internally or externally?) _____

You will be looking for the **sign** and the **signified** in this poem.[5] The sign is an indicator, and the signified is the meaning of that indicator.

5a) What is the "sign" (the indicator) in lines 1 and 2? _____
_____

5b) What does the sign make known? _____

5c) Considering the Persian influence on the poem (its ghazal form), why do you suppose the wind comes from the east? _____
_____

The "fragrance from the east" may refer not only to the traditional tropes of love and beauty of the ghazal, but also to the freedom of ideas that the German Romantics, in this case Rückert, found in the poems of Hafez and Rumi. This image had a metaphorical meaning in the poems of Persia, for whom "the east is considered to be a spiritual source and the *saba* [east wind] not simply a wind but a communication channel which carries symbolic messages."[6] So stay on the lookout for more "symbolic messages" in this poem!

Stanza 2

6a) What is the subject of the first two lines of stanza 2? _____ To whom do you think they belong? _____

What emotion is invoked? _____ Is this emotion generally positive or negative? _____ Could anyone notice this emotion if they were there; that is, is it primarily external or internal? _____

6b) What is announced in the second strophe? _____

6c) What are the two ways of "announcement" or "knowing" suggested in stanza 2? (What words are used to convey this idea?) _____

Which is external and which is internal? _____
_____

The phrase "wirst du innen" means "you become aware of" (from the verb "innewerden"), while the "kund" in the next line means "know."

6d) What is the "sign" of stanza 2? _____ What do they indicate and to whom?
_____

Compare the two types of "knowing" in this stanza; how are they different? _____
_____
_____

6e) Compare the final line of each of the first two stanzas: What connections and contrasts does the poet set up for us? Write the sign and the person named for each stanza, along with the affect expressed for each:

1) _____

2) _____

3) _____

Stanza 3

7a) In stanza 3, what are the subjects of the first line? _____

7b) Which is external, and which internal? _____
_____

288   *Chapter 22*

7c) Can either remain hidden? _____ How do strophes 1 and 2 answer this question?
_____
_____

7d) How do lines 4 and 5 answer the question? _____
_____

  The last line of strophe 3 actually refers to the subjects of this stanza, Beauty or Love. (I capitalize them because they are philosophical ideals.) "Sie" can mean "she," but in this case means "it," as in line 2. Thus, the final line of the poem, as well as the title, should read as **"That it [Beauty or Love] has been here!"** In common English we might write "that they have been here" as a translation.

8a) Does stanza 3 follow the same opening form as stanzas 1 and 2? _____What part of speech do we begin with here, and how does it function in the sentence? _____
_____

  Why do you think Rückert makes this change? _____
_____
_____

  What is the meaning of "sie" in line 2? _____

8b) How does the line "Schönheit oder Liebe" refer back to stanzas 1 and 2? _____
_____

  Rückert's poem follows many of the traditions of the Persian ghazal in terms of its structure, images, and subject. As noted above, the "fragrance from the east" brings symbolic messages. Many performers may think of this as a song about love relationships (which it is also), but Rückert very carefully distinguishes among ways of communication and perception, beginning with announcing, becoming aware, and knowing.[7] So what is the message being brought by the east wind? _____
_____
_____
_____

MUSIC

9a) What is the mood of this song? _____
_____
_____

Why do you think? _____
_____
_____

9b) Listen to the piece several times. Write down the measure numbers in which the refrain appears in the voice part, and sing them. Refrains: _____

9c) Is the refrain easier to sing and understand than the rest? _____ Is the refrain set diatonically or chromatically? _____ Is the refrain set with downbeat phrases or upbeat phrases and why? _____
_____
_____

9d) Why do you think the refrain is set in this way? _____
_____
_____

9e) What other words are set to the refrain melody and in which measures? _____
_____
_____

9f) Why do you think Schubert distinguishes these lines by linking them musically to the refrain? _____
_____
_____

9g) Which sections feel a bit confusing? _____
_____
_____

10a) How are the musical settings of stanzas 1 and 2 related? _____
_____

10b) What is the form called when stanzas are set with the same music? _____

10c) What is different between the two musical strophes? _____

Tonal Structure and Harmony

11a) The poet and theorist C. F. D. Schubart describes C major as "completely pure. Its character is innocence, simplicity, naivety, children's talk."[8] Does this sound like it fits the poem? Why do you think Schubert chose this key? _____
_____

11b) Are you surprised by the opening chords? _____ Does this sound like Schubert, or rather a little like *Tristan and Isolde*?

11c) Does the piece sound like it's in C major for the first eleven bars? _____

11d) Listen to the songs several times and make a tonal map (circle the cadences and then write in the cadence levels [e.g., B♭] on your text and translation of the poem). To what tonal levels do you find authentic cadences, and where do they occur in relation to the text? _____
_____
_____

Part 1 (mm. 1–18)

12a) Songs usually begin in the tonic area of the key; does this one? _____ Why do you think? _____

12b) Now fill out the letter names of the following chords in this key. The first two are done for you:

I: C,   V: G   ii: ___ , IV: ___ , vi: ___

12c) Where do you first see any of these chords? List the measure number, chord, and chord function. (Note: the note E in m. 5 is an appoggiatura—not part of the chord—which resolves to D in m. 6.) _____

12d) What is this type of cadence in m. 8 called? _____

12e) Which word of the poem does this chord set, and where does it occur in the poem? _____

12f) So why do you think an important chord in the key appears at this point? _____

12g) Where is the next time one of these basic chords appears? List the measure number, chord, and chord function. (Note: the note E in m. 12 is an appoggiatura—not part of the chord—which resolves to the note D.) _____

12h) Which word of the poem does this chord set, and where does it occur in the poem? _____
_____

13a) Now let's tackle the tricky opening. Would you say the first four bars are consonant or dissonant? _____

13b) Starting at m. 5 will help to put things in perspective. Name the chord and function in mm. 5–6 (the note E in m. 5 is an accented dissonance): ____, ____

13c) Now go to the beginning and name the chord on the second beat of m. 1: _____

13d) A diminished chord in a major key usually functions how (which Roman numeral)? _____

13e) So if this chord is not in C major, it is a secondary chord; name its function: ___/___

13f) In what measure do we arrive at the resolution to this secondary chord? _____

13g) Follow the same process for the chord on the second beat of m. 2 (name the chord and its function): _____ ___/___

13h) Compare the piano part in mm. 1–2 to that in mm. 3–4. How do they compare? ___
_____

13i) Do you see that we've been trying to get to the chord in m. 5 for the first four bars?

13j) Now we can figure out that very dissonant opening chord in m. 1. What kind of chord does it sound like? (What is the chord quality?) _____

What is the difference between the two chords in m. 1? (What note moves to what note?) _____ The F in the first chord is an appoggiatura which resolves by semitone to the E in the second chord. Looks like we may have ourselves a *semitone motive*! (Note how the accents in mm. 1–2 emphasize each semitone.) If you combine the two semitones, you get the **four-note motive** F-E, D-C♯. Remember this, as it will turn up again soon.

13k) Do the same thing for bar 2. What are the two moving notes? ____ ____ Semitone motive confirmed!

14a) If you look at mm. 1–8 you can see that the first four bars are trying to get to the chord in mm. 5–6, which prepare for the half cadence in m. 8. Let's see what happens in mm. 9–12. Name the chord and function of the first beat of m. 9: ____, ____/____

Notice that this time there is no dissonant appoggiatura. Does it resolve in the next chord (beat 2)? _____ If not, name the chord and function: ____, ____/____

Are you surprised? What is it called when we think we are going to resolve a chord but it moves somewhere else? _____

14b) These same chords are repeated again in m. 10: we try to get to ii, but again are put off. Is the third time the charm (mm. 11–12)? _____ Note that in these two measures, the semitone motive becomes functional, moving from a melodic semitone to a harmonic one (vii°$^6_5$/ii → ii).

14c) If you were going to think of the first twelve bars of this piece as a prolongation of one tonal level, which would it be (as a Roman numeral)? _____

14d) Why do you think that, in a supposedly C major piece, Schubert leaves us floating in the air, often unaware of where we are tonally? _____
_____
_____

14e) Do mm. 1–12 set the sign or the signified? _____

Is the sign clear or ambiguous? _____

15a) The harmonies in mm. 13–16 come as a contrast to the ethereal opening section. Write the functions (Roman numerals) of the chords in mm. 13–16: ___-___, ___-___

How does this make you feel? _____
_____

15b) Why do you suppose Schubert suddenly clarifies the key with such simple harmonies at this point? _____
_____

15c) Do measures 13–19 set the sign or the signified? _____
_____

Compare the four-note motive in mm. 2–4 (F-E-D-C♯) with the "new and improved" four-note motive in m. 13 (C-B-A-G). Notice how the dissonant interval (a diminished fourth) is altered to a consonant interval (a perfect fourth).

In "Dass sie hier gewesen!" Schubert sets the sign, the fragrance from the east, with a dissonant interval and ambiguous harmonies, so that the listener is not using rational faculties but is lost in the beauty of the music, enjoying the eastern spirit so beloved by the German Romantics. In contrast, the refrain, the signified ("that you have been here"), is set with a perfect fourth and strong and clear cadences, letting us know ("kunden") musically that this, at least, is knowable.

Voice part

16a) Is the voice part primarily chromatic or diatonic in mm. 2–4 and 9–12? _____

16b) What is the interval outlined in the four-note motive in mm. 3–4? _____

How does this interval add to the hazy and floating feeling of the song's opening? ____
_____

"Dass sie hier gewesen!"

What key (note and function) might it suggest? _____ _____ One wonders if Schubert may have been intending to suggest a Persian sound to the opening melody.

16c) How does the four-note motive change in mm. 5–8? (Hint: What is the interval now?) _____

16d) The four-note motive returns in mm. 9–12, but what has happened to it? _____
_____

The "east wind's fragrance" has now been broken up, though the diminished fourth interval still remains in m. 10.

16e) How does the melody change in mm. 13–16? _____
_____

What interval does the descending four-note motive in m. 13 outline now? _____

16f) What words does the four-note motive in mm. 3–4 set? _____
_____

16g) What words does the four-note motive in m. 13 set (include the text in m. 14 also)?
_____

Do you see how the four-note motive connects the sign and the signified?[9]

17a) How does the swell in mm. 14 and 16 make you feel? _____
_____

Contrast that with the mystery of the opening bars. Do you see how we are being pulled from a vague sensing to a clear knowing?

17b) The piano combines with the voice (in octaves!) and then takes over, but then is suddenly cut off with a measure of rest.[10] Does the phrase feel ended? _____

What is the chord in m. 17? _____ Why do you think Schubert does this? (Hint: What text follows in the next refrain?) _____
_____

17c) How will you perform this passage? _____
_____
_____

Part 2 (mm. 19–35)

18) Is the musical setting of part 2 exactly the same as part 1, up to m. 35? _____

Part 3 (mm. 35–67)

19a) Compare what happens in mm. 35–37 with mm. 17–18: _____
_____

What motive do you recognize in mm. 35–37 (in the right hand of the piano) and 38–39 (in the voice part), and what interval is it now? _____
_____

What words are set to this motive? _____

19b) Why do you think Schubert begins this stanza with the refrain motive set with a clear C major tonality, when the previous openings were dissonant and ambiguous?
_____
_____
_____

19c) We now reach the highest vocal note in the piece, G. **Always pay attention to the text which includes the high point of a song.** Write out the two text lines (and their translation) which are set in mm. 38–41: _____
_____
_____
_____

Why do you think this line is set with the highest note? _____
_____
_____

19d) Schubert adds extra dissonance to the V^7 chord in mm. 40–41. How would you describe the chord on the downbeat of m. 40? (Hint: notice that the G sustains across the two bars.) _____
_____
_____

(A joke I often tell my students is "How do nineteenth-century composers resolve a dissonance? With an even stronger dissonance!" Here it's just an embellishment, but see "Gretchen am Spinnrade" for a memorable example.)

19e) Notice the pedal point on G in mm. 35–41; was there a long pedal point in the first verse? _____ Why do you think Schubert adds it here? What important words does it underlie? _____
_____

20a) What are the chords on the second beat of mm. 42 and 43 (chord and function): ____
_____, _____ In what ways is this different from the opening (compare the type of chords and what tonal area they are secondary to)? _____
_____
_____

How does this feel in comparison to the opening dissonances? _____
_____

20b) The four-note motive appears again in the top line of mm. 42–43. Compare the motive here with its appearance in mm. 1–2. Name the notes and interval. What's different?
_____

What happens in the piano part in mm. 43–44? _____
_____

20c) Why do you think Schubert sets the word "Düfte" (perfume) with such a long note?
_____

21a) What are the chords and their functions in mm. 46–47? (Hint: the first chord contains a dissonant appoggiatura, as in the opening; the G is not part of the chord.)
_____

21b) What happens to this key in m. 50? Name the chord and how the key is altered:
_____

21c) What text is set from mm. 44–50, and what do you think inspired this shift? _____
_____
_____
_____

21d) The four-note motive appears in the voice part in m. 47; which version is it: the diminished or the perfect fourth? _____ Note that it uses the same notes as mm. 42–43.

In parts 1 and 2 of the song, the diminished fourth set signs (fragrance and tears) and the perfect fourth set the signified (that you or I have been here), but now the signs and the signified are united, both now represented by a perfect fourth interval across the four-note motive.

22a) The refrain text returns in m. 51; what has happened to the four-note motive (direction and interval)? _____

Notice that the two motives (four-note and semitone) alternate in mm. 51–54. Why do you think Schubert does this? _____
_____

22b) Notice that the voice and piano are no longer doubled, as in the previous refrain settings, but now in imitation, singing to each other, as it were. What might this suggest? _____
_____

22c) For the first time, the refrain is not in C major (mm. 51–54). Write the chord names and functions of mm. 51–52: ___, ___, (___/___), (___/___)

22d) To what key do we expect to cadence? _____ Do we arrive there? _____ Notice that instead of authentic cadences, as in strophes 1 and 2 (mm. 14 and 16 and 32 and 34), these are half cadences.[11]

22e) What is the relationship of this key to C major (i.e., what interval is it from C?)? Unexpected, perhaps, but is this an unusual tonal relationship in the nineteenth century?
_____
_____

22f) Compare the chord in mm. 52–54 with the downbeat of m. 55. What note has changed to what other note? _____ What motive does this create? _____
_____

23a) Write the chords and functions of m. 55: ___, ___ (___/___, ___/___)

23b) Write the chords and functions of m. 57: ___, ___ (___/___, ___/___)

23c) What secondary tonal area (note and function) is implied in m. 55? _____
In m. 57? _____

Notice that the word "Düfte" in m. 57 is set to the same chord as sets this word in m. 4. That exquisite half-diminished seventh color leaves you hanging in the air for just a moment, and the sighing semitone motive fills it with longing. Notice, too, that the four-note motive in mm. 57–58 is a permutation of mm. 3–4: D-C♯-F-E instead of F-E-D-C♯.

24a) The song emphasizes ii in the majority of parts 1 and 2 (mm. 1–12 and 19–30), and IV in part 3 (mm. 42–58). Which one wins? Do mm. 59–60 clearly confirm either one?
_____
_____
_____

24b) But whether ii or IV, both function as a predominant to get us to the cadences from 61 to the end, where the refrain finally returns in the "correct" key. Compare mm. 61–67 with mm. 13–18; what is different? _____
_____
_____

* * *

This song is about ways of knowing things that cannot necessarily be seen. The fragrance from the east wind (inspiring poetry from Persia) brought symbolic messages of new ways of thinking and feeling for the German Romantics, both poets and composers. The vague signs (a perfumed breeze and tears) appear as ambiguous and dissonant harmonies linked with the diminished fourth four-note motive, in contrast to the signified (Love and Beauty), presented with clear C-major harmony and a perfect fourth motive. Beauty and love in ancient and modern poetry—as well as in Schubert songs—can never be hidden.

25a) What have you learned about the meaning of the song from your analysis? _____
_____
_____
_____
_____

25b) How will you express it through your performance? _____
_____
_____
_____
_____

NOTES

1. Harry Seelig, "The Literary Context: Goethe as Source and Catalyst," in *German Lieder in the Nineteenth Century*, edited by Rufus Hallmark (New York: Schirmer Books, 1996), 18.

2. Charlotte El-Shabrawy, "German Ghazals: An Experiment in Cross-Cultural Literary Synthesis," *Alif: Journal of Comparative Poetics*, no. 3 (Spring, 1983): 59–61, 67.

3. El-Shabrawy, "German Ghazals," 61, 69.

4. I am grateful for Richard Law's revealing and engaging discourse on this poem. Richard Law, "'Dass sie hier gewesen' D 775: Rückert and Schubert," *Figures of Speech* (blog), January 16, 2019, http://figures-of-speech.com/2019/01/hier-gewesen.htm.

5. Carl Schachter, "Motive and Text in Four Schubert Songs," in *Aspects of Schenkerian Theory*, ed. D. W. Beach (New Haven: Yale University Press, 1983), 64–66.

6. Law, "Dass sie hier gewesen" (blog).

7. In his analysis of the poem, Richard Law points out the gradual transition from "announcing" ("kundtun") in stanza 1 to "becoming aware of" ("innewerden") and finally "knowing" ("kund sein") in stanza 2. Law, "Dass sie hier gewesen" (blog).

8. Christian Friedrich Daniel Schubart, *Ideen zu einer Ästhetik der Tonkunst* (Vienna: Degen, 1806), reprint, ed. P. A. Merbach (Leipzig: Wolkenwander-Verlag, 1924), quoted in Rita Steblin, *A History of Key Characteristics in the Eighteenth and Early Nineteenth Centuries* (Ann Arbor: UMI Research Press, 1983), 124–25.

9. Schachter, "Motive and Text," 66–67.

10. Graham Johnson suggests the piano doubling beginning in m. 15 could be the voice of the lover. Graham Johnson, *Schubert: The Complete Songs* (New Haven: Yale University Press, 2014), 1:403.

11. Kofi Agawu associates the shift to A♭ in mm. 51–54 to the A♭ on the word "Tränen" (tears) in m. 48. V. Kofi Agawu, "Schubert's Harmony Revisited: The Songs 'Du liebst mich nicht' and 'Dass sie hier gewesen,'" *Journal of Musicological Research* 9 (1989): 34.

23

"Erlkönig"

Everyone knows and loves this most famous of Schubert's songs. "Erlkönig" is beloved for its four distinct characters, virtuosic piano part, and dramatic and tragic story. Goethe's poem, which appeared in his Singspiel *Die Fischerin*, was inspired by Herder's translation of the Danish "King of the Elves" ballad. Schubert set it to music immediately after reading the poem out loud to friends and—because he didn't have a piano at home—they all had to go to his school to play through it.[1] It is hard to believe that Schubert was only around eighteen years old when he composed this song, for it displays a mastery of motivic structure and manipulation.

In this song you will find **alliteration**, musical expression of the physical and emotional, the piano as a character, obsessive **motives**, **tonal areas associated with the characters**, and **motivic parallelism**.

* * *

TEXT

1a) Summarize the story of this ballad: _____
_____
_____
_____
_____

1b) How does the story express ideas of German Romanticism? _____
_____
_____

1c) Name the four characters: _____
_____

1d) In your text and translation, write the name of each character before the lines they speak (each time they appear or reappear).

1e) How does Goethe distinguish among the different characters? _____
_____
_____
_____

1f) What do you think the Erlking symbolizes in this poem? _____

2a) How many stanzas are in this poem? ____ Number them.

2b) What is the structure of the stanzas? Which stanza numbers feature the narrator? ____

Which feature the Erlking? _____ Which feature the father and son talking to each other? _____ Do you see how Goethe carefully structured the poem with narration at the beginning and end, and stanzas for the father and son alternating with those of the Erlking?

2c) Notice that in stanzas 2, 4, and 6 the father and son are together, while the Erlking gets his own strophes in stanzas 3 and 5. What happens in stanza 7 that is different? _____
_____

What do you think Goethe may be suggesting by this? _____
_____

How do the last two lines of stanza 7 support this? _____
_____

2d) What is the rhyme scheme? _____

3) Look closely at stanza 3, the Erlking's first introduction.[2]

»Du liebes Kind, komm, geh mit mir!	"You dear child, come, go with me!
Gar schöne Spiele spiel ich mit dir;	Very fine games I will play with you;
Manch' bunte Blumen sind an dem Strand,	Many colorful flowers are along the shore;
Meine Mutter hat manch gülden Gewand«	my mother has many golden garments."

Circle every example of **alliteration** (repetition of the same letter or sound in nearby words) in your text; which letters do you find? _____

Goethe appears to be infusing the Erlking's speech with ancient poetic devices to make him sound mythical.[3]

MUSIC

4a) Listen to the song while following the text and translation. What is the general mood of the song? _____

What musical effects create this mood? _____

4b) The poet and music theorist C. F. D. Schubart described the key of G minor as expressing "discontent, uneasiness, worry . . . bad-tempered gnashing of teeth."[4] How appropriate do you find Schubert's choice of key for this poem? _____

4c) Does Schubert follow the stanza structure of the poem? _____

4d) How does Schubert distinguish the characters through vocal range? List each character and describe its vocal range: _____

4e) What do the pounding octave triplet figures in the piano represent in the story? _____

Schubert always has a double meaning for his pictorial piano representations: a surface meaning and a deeper emotional one. In "Gretchen am Spinnrade," for example, the winding sixteenth note motives represent both the spinning wheel and her spinning emotions. What emotion do you think the pounding triplets represent? _____

Do you think the piano represents its own character? Why or why not? _____

4f) Why do you think Schubert included the sudden recitative in the last three bars of the song? _____

What is the effect of the rest on the second beat of m. 147? _____

Motives

Motives play an extremely important role in telling the story of the Erlking. **Four motives** are each associated with a different character or problem. The rising line in the left hand of m. 2, sometimes referred to as the riding motive, contains two of these. If you have already analyzed a few Schubert songs (or works by any nineteenth-century composer) you will not be surprised to find that a semitone motive is one: the **D-E♭-D upper neighbor**, associated with the son. Also in m. 2 is the **sixth motive (G-E♭)**, linked with the Erlking. Of course, you don't know if something is motivic until you look closely through the song; in nineteenth-century music, however, it's a good bet that a distinctive interval or musical figure introduced early on will turn out to be motivic. Another motive is the **passing tone motive**, appearing originally as C-C♯-D in mm. 6–7 and suggesting worry. The final motive is the **fourth motive**, a perfect fourth associated with the father, heard first in m. 21 as D-G. Though the father, son, and Erlking each have their own motives, the Erlking famously imitates other characters in the drama, as you will discover. The motives actually link up at the climax of the song in stanza 7, and throughout the song one can see the Erlking moving into the territory of the other characters by using their motives and tonal areas.[5]

For this analysis you will be looking for these four motives in the song and then seeing how and why they interact. Then you will look at the harmonic structure of the song itself and discover Schubert's use of **motivic parallelism**, which is when a motive appears at more than one level of structure.

The upper neighbor motive (the son)

5a) Look through the song and circle the upper neighbor motive throughout the voice part of the song, then add the information to the chart. The first two are done for you.

mm.	notes	char.	text
2	D-E♭-D	piano	none (origin of motive)
15–16	A-B♭-A	Narr.	"Who rides so late"
42–45	(1) D-E♭-D-E♭	Son	"Father, don't you see the Erlking?"
46–50			
72–76	(2)		
76–77			
97–101	(3)		
101–02			
116–19			
123–27	(4)		

Note that with one exception (highlighted in gray), the only person singing this motive is the son. In mm. 116–19, the Erlking finally loses patience and **steals the child's motive**, singing D-C♯-D-E♭.

5b) The four lines that are boxed (mm. 42–45, 72–76, 97–101, and 123–27) each set the son calling out to his father and are numbered as groups 1–4. The first two begin at the same level, but then begin to change. In what direction are they moving, and how does this express the character's emotion and the drama of the song? _____

_____

5c) Notice that each callout to the father except for the last is followed by a second line of text that also contains the neighbor-tone motive at a lower level, creating three groups of musical phrases. Do you see that group numbers 2 and 3 are exact transpositions of each other (2: D-E♭, A-B♭ vs. 3: E-F, B-C)? Which of the two fit into G minor, no. 2 or no. 3?

Do you see how the Erlking is pulling the son out of his home key of G minor and into other tonal areas? (We will see more examples of this later.)

5d) The child's final call to his father has no second line of text set at a lower level, as in groups 1–3. Why do you think this is? _____

_____

You will see in the next chart how Schubert combines two motives in this climactic section. But if you move from the son's mention of the Erlking in m. 46 (on a C, the lowest note of this particular neighbor tone figure) to the top note of the highest neighbor tone figure in m 126 (G♭), you will see that Schubert has outlined a tritone, foreshadowing bad news in a way similar to that in "Meeres Stille." See the section on pedal points below for a more immediately recognizable use of melodic tritones in the bassline.

The passing tone motive (rising chromatic motion)

In the prelude, Schubert distinguishes his use of triplet octaves in the right hand from that of the triplet chords. Listen to the opening piano prelude (mm. 1–15) carefully with this in mind.

6a) In what measures do the chords appear? _____

What is happening in the bassline in these two passages? _____

_____

Could this be a motive? _____ We don't know for sure until we examine the song closely, as you will be doing below.

6b) Look for this **rising chromatic motive** in the vocal part throughout the song, and in the piano part in the postlude. In what measures do you find it? Include the measure numbers, notes, character, and what they're saying. The first two are done for you:

mm.	no.	notes	char.	text
6–7	1a)	C-C♯-D	piano	[no text]
39–40	1b)	B♭-B♮-C	Father	"why do you hide your face so fearfully?"
66–67	2a)	_____	_____	_____
67–68	2b)	_____	_____	_____
77–79	3ab)	_____	_____	_____
87–88	4)	_____	_____	_____
102–04	5)	_____	_____	_____
119–20		_____	_____	_____
128–29		_____	_____	_____
141–42	6)	_____	piano	[no text]
146–47	7)	_____	piano	[no text]

6c) Look at the chart above and compare the notes in mm. 66–67 and 87–88 with mm. 6–7. What do you notice? _____

Who is speaking in the latter two? _____ So to whom does the rising chromatic motive in mm. 6–7 refer? _____

6d) Highlight or circle around each C-C♯-D in the chart above. What do you notice?
_____

6e) Notice that the first two presentations of the rising chromatic motive appear as C-C♯-D and B♭-B♮-C (piano and the father). How does the father feel at the moment he is singing this motive in mm. 39–40? _____

Who sings the next two iterations (mm. 66–68)? _____ Do you see how he has stolen the father's worry motive? _____

6f) The third set of the paired motives appear in mm. 77–79. Who sings them, and what is he describing? _____

Notice how instead of the paired motives as in 1a and b and 2a and b, he combines them as 3ab, doubling the worry and increasing the tension through the long-rising chromatic line.

6g) The fourth and fifth presentations of the C-C♯-D motive are sung by the Erlking and the son, the latter in an extended form. Compare the extended motive in mm. 102–4 with that in 77–79. What do you notice? _____
_____

How does this convey the emotion of the child and the drama of the song? _____
_____

Observe that in both these sections the neighbor motive and the rising chromatic motives are combined, and as mentioned in the section above, the Erlking is pulling the child out of the key of G minor.

6h) What happens to the motive in mm. 119–20, and what is the Erlking saying at this point?
_____
_____

Notice that while the son rises up chromatically from B to E in mm. 102–4, the Erlking picks it up a semitone below (on E♭) and descends, pulling him down.

6i) Compare the son's transposed statement of the motive (mm. 128–29)—the climax of the song—with the previous versions. What do you notice and what do you think this means?
_____
_____

Do you see how this version continues up the pattern of rising chromatic motion from the second version? The son's presentation of this motive rises from A in m. 77 up nearly an octave to G in m. 129. Again Schubert combines the neighbor and rising chromatic motives in mm. 123–31. Deborah Stein points out the irony in the child finally returning home to G minor exactly at the moment he is being permanently pulled away from his father by the Erlking (Death).[6]

The perfect fourth motive (the father)

In her analysis of this song, Deborah Stein associates a **perfect fourth motive** with the father, noting how the Erlking mimics him later in the song.[7] The boldfaced measure numbers will help you find a pattern.

7a) Fill out the chart and note if the motive is inverted by writing "inv" next to the note names.

mm.	notes	char.	text
21	D-G	Narr.	"It is the father"
24–27	B♭-E♭, B♭-E♭	Narr.	"He has the boy in his arm"
29	D-A (inv)	Narr.	"he holds him securely."
36–40	D-G, D-G, G-C	Father	**"My son, why do you hide your face so fearfully?"**
51–53	_____	_____	_____
69–70	_____	_____	_____
76–79	_____	_____	_____
80–81	_____	_____	_____
105–06	_____	_____	_____
108–09	_____	_____	_____
117	_____	_____	_____
129–30	_____	_____	_____
133–34	_____	_____	_____
139	_____	_____	_____
143–45	_____	_____	_____
146–47	_____	_____	_____

7b) The perfect fourth motive appears no fewer than four times in mm. 21–29 (boxed). Who sings this passage, and about whom are they singing? _____
_____
_____

Do you see how this motive is clearly linked with the father?

7c) How many times does the father use the P4 motive in mm. 36–40 and 51–53? _____

7d) Who sings the P4 motive in mm. 69–70, and what word does it set? _____
_____

What is the significance of this? _____
_____

Do you see how and why the Erlking has stolen the father's motive?

7e) Compare the notes of the father's P4 motives in mm. 80–81, 105–6, and 108–9. What is happening and why? _____
_____

7f) Write the P4 motive notes in mm. 105–6 and 108–9: _____

Do these notes fit into G minor, the home key? _____ We are traveling to more difficult tonal areas, which will be discussed further, below.

7g) What happens in m. 117 and why? _____
_____
_____
_____

7h) Who sings the final four iterations in mm. 132–47, and who is it about? _____
_____

Compare the motives in mm. 133–34 and 139 with that in m. 21. Do you see how Schubert frames the song, relating back musically and motivically to the setting of the first stanza?

7i) Compare the first note of the motive in m. 143 with that of m. 147. What is the interval between these two notes and its significance in this song? _____
_____

The sixth motive (Erlking)

Another important motive is the interval of the sixth, which is clearly associated with the Erlking. As with the neighbor tone motive, it appears first in m. 2, rising from G to E♭. Yet the first time we hear anyone sing it is in mm. 46–48, where the son sings the word "Erlenkönig" (a longer version of "Erlkönig"). And shortly after that, the Erlking sings a song full of sixths.

8a) Fill out the chart for the song, and note if it is inverted by writing "inv" next to the notes.

mm.	notes	char.	text
2	G-E♭	piano	[none]
42–45	G-E♭, G-E♭	Son	"Father, don't you see the Erlking?"
47–48	D♭-F (inv)	Son	"Erlenkönig"
58–59	_____	_____	_____
60–61	_____	_____	_____
64	_____	_____	_____
65–67	_____	_____	_____
68–69	_____	_____	_____
70–71	_____	_____	_____
87–88	_____	_____	_____
88–90	_____	_____	_____
92	_____	_____	_____

Notice that the no one else sings the sixth motive except the son (twice in one phrase and then inverted in another, both times saying the Erlking's name!) and the Erlking (ten times). The sixth motive appears to be intended to give a singsong quality to the utterance of the Erlking. Yet the instant the Erlking grows impatient and angry, it completely disappears—he drops the fake singing and takes over both the father's and the son's motive. As we have seen, the Erlking steals the father's fourth (now inverted) in E♭-B♭ ("I love you") and the semitone motive of the son on E♭-D-E♭-D-E♭, followed by the passing tone motive (now inverted) on E♭-D-C♯.

8b) Compare the motive notes in mm. 2 and 42–45 with those in mm. 87–90. What do you notice? _____

Pedal Points

9a) What do you think is the psychological and emotional effect of the pounding triplet octave G's that carry the listener (and the riders) through this harrowing song? _____

In addition to the repeated triplets, pedal points in the left hand also serve an important function, providing a sense of stability in the music, and thus in the character who is being presented.

9b) For each section, list the note which is prolonged as a pedal point. The gray highlighting will show you something about the structure of the song.

mm.	note	no. bars	char.	talking about?
1–12	G	12'	[prelude]	
15–20	D	6	narr.	about the father
24–28	B♭	5	narr.	about the child
33–39	___	___	___	___
40–45	___	___	___	___
46–53	___	___	___	___
57–62	___	___	___	___
65–66	___	___	___	___
87–88	___	___	___	___
112–16	___		[interlude]	___
117–19	___	___	___	___
131–39	___	___	___	___

9c) What happens to the length of the pedal points after measure 62? _____
_____

9d) Do you find any pedal points for the father and son after the Erlkonig's first "song" (mm. 57–72)? _____ Why or why not? _____
_____

9e) What interval and chords are outlined in the bassline in mm. 73–76, 97–101, and 124–27, right underneath the neighbor motives to set "My father, my father"? What emotion does this express? _____
_____
_____

Do you see how Schubert moves from a more stable bassline in the first half of the song to a more active one (except for the Erlking) as the father and son become more panicked? Notice how stability returns in the final narration via a pedal point on tonic to create a frame.

9f) How will you convey these changes in your performance? _____
_____
_____
_____

Tonal Structure and Motivic Parallelism

10a) Make a cadence map of this song. Listen with the score and circle the cadences. Then write in the cadence names next to your text and translation so you can see what is happening in the song when the piece modulates.

10b) After two cadences to G minor in the piano prelude, the song then cadences to a new area in m. 24. Name the cadence level (key), its function in the key of G minor, and the word it sets: _____

_____

Is modulation to this area unusual or common in this key? _____

What measure and chord (name and function in g) begins the modulation back to G minor? _____

10c) In what key does the Erlking first sing? (Hint: see cadence in m. 58.) _____

Do you see that the Erlking sings in the same key in which the "child" was first mentioned in m. 24? Why do you think the Erlking "steals" the key of the child? _____

_____

10d) Compare the structure of Erlking's first "song" (mm. 57–72) with the narrator's introduction (mm. 14–32). Compare and contrast the modulation: Does each move to a closely related key or a distant one? Explain the relationships. _____

_____

_____

10e) Compare the cadence in m. 81 to the previous cadence in m. 72. Name them and explain the interval between them: _____

Do you see how the melodic semitone (neighbor) motive now appears at the tonal level? This technique is known as **motivic parallelism**, when motives appear at different levels of structure.

10f) Why do you think the father cadences to G major in m. 85? _____

_____

_____

In what key does Erlking sing his next song (mm. 86–96)?[8] _____ Compare the cadence in m. 96 with the previous cadences in m. 72 and 81 and write them here:

_____

Does this look familiar? _____

Now write in the chord name of the next cadences in mm. 106 and 112: _____

List the cadence levels from mm. 72–112: ____ ____ ____ ____ Do you see how Schubert is using tonal structure to express the rising chromatic motive, and creating tension at the same time?

10g) What temporary tonal area governs mm. 117–19? _____ What is this chord in relationship to D minor (our previous cadence)? _____

Do you see how the cadences on D minor in mm. 112 and 122 sandwich an area in E♭ in mm. 117–19, creating a larger-scale neighbor tone motive? List the tonal areas (cadences plus the E♭ tonal area and d cadence in m. 123.) from mm. 72–123: ___ ___ ___ ___ ___ ___ ___ And this is not the last example of motivic parallelism in the song!

10h) What is the chord in m. 146? _____ What is its function in G minor? _____

How does this chord express one of the motives? _____
_____

10i) Another example of motive parallelism occurs in the narrator's description of the father arriving home at last. Can you find the rising motive (G-E♭) from m. 2 distributed across mm. 134–40? Write each note and the measure in which it appears. The first two are done for you: G (134), A (135), _____ _____ _____ _____ What is the interval from G to E♭? _____ Is this the Erlking having the last laugh?

One more amazing example of motivic parallelism awaits. Charles Burkhart showed that a large-scale tonal structure across the song reproduces a version of the rising motive:[9]

tonal level:	g	B♭	C	D	E♭	D	G
mm.:	1	58	87	112	117	123	131

The final two text lines (mm. 143–end) are full of motives, as you have seen, particularly semitone relationships, including the C-D♭ (mm. 143–44), A♭-G (mm. 144 and 146), C♯-D (m. 146), and F♯-G (mm. 147–48). And finally, the bassline presents the rising chromatic motion in mm. 146–47 to end where it began in the piano prelude.

11a) What have you learned about the meaning of the song from your analysis? _____
_____
_____
_____
_____

11b) How will you express it through your performance? _____
_____
_____
_____
_____

*   *   *

Can you imagine such a feat of motivic genius on the part of the composer? Yet, despite the fact that Schubert had sent Goethe some of his musical settings, including "Erlkönig," they were sent back unopened. Tragically, Goethe finally heard (and appreciated) this song only after Schubert's death.[10] But the rest of us have been moved by this powerful song for over two hundred years.

NOTES

1. Graham Johnson, *Schubert: The Complete Songs* (New Haven: Yale University Press, 2014), 1:519–520.

2. Translation of this stanza and several other lines are by Martha Gerhart, in Franz Schubert, *100 Songs: High Voice,* ed. Steven Stolen and Richard Walters, trans. Martha Gerhart (Milwaukie, WI: Hal Leonard Corp, 2000).

3. Ancient Germanic poetry featured alliteration as part of its structure, and you will also find it in the works of J. R. R. Tolkien, author of *The Lord of the Rings* and a scholar of Medieval literature.

4. Christian Friedrich Daniel Schubart, *Ideen zu einer Ästhetik der Tonkunst* (Vienna: Degen, 1806), reprint, ed. P. A. Merbach (Leipzig: Wolkenwander-Verlag, 1924), quoted in Rita Steblin, *A History of Key Characteristics in the Eighteenth and Early Nineteenth Centuries* (Ann Arbor: UMI Research Press, 1983), 124–25.

5. Many scholars have weighed in on the motives and structure of Erlkönig. Charles Burkhart observed the motivic parallelism between the opening rising triplets (G-B♭-D-E♭-D-G) in m. 2 (containing the upper neighbor) and the tonal organization of the song, relating it to the dramatic events in the poem, while Ann K. McNamee discussed the passing tone motive (C-C♯-D), and noted the "metamorphosis" through enharmonic motion at the climax in mm. 128–29 (at the moment Erlkönig's name is sung) and the linking of the neighbor tone and passing tone motives. Harald Krebs pointed out its frequency, association with the Erlkönig in earlier appearances (including "incomplete" appearances such as C-D♭ and C♯-D motion in mm. 46–47 and 106–9), and appearance at deeper levels of structure. Deborah Stein added discussion of the many transpositions of this figure, and the different ways in which the motives work together with the harmonic structure to create the drama in this song, detailing "the systemic encroachment of the Erlking into, and his ultimate destruction of, the world of the father and his child." The discovery of the sixth motive and its close association with the Erlking is my own. Charles Burkhart, "Schenker's 'Motivic Parallelisms,'" *Journal of Music Theory* 22 (1978): 145–75; Ann K. McNamee, "The Role of the Piano Introduction in Schubert's *Lieder*," *Music Analysis* 4 (1985): 95–106; Harald Krebs, "Some Addenda to McNamee's Remarks on 'Erlkönig,'" *Music Analysis* (1988): 53–57; and Deborah Stein, "Schubert's 'Erlkönig': Motivic Parallelism and Motivic Transformation,"*19th-Century Music* 13, no. 2 (Autumn, 1989): 145–58 (the quote is from p. 157). A summary of Deborah Stein's article on "Erlkönig" may be found in Deborah Stein and Robert Spillman, *Poetry into Song: Performance and Analysis of Lieder* (New York: Oxford University Press, 1996), 157–61.

6. D. Stein, "Schubert's 'Erlkönig,'" 148.

7. D. Stein, "Schubert's 'Erlkönig,'" 150.

8. Deborah Stein points out that the Erlking steals both the father's fourth motive as well as his C minor tonality, transforming it into the fake C major. D. Stein, "Schubert's 'Erlkönig,'" 157.

9. Burkhart, "Schenker's 'Motivic Parallelisms,'" 160.

10. Johnson, *Schubert: The Complete Songs*, 1:520.

Appendix

Templates for Song Analysis (Long Version)

THE POEM

General Meaning

- Do a **dramatic reading** of the poem to assess its general meaning. Which words are particularly important? Try several different readings with different emphases and emotion.
- Summarize the poem's **general story** or idea.
- What is the **mood** of the poem, and how is it created? Are there any shifts in the mood?
- What themes of nineteenth-century **Romanticism** are expressed in the poem? (Look for a focus inward on the individual, the wanderer, nostalgia for ancient times, ambiguity, nature, mysticism, transcendence or yearning for death, along with love and other strong emotions.) Do you find any ways of escaping the rational mind such as sleep, dreams, fantasy, or insanity?
- Look for **imagery** (the pictures created in the reader's mind) and **metaphor** (the use of one object to stand in for a person or idea).
- Who is speaking (**the *persona***)? Who are the characters (which may include natural elements)? Does the narrator change? Is the narrator believable?
- Who is the speaker addressing (**mode of address**), and what is the **subject**? Do either change?

Structure and Sound

- How many **stanzas** (paragraphs) are set in the song?
- Does the poem have a **refrain** (a repeating line or lines)? How does the meaning and/or emotion of the refrain change throughout the poem? Does the structure of the poem tell you something about its meaning?
- Summarize the **action** and **affect** (emotion) of each stanza. How does it change throughout the poem? Is there a predominant emotion or strong emotional contrasts? How are they expressed? Are there any dramatic high points or twists in the poem? Are there any **metaphors** that suggest meanings other than the superficial?

- What is the **meter** (type of accent pattern and number of feet per line)? Does it change; if so, why?
- What is the **rhyme scheme**? Do any words stick out (e.g., only non-rhymed lines in a rhymed poem or only rhymed lines in free-verse)? Is there any internal rhyme?
- What kind of **special word sounds** do you find? Some examples might be **alliteration** (repetition of the same letter or sound at the beginning of words) or **consonance** (same as alliteration, but not at the beginning of words), **assonance** (repetition of vowel sounds), **cacophony** (harsh or noisy sounds), **onomatopoeia** (a word that sounds like its meaning), or **bright vs. dark** vowel sounds.

THE MUSICAL SETTING

Mood

- What is the mood of the musical setting? How do you feel while listening to the song? Does the mood change at any point, and if so, to what other mood or moods?
- How is the mood conveyed? As you are listening, try to sense in a general way what features of the setting make you feel this way: Is it the shape of the melody, the chords, the range of the melody or piano part, the rhythm, the repetition of a refrain, or something else?
- Does the mood express what you felt when you studied the poem? Are there slight changes (or even surprising differences) between the poem and the mood expressed by the music?
- Does the melody sound like the words? For instance, is the music trying to represent something nonmusical, like Gretchen's spinning wheel or the brook in "Die Forelle"? You will do a more detailed examination below, so just get a general sense for it here.

Piano Part

- Singers need to listen over and over to the piano part while studying the score, and pianists should similarly sing through the vocal part, so that both of you can communicate and coordinate your performance.
- Make sure that you explain how you will be shaping the melody that you sing, in terms of breath, dynamics, tempo, tone quality, and mood.
- How does the piano prelude tell the story of the song? Does it present any questions or complexity? How are these developed in the rest of the song?
- Does the piano part represent a character that is independent from the voice part?
- Is there a piano interlude? What mood does it express?
- How does the piano postlude compare to the prelude? Is it the same, or are there conspicuous changes? Sometimes the true meaning of the song, the answer to the question posed in the prelude, may appear in the postlude.
- Where does the piano double the voice part (play the same notes), and where is the voice singing its own line? How will the two of you coordinate the doubled sections?
- Does the piano part feature a representation of nature or a physical object? If so, how is it expressed? What emotion might it represent?

Form

- Does your text repeat? If so, is it set to a repeat of the same or different music?
- What is the large-scale structure of the poem? What is the structure of the music? Does the music follow the structure of the poem? If not, why not? Does the change in structure add to or change the meaning of the poem in any way?
- How will the form of the song affect the audience? Is it a comforting repetitive form, a contrasting section with a return, or is it a completely through-composed song, moving ever forward?
- If strophic, how will you perform each strophe so that each is different?
- If your song is modified strophic (strophic with variations), why do you think the composer made these changes? How will that affect your performance?
- If your song features a return, is it the same as the original or are there changes? If so, why? How will you present this gift to your audience?
- If your song is through-composed, how will you distinguish the mood of each section?
- Does anything interesting happen at the midpoint of the song?

Phrasing

- After listening to your song many times, mark out the phrases by writing an arc over each one in your score. Small phrases are often combined to form medium-sized ones. Go through and also mark the medium-sized phrases in your score.
- How do the musical phrases compare to the text lines of the poem? Does the composer follow the structure of the poem? Take your poem and write in an arc over each text line or lines that the composer has set as a musical phrase; make a larger arc to indicate a medium section composed of two or more phrases.
- What are the shapes of each phrase? How will you emphasize this when you sing or play the song?
- For each phrase, find the most important word or words and decide how you will bring it (them) out in your performance.
- Practice singing or playing your phrase with direction, moving forward until you find a resolution.
- Go through the phrases in your score and get a sense for which ones are the most important (containing a high point, revealing something important in the story). This will help you to build up to this point when performing the song.
- Find all the cadences in your song and circle them. Are they strong, medium, or weak? How will you express the variety? Which ones are deceptive, and how will your performance make the audience feel the pain of disappointment?

Melody

- Where are the high and low points and what words do they emphasize? Why does the composer set them in these places?
- Is the range wide or narrow? How does this express the mood of the character or the text in the poem?
- What shapes does the melody create? How do they add to the drama of the song, and how will you bring them out in performance?

- Are there any unusually shaped melodies such as a monotone (melody on one note or with a limited range)?
- For each phrase, note the beginning and ending notes. Which phrases progress (end on a different note) and in which direction? Which phrases don't progress (end on the same note)? Why do you think the composer has written it this way? Which phrase or phrases have the most melodic progression (change from beginning to end of the phrase)?
- Note any particularly wide or narrow intervals and any dissonant ones. What words do they set, and why do you think the composer did this?
- Is the melody simple or is it highly ornamented? Be sure you understand how the underlying melody works and how to bring it out in performance.
- Is anything missing in the melody? Are any notes left out until later (withholding)?

Motive

- What melodic and rhythmic motives appear?
- Are they associated with a word or idea from the poem? How will you bring them out?
- If it is a repeating motive, how will you give it shape so that it is not always the same?
- Where does the motive *not* appear and why? How will you distinguish this section?

Tempo

- Does the song have tempo designation? What does it mean?
- Does it have an original (designated by the composer) metronome marking?
- Are there any changes in tempo? If so, what is its purpose?
- What note gets the beat?
- How many levels of subdivision do you hear? (If a quarter note gets the beat, are eighth notes common? Sixteenth notes? Or are the rhythms mostly half notes, making it sound slow?) Are there any changes in the subdivision of the beat? How does it affect the mood?
- How can you use tempo to express the mood of the song?

Meter and Rhythm

- What type of message does the meter of your song send? How does it affect the mood?
- Does the song feel like a march, a waltz, or a neutral background for a variety of rhythms? Are there changes of meter or style?
- Does your song use all upbeat phrases, all downbeat phrases, or is it mixed? Why?
- How will you bring out the characteristic of this type of song and any shift between upbeat and downbeat phrases?
- How is the personality of your song expressed through rhythm? Is it generally varied or monotonous?
- How are rests used in your song, and what do they evoke?
- How are rhythmic shifts used to express contrast? What ideas or emotions are being juxtaposed?
- How does rhythm speed up or slow down sections of the song?

Accents

- What is the function of the accents in your song? Do they emphasize important words or chords, imitate the natural world, express a mood, or show the piano emerging from the vocal line?

- Did you find any "stingers" (offbeat accents in the piano part expressing sudden pain in the protagonist)? Make sure the pianist brings them out in performance.
- How will the accents help you to express the meaning of the song in performance?

Texture

- Does the texture remain the same throughout the song?
- If it changes, why? How will you bring out the change?
- How will the texture affect your listeners' understanding of the song's meaning?

Dynamics

- What is the predominant dynamic level? What is the total range?
- Are there any sudden changes or extremes of dynamic level; if so, why?

Cadence Map

- After listening many times to your song, circle the cadences in the score.
- Now write in the cadence levels on your translation of the poem.
- What type of cadence map do you see: is it a warm bath (cadences always on the same level), a sinking ship (cadences all over the place or else sinking stepwise), or does it follow the more typical path and modulate to one or two other tonal levels?
- Is there a particular pattern of cadences? How would you characterize the ordering of cadences?
- Does it avoid any important cadence level?
- Are there any deceptive or avoided cadences?
- Does the song end in the same key in which it began? If not, why not?

Choice of Key

- In what key is your song?
- How does the choice of key relate to its meaning?
- If the song moves through different keys, how do they express meaning?

Linear Motion

- Look for linear motion in your song. Does the composer outline any important intervals? If so, is the interval consonant or dissonant?
- Are there any surprises, where the composer moves farther than the expected interval being outlined?
- Is the linear motion diatonic or chromatic? In which direction does it move?
- What does linear motion tell you about the composer's viewpoint of the story being told and how will you bring it out?

Pedal Points

- Does your song have a pedal point?
- If so, why do you think the composer included it? Is it used to express a word or phrase? To create a feeling of being stuck? To create tension by sitting on the dominant? To assist in modulation? Or to create a stark or negative mood?
- How does the pedal point express the meaning of the poem?

Harmony: Chord Function and Modulation

Dissonance and appoggiaturas

- Listen to your song with the score. Where are the dissonances? What words do they set? How does this tell you more about the song's meaning?
- Listen for appoggiaturas in your song. Where do they occur? How do they make you feel? Practice performing them so that each one sounds like a musical sigh.

Modulation

- Look at your cadence map to see where your song travels.
- In a modulating passage, look for a pivot chord, a chord that works in both keys.
- Keep an eye out for secondary dominants. Remember that in a major key the chord on $\hat{2}$ is minor; if this chord is major it is probably functioning as V/V, not II.
- Another sign of modulation is a I_4^6 chord in a new key; the appearance of a I_4^6 is often a way of putting a floor under a new key; it wants to move to V and then to cadence on I.
- Look for temporary tonicizations, in which a few secondary harmonies highlight a new area for a brief time. Ask yourself why the composer is moving into this area. (Hint: check the text!)

Augmented and Neapolitan sixth chords

- Do augmented sixth or Neapolitan sixth chords appear in your song? If so, why? How do they affect the emotion expressed?

Enharmonic shift and sudden shift to a new key

- Does your song have an enharmonic shift, in which the same chord is spelled differently? If so, what is its purpose?
- Does your song feature any sudden shifts to a new key, and if so, why?

Third relationships and chromatic mediants

- Does your song contain chromatic mediants (a third-related chord that has been altered chromatically) or a shift to a third-related key (such as C major to E major)? How does it sound, and why do you think the composer sets the text this way?

Oscillation and circling

- Do you find any **oscillation** in your song (when a note or chord goes back and forth between two or several notes, resulting in a static or hypnotic quality)?
- Is there any **melodic circling** (emphasizing an important note by ringing it with an upper and lower neighbor) in your song? If so, what is it suggesting about the meaning of the text?

Appendix

Templates for Song Analysis (Short Version)

THE POEM

General Meaning

- Dramatic reading, summarize general story, determine mood (and any shifts)?
- Themes of German Romanticism, imagery, metaphor?
- Persona, characters, narrator, mode of address, subject?

Structure and Sound

- Number of stanzas, refrain? Action and emotion of each stanza? Any sudden shifts?
- Meter and rhyme scheme (look for words that stick out by being the only rhyme or non-rhyme)?
- Special words sounds (alliteration, consonance, assonance, cacophony, onomatopoeia, bright/dark vowel sounds)?

THE MUSICAL SETTING

Mood and Piano Part

- General mood, how created, change in mood?
- Learn both parts! How does the piano tell the story?
- Is there a prelude/interlude/postlude? How do they compare; if different, why?
- Piano doubling of voice? Where and why?
- Any musical representation of nature?

Form and Phrasing

- Does text repeat? To new or same music?
- Large-scale structure? Does music follow this structure? If not, why not?

- How will the form of the song affect the audience (repetitive, or changing)? Review ch. 2.
- Write in all the musical phrases. Compare with the text lines of the poem.
- What are the shapes of each phrase? What is the most important word in each phrase?
- Are you singing each phrase with direction?
- Listen for all the cadences and circle them in your score. Are they strong, medium, or weak?

Melody and Motive

- Where are the high and low points, and what words do they emphasize?
- Is the range wide or narrow, and how does this express the mood?
- What melodic shapes do you find, and how does this create drama? Any monotone?
- Do the phrases progress (end on a different note) or return to the same note, and why?
- What words are set by particularly wide/narrow or dissonant intervals?
- Is the melody simple or is it highly ornamented? Are any notes left out (withholding)?
- What melodic and rhythmic motives appear? How do they relate to the poem? Where are they missing?

Tempo, Meter, and Rhythm

- What is the tempo, and what does it mean? Are the metronome markings original to the composer? Are there changes in tempo, and if so, why?
- What note gets the beat and what subdivisions are present? How does tempo affect mood?
- What does the meter of your song tell you about the mood? Does it change?
- Does your song use all upbeat phrases, all downbeat phrases, or is it mixed? Why?
- Is the rhythm varied or monotonous? How does it express the song's personality?
- How are rests or rhythmic shifts used in your song?

Accents, Texture, and Dynamics

- How do accents function in your song? Are there any "stingers" (offbeat accents in the piano part)?
- What is the texture? How does it affect the mood? Does it change?
- What is the general dynamic level? Any sudden changes? If so, why?

Cadence Map and Choice of Key

- Make a cadence map to understand where you are traveling in the song. Is it a warm bath (cadences on same level) or a sinking ship (all over the place), or something simpler?
- How does your song's key relate to its meaning? Does it modulate? If so, why?

Linear Motion and Pedal Points

- Does the composer outline any important intervals? Are they consonant or dissonant? Diatonic or chromatic? In what direction does it move? What does this tell you about the song and how will you bring them out in your performance?
- Does your song have any pedal points? If so, how do they function to express the meaning?

Dissonance, Appoggiaturas, Modulation, Augmented and Neapolitan Sixth Chords

- What words are set by dissonances? By appoggiaturas? Make sure the latter sound like a sigh!
- Listen for modulation; how did you arrive in the new key? Look for a pivot chord, secondary dominants, and I_4^6 chords, as well as temporary tonicizations. Ask yourself why we are in this new key.
- Do augmented sixth or Neapolitan sixth chords appear in your song? If so, why? How do they affect the emotion expressed?

Enharmonic Shift, Sudden Shift to a New Key, Third Relationships, Chromatic Mediants

- Do you find any sudden shifts to a new key or any enharmonic shifts? If so, why?
- Do you find any chromatic mediants (a third-related chord that has been altered chromatically) or a shift to a third-related key (such as C major to E major)? What emotion does it express?

Oscillation and Circling

- Do you find any oscillation in your song (when a note or chord goes back and forth between two or several notes, resulting in a static or hypnotic quality)?
- Is there any melodic circling (emphasizing an important note by ringing it with an upper and lower neighbor) in your song? If so, what is it suggesting about the meaning of the text?

Bibliography

For scores: International Music Score Library Project at https://imslp.org/wiki/Main_Page.
For translations: search online for "Oxford International Song Festival" and the name of your song, or go to the LiederNet Archive at https://www.lieder.net.

Agawu, V. Kofi. "Schubert's Harmony Revisited: The Songs 'Du liebst mich nicht' and 'Dass sie hier gewesen.'" *Journal of Musicological Research* 9 (1989): 34.
Bodley, Lorraine Byrne, and Julian Horton. *Rethinking Schubert*. Oxford: Oxford University Press, 2016.
Brown, Clive. "Schubert's Tempo Conventions." In *Schubert Studies*, edited by Brian Newbould, 1–15. Burlington, VT: Ashgate, 1998.
Brown, Jane K. "In the Beginning Was Poetry." In *The Cambridge Companion to the Lied*, edited by James Parsons, 12–32. Cambridge: Cambridge University Press, 2004.
Brown, Jane K. "The Poetry of Schubert's Songs." In *Schubert's Vienna*, edited by Raymond Erickson, 183–213. New Haven: Yale University Press, 1997.
Burkhart, Charles. "Schenker's 'Motivic Parallelisms.'" *Journal of Music Theory* 22 (1978): 145–75.
Chafe, Eric. *Tonal Allegory in the Vocal Music of J. S. Bach*. Berkeley: University of California Press, 1991.
Clark, Susannah. *Analyzing Schubert*. Cambridge: Cambridge University Press, 2011.
Damschroder, David. *Harmony in Schubert*. Cambridge: Cambridge University Press, 2010.
DeBoer, Katharine. "Schubert for Starters: Songs for the Lieder Novice." *Journal of Singing* 69, no. 3 (January/February 2013): 353–60.
Dittrich, Marie-Agnes. "The Lieder of Schubert." Translated by Sven Hansell, revised by editor. In *The Cambridge Companion to the Lied*, edited by James Parsons, 85–100. Cambridge: Cambridge University Press, 2004.
Dürr, Walther. "Schubert's Songs and their Poetry: Reflections on Poetic Aspects of Song Composition." In *Schubert Studies: Problems of Style and Chronology*, edited by Eva Badura-Skoda and Peter Branscombe, 25–46. Cambridge: Cambridge University Press, 1982.
El-Shabrawy, Charlotte. "German Ghazals: An Experiment in Cross-Cultural Literary Synthesis." *Alif: Journal of Comparative Poetics*, no. 3 (Spring, 1983): 55–79.
Erickson, Raymond. *Schubert's Vienna*. New Haven: Yale University Press, 1997.
Feurzeig, Lisa. *Schubert's Lieder and the Philosophy of Early German Romanticism*. Burlington, VT: Ashgate, 2014; New York: Routledge, 2016.
Garland, Henry, and Mary Garland, eds. *The Oxford Companion to German Literature*. Third edition. Oxford: Oxford University Press, 1997.

Gibbs, Christopher. *The Life of Schubert*. Cambridge: Cambridge University Press, 2000.
Gibbs, Christopher, and Morten Solvik. *Franz Schubert and His World*. Princeton: Princeton University Press, 2014.
Gingerich, John H. *Schubert's Beethoven Project*. Cambridge: Cambridge University Press, 2014.
Gorrell, Lorraine. *The Nineteenth-Century German Lied*. Portland: Amadeus, 1993.
Gramit, David. "Orientalism and the Lied: Schubert's 'Du liebst mich nicht.'" *19th-Century Music* 27, no. 2 (2003): 104.
Hallmark, Rufus. "Schubert's 'Auf dem Strom.'" In *Schubert Studies: Problems of Style and Chronology*, edited by Eva Badura-Skoda and Peter Branscombe, 1–24. Cambridge: Cambridge University Press, 1982.
Hisch, Marjorie Wing. *Schubert's Dramatic Lieder*. Cambridge: Cambridge University Press, 1993.
Hollander, John. *Rhyme's Reason: A Guide to English Verse*. Fourth edition. New Haven: Yale University Press, 2014.
Johnson, Graham. *Schubert: The Complete Songs*. 3 vols. New Haven: Yale University Press, 2014.
Kimball, Carol. *Art Song: Linking Poetry and Music*. Lanham, MD: Rowman & Littlefield, 2013.
Kimball, Carol. *Song: A Guide to Art Song Style and Literature*. Revised edition. Milwaukee: Hal Leonard Corporation, 2006.
Kinderman, William. "Schubert's Tragic Perspective." In *Schubert: Critical and Analytical Studies*, edited by Walter Frisch, 65–83. Lincoln: University of Nebraska Press, 1996.
Kopp, David. *Chromatic Transformations in Nineteenth-Century Music*. Cambridge: Cambridge University Press, 2002.
Kramer, Lawrence. *Franz Schubert: Sexuality, Subjectivity, Song*. Cambridge: Cambridge University Press, 1998.
Kramer, Lawrence. "The Schubert Lied: Romantic Form and Romantic Consciousness." In *Schubert: Critical and Analytical Studies*, edited by Walter Frisch, 200–236. Lincoln: University of Nebraska Press, 1996.
Kramer, Richard. *Distant Cycles: Schubert and the Conceiving of Song*. Chicago: University of Chicago Press, 1994.
Krebs, Harald. "Some Addenda to McNamee's Remarks on 'Erlkönig.'" *Music Analysis* (1988): 53–57.
Krebs, Harald. "Some Early Examples of Tonal Pairing: Schubert's 'Meeres Stille' and 'Der Wanderer.'" In *The Second Practice of Nineteenth-Century Tonality*, edited by William Kinderman and Harald Krebs, 17–33. Lincoln: University of Nebraska Press, 1996.
Laitz, Steven. "The Submediant Complex: Its Musical and Poetic Roles in Schubert's Songs." In *Theory and Practice* 21 (1996): 123–65.
Lambert. Sterling. *Re-Reading Poetry: Schubert's Multiple Settings of Goethe*. Rochester, NY: Boydell & Brewer, 2009.
Law, Richard. "Christian Schubart: The Trout." *Figures of Speech* (blog). February 7, 2016, http://figures-of-speech.com/2016/02/die-forelle-5.htm.
Law, Richard. "'Dass sie hier gewesen' D 775: Rückert and Schubert." *Figures of Speech* (blog). January 16, 2019, http://figures-of-speech.com/2019/01/hier-gewesen.htm.
Law, Richard. "Du bist die Ruh D776." *Figures of Speech* (blog). February 20, 2020, http://figures-of-speech.com/2020/02/du-bist-die-ruh_1.htm.
Law, Richard. "Goethe's Heidenröslein." *Figures of Speech* (blog). July 25, 2017, http://figures-of-speech.com/2017/06/röslein.htm#update-3.
Mahoney, Dennis F., ed. *The Literature of German Romanticism*. Rochester, NY: Camden House, 2003.
McClelland, Clive. "Death and the Composer: The Context of Schubert's Supernatural Lieder." In *Schubert the Progressive: History, Performance Practice, Analysis*, edited by Brian Newbould, 21–36. Abingdon, Oxfordshire: Routledge, 2003.
McNamee, Ann K. "The Role of the Piano Introduction in Schubert's *Lieder*." *Music Analysis* 4 (1985): 95–106.

Muxfeldt, Kristina. "Schubert, Platen, and the Myth of Narcissus." *Journal of the American Musicological Society* 49, no. 3 (Autumn, 1996): 480–527.

Muxfeldt, Kristina. "Schubert's Songs: The Transformation of a Genre." In *The Cambridge Companion to Schubert*, edited by Christopher H. Gibbs, 119–37. Cambridge: Cambridge University Press, 1997.

Muxfeldt, Kristina. *Vanishing Sensibilities: Schubert, Beethoven, Schumann.* Oxford: Oxford University Press, 2011.

Newbould, Brian. *Schubert, the Music, and the Man.* Berkeley: University of California Press, 1997.

Porhansl, Lucia. "Schuberts Textvorlagen nach Friedrich Wilhelm Gotter und Christian Friedrich Daniel Schubart." *Schubert durch die Brille* 10 (1993): 69–74.

Reed, John. *The Schubert Song Companion.* Manchester: Manchester University Press, 1997.

Ronyak, Jennifer. *Intimacy, Performance, and the Lied in the Early Nineteenth Century.* Bloomington: Indiana University Press, 2018.

Rosen, Charles. "Schubert's Inflections of Classical Form." In *The Cambridge Companion to Schubert*, edited by Christopher H. Gibbs, 72–98. Cambridge: Cambridge University Press, 1997.

Schachter, Carl. "Motive and Text in Four Schubert Songs." In *Aspects of Schenkerian Theory*, edited by D. W. Beach, 61–76. New Haven: Yale University Press, 1983.

Schubart, Christian Friedrich Daniel. *Ideen zu einer Ästhetik der Tonkunst.* Vienna: Degen, 1806. Reprint, ed. P. A. Merbach. Leipzig: Wolkenwander-Verlag, 1924. Quoted in Rita Steblin, *A History of Key Characteristics in the Eighteenth and Early Nineteenth Centuries.* Ann Arbor: UMI Research Press, 1983.

Seelig, Harry. "The Literary Context: Goethe as Source and Catalyst." In *German Lieder in the Nineteenth Century*, edited by Rufus Hallmark, 1–30. New York: Schirmer, 1996.

Steblin, Rita. *A History of Key Characteristics in the Eighteenth and Early Nineteenth Centuries.* Ann Arbor: UMI Research Press, 1983.

Stein, Beverly. "Between Key and Mode: Tonal Practice in the Music of Giacomo Carissimi," PhD diss. Brandeis University, 1994.

Stein, Deborah. "Schubert's 'Erlkönig': Motivic Parallelism and Motivic Transformation." *19th-Century Music* 13, no. 2 (Autumn, 1989): 145–58.

Stein, Deborah, and Robert Spillman. *Poetry into Song: Performance and Analysis of Lieder.* New York: Oxford University Press, 1996.

Steinbron, Matthew. "Polyfocal Structures in Franz Schubert's Lieder." PhD diss. Louisiana State University, 2011.

Suurpää, Lauri. *Death in Winterreise: Musical-Poetic Associations in Schubert's Song Cycle.* Bloomington: Indiana University Press, 2014.

Watanabe-O'Kelly, Helen, ed. *The Cambridge History of German Literature.* Cambridge: Cambridge University Press, 1997.

Whitton, Kenneth S. *Goethe and Schubert: The Unseen Bond.* Portland: Amadeus, 2003.

Wigmore, Richard. *The Complete Schubert Texts.* London: Orion, 1992.

Wolff, Christoph. "Schubert's 'Der Tod und das Mädchen': Analytical and Explanatory Notes on the Song D 531 and the Quartet D 810." In *Schubert Studies: Problems of Style and Chronology*, edited by Eva Badura-Skoda and Peter Branscombe, 143–72. Cambridge: Cambridge University Press, 1982.

Youens, Susan. *Die schöne Müllerin.* Cambridge: Cambridge University Press, 1992.

Youens, Susan. "Franz Schubert: The Prince of Song." In *German Lieder in the Nineteenth Century*, edited by Rufus Hallmark, 31–74. New York: Schirmer, 1996.

Youens, Susan. *Retracing a Winter's Journey: Schubert's Winterreise.* Ithaca: Cornell University Press, 1991.

Youens, Susan. "Schubert and His Poets: Issues and Conundrums." In *The Cambridge Companion to Schubert*, edited by Christopher H. Gibbs, 99–118. Cambridge: Cambridge University Press, 1997.

Youens, Susan. *Schubert, Müller, and Die schöne Müllerin.* Cambridge: Cambridge University Press, 1997.

Youens, Susan. *Schubert's Poets and the Making of Lieder.* Cambridge: Cambridge University Press, 1999.

Glossary

TERMS USED TO DISCUSS POETRY

affect: the emotion created by a poem or song
alliteration: the repetition of the same letter or sound at the beginning of words that are near each other
assonance: the repetition of a similar vowel
cacophony: when harsh sounds are created by plosive consonants such as K, G, P, B, or T
consonance: the repetition of the same letter or sound in the middle of a word
foot: the basic pattern of stressed and accented syllables in a poem
imagery: the pictures created in the reader's mind
internal rhyme: a rhyme that occurs within a line of poetry, rather than at the end of a line
metaphor: the use of one object to stand in for a person or idea
onomatopoeia: when a word sounds like its meaning (as in the word "plunk")
poetic meter: the combination of poetic feet in a line of poetry, named by combining foot with the number of feet per line (as in iambic pentameter)
refrain: a repeating text line in a poem or song
rhyme scheme: the rhyme pattern created by the ends of lines of poetry
stanza: a paragraph of text in a poem
strong ending: a line of poetry that ends on a stressed syllable
weak ending: a line of poetry that ends on an unstressed syllable

TERMS USED TO DISCUSS MUSIC

appoggiatura: an ornament in which an accented dissonance resolves down to a consonant note, emphasizing it (Technically, they are approached by leap, but an accented passing tone can informally be called an appoggiatura.)
augmented sixth chords: chords which push very strongly in contrary motion (by semitone) to the octave, usually to the I_4^6 or V chord
binary form: a song in two main parts

cadence map: a chart of the cadences in a song that tells you where it is traveling

chromatic mediant: a third-related chord that has been altered chromatically; it does not appear naturally in the key, as in moving from C major to E major

circling: a way of emphasizing an important note by ringing it with an upper and lower neighbor (sometimes called a "double neighbor," "changing tone," or "neighbor group")

deceptive cadence: a cadence which doesn't resolve the way you think it will

enharmonic shift: crossing from a key written in flats to one in sharps (or vice versa); one chord may be spelled two different ways, depending on the signature

key characteristic: association of emotions or personalities with a particular key

linear motion: movement of a bassline or other line which can outline an important interval that may express the meaning of the poem, such as a tritone or perfect fifth.

modulation: movement to a new tonal area which is established as a new tonic

motive: the smallest recognizable part of a melody, often used to structure a song through its frequent appearance

motivic parallelism: the appearance of a motive at different levels of scale

Neapolitan sixth: the chord in first inversion based on $\flat\hat{2}$ in the key that pushes very strongly to the I_4^6 or V chord

oscillation: when a note or chord goes back and forth between two or several notes, resulting in a static or hypnotic quality

pedal point: when a bassline stays on one note for a while

pivot chord: in tonicization or modulation, a pivot chord functions in both the original and the new key, allowing for a shift to the new key

secondary dominant: the dominant of another tonal level in the key of the piece, often V/V

strophic form: a song in which each stanza of the poem is set to the same music

ternary form: a song in three main parts, often ABA or ABA'

through-composed: a song structure without large repeated sections

tonal structure: the organization of tonal areas in a song

tonicization: a temporary movement to a new tonal area

withholding or tonal withholding: when a note, chord, or cadence area is intentionally avoided

Index

Page reference for tables and figures are italicized.

accents, 18, 31, 34–36, 101, 112, 120n4
accompaniment. *See* piano part
action. *See* poetry analysis
affect. *See* poetry analysis
alliteration. *See* poetry analysis
appoggiatura, 34, 57, 61, 65, 78n19, 87, 115
assonance. *See* poetry analysis
augmented sixth chords, 20, 26, 61, 67–72, 138, 190, 227, 241
avoidance (of note, cadence, or tonal area), 41, 43–44, 46, 51, 227–28. *See also* withholding

binary form. *See* form

cacophony. *See* poetry analysis
cadence, 23, 25–26, 38–44, 46–47, 49–52, 57, 61, 63–65, 67, 69, 72–76, 77nn2–3, 77n5, 90, 217, 219
cadence levels. *See* cadence map
cadence map, 38–47, 90
characters. *See* poetry analysis
chiastic structure. *See* poetry analysis
chord progressions, 60–77, 83
chromatic mediant, 74–75, 111, 117. *See also* third relationships
chromatic motion, 52–56, 76
circling. *See* melodic circling
Claudius, Matthias, 46, 121–22
consonance (in poetry). *See* poetry analysis
contrary motion, 35, 54, 67, 69, 72, 76, 138

deceptive cadence, 25–26, 38, 40–41, 44, 61, 65
directional tonality, 46
dissonance, 21, 61, 68, 76, 115, 216
dramatic reading. *See* poetry analysis
drone, 58, *59*, 76
dynamics, 21–22, 35–36

endings, strong and weak. *See* poetry analysis, line endings (strong/weak)
enharmonic shift, *71*, 72–73, *73*

folklike style, 8–9, 32, 94, 113, 121
foot/feet (poetic). *See* poetry analysis
form, 22–25;
 binary form, 22–23;
 modified strophic form, 22–23;
 rondo form, 22–23;
 strophic form, 22–23, 65, 82;
 ternary form, 22–23;
 through-composed form, 22–25

ghazal. *See* poetry analysis
Goethe, Johann Wolfgang von, 6–9, 12, 15, 16n1, 16n3, 24, 43–44, 54, 150, 158, 213, 228, 231, 271, 283n1, 284, 298

half cadence, 39, 41, 44, 64, 65, 69, 219
harmonic progression. *See* chord progression
harmony, 18, 26, 38, *50*, 52, 54, 60–75, 166
Heine, Heinrich, 36n1, 150

internal rhyme. *See* poetry analysis
I64 chord (used to modulate), 52, 58, 63–64, *64*, 67–69, *68*, 74, 76, 78n14, 119, 138, 217

key ambiguity, 44–45, *46*, 63–64, 133
key characteristics (according to C. F. D. Schubart), 47–51, *71*, 71–72, 74, 78nn7–11, 201–2, 208, 217, 251, 271

linear motion, 18, 20, 38, 52–56, 63, 69, 87
line endings (strong/weak). *See* poetry analysis
line length (in poetry). *See* poetry analysis

major vs. minor key contrast, 155, 270n8
melodic circling, *53*, *55*, *64*, 76–77, 118, 155, 162
melody, 18–22, 25, 26–28, 33, 38, 52, 56, 61, 66, 185
metaphor. *See* poetry analysis
meter (musical), 28, 30, 31–32, 33, 35–36
meter (poetic). *See* poetry analysis
mode of address. *See* poetry analysis
mode mixture, 111
modified strophic form. *See* form
modulation, 57, 60, 63–67, 71, 73–74, 119, 217
monotone, 26, 153, 216
mood, 7, 14, 18–19, 23–24, 34–36, 38, 42, 49, 58, *65*, 71, 201
motive:
    rhythmic motive, 27, 30;
    melodic motive, 27, 34, *39*, *45*, 52, 54, 56, 58, 69, *70*, 74, 76, 87, 114, 118, 155, 163, 201, 216, 301, 310n5;
    semitone motive, 27–28, 34, *39*, *45*, 56, 58, 69, 74, 76, 118, 155–56, 163, 216
motivic parallelism, 52–56, 118, 155, 163, 201, 216, 310n5

narrator. *See* poetry analysis
Neapolitan sixth chords, 34, 49, 63, 67–73, *69–72*, 74
nostalgia. *See* poetry analysis

onomatopoeia. *See* poetry analysis
oscillation (melodic and harmonic), 73, 76, 118, 165

pedal points, *41*, *55*, 57–58, *57–59*, 69, *70*, 73, 76–78n17
persona. *See* poetry analysis
phrasing, 25, 28, 35

piano part (accompaniment), 19–22, 34–35, 52, 54, 64, 76
piano postlude, 19–22, *20–21*, 40, 42, 44, 51, 66, 76, 86
piano prelude, 19–22, *21*, 27, 30–31, 33, 40, 42, 46, 58, 69, 76, 86, 185, 274
plagal tonal area, 73
Platen, Karl August Graf von Platen-Hallermünde, 150, 257–58, 284
pivot chord, 63, 158
poetry analysis, 5–16;
    action, 8, 74;
    affect, 9, 153;
    alliteration, 12–15, 310n3;
    assonance, 11–12, 14;
    cacophony, 12–13, 15;
    characters, 6–8, 12, 15, 19, 26, 29, 32, 36n1, 94, 139, 153;
    chiastic structure, 141;
    consonance, 12–13;
    dramatic reading, 7;
    foot/feet, *10*, 10–11, 14;
    ghazal, 150, 153, 284;
    internal rhyme, 11–12, 150;
    line endings (strong/weak), 11, 14, 123, 141;
    line length, 14;
    metaphor, 8, 14, 49, 94, 101, 122;
    meter (poetic), 10–12, 14–15, 24, 112, 122, 184;
    mode of address, 6, 8;
    narrator, 8;
    nostalgia, 15, 101;
    onomatopoeia, 12, 14;
    persona, 6;
    refrain, 6–9, 11, 22–23, 32, 34, 41, 50, 57–58, 66, 284, 292;
    rhyme scheme, 11–12, 141;
    stanza, 5–9, 11–16, 24, 69;
    structure, 6, 9–10, 14, 25, 141, 310n3, 310n5;
    subject, 13, 33, 122, 257, 284;
    unreliable narrator, 6;
    vowel patterns, 14, 36, 123
postlude. *See* piano postlude
prelude. *See* piano prelude
progressive tonality. *See* directional tonality

refrain. *See* poetry analysis
rhyme scheme. *See* poetry analysis
rhythm, 27, 30–36, 61, 164, 208, 254
rhythmic motive. *See* motive

Roman numeral analysis, 61–63
romanticism, 15, 19, 45, 67, 139, 150, 181, 284, 292, 297
rondo form. *See* form
Rückert, Friedrich, 24, 65, 150, 180n1, 284

Schubart, Christian Fridrich Daniel (poet and theorist), 8, 16n4, 47–49, 72, 78nn8–9, 94–96, 127, 129, 160, 185, 202, 209n1, 217, 251, 260
Schubert songs:
    "An die Musik," 15, 29–30, 32, 35, 39, 50, 52, *54*, 61, 93n1;
    "An die Nachtigall," 6, 29, 31, 33, 35, 45, *46*, 63, 68, 76;
    "Ave Maria" (Ellens Gesang III), 15, 29, 32–33, 35, 49, 58, 139;
    "Dass sie hier gewesen," 15, 27, 29, 32–35, 49–50, *50*, 57, 65, *66*, 169, 284–85;
    "Der Neugierige" (from *Die schöne Müllerin*), 19–21, *20*, 23–24, 27, 29, 31–33, 50, 63, *64*, 74, 76, 111, 113;
    "Der Tod und das Mädchen," 15, 23–24, 26–32, *28*, 48–49, 121, 202;
    "Die Forelle," 8, 19, 23, 29, 32–34, 47, 49, 65–66, *66*, 94, 96;
    "Die junge Nonne," 13–16, 19–20, 29, 31–32, 34–35, 49, 57, 68, *73*, 73–74, 78n10, 241;
    "Die Liebe hat gelogen," 13, 15–16, 27, 29–30, 32–34, 36, 49, 51, 69, 75, 77n2, 257;
    "Du bist die Ruh," 6, 15, 20, 24, 29, 31–33, 36, 49, 52, 69, *70*, 74, 169, 284;
    "Du liebst mich nicht," 16, 19–20, 24, 26–30, 32–36, 40, 42, 44, 48–49, 51, 61, *62*, 65, 69, 127, 150, 163, 202, 257–58, 271, 284;
    "Erlkönig," 12, 30, 56, 201, 298, 305–6;
    "Erster Verlust," 15–16, 19, 23, 28–30, 32, 34, 36, 37n7, 44–45, *45*, 49, 56, 63, 68, 213;
    "Frühlingstraum" (from *Winterreise*), 15, 27, 29, 31–33, 50, 69, *70*, 181;
    "Ganymed," 15, 20, *21*, 24, 29, 33–36, 46, 49, 65, 69, 71–72, *71–72*, 202, 271;
    "Gretchen am Spinnrade," 15–16, 19, 23, 27, 29–32, 36, 41, 48–49, 52, *53*, 58, *59*, 74, 76, 127, 190;
    "Gute Nacht," 15, 20, 23, 27–29, 32, 34–35, 101, 185;
    "Heidenröslein," 6, 8–12, 14, 22, 26, 29–30, 32–33, 50, 60, 63, 81, 86;
    "Meeres Stille," 9, 23, 27, 29–30, 32–33, 35, 37n7, 40, 43, 50, 54, 68, 153, 161, 231;
    "Nur wer die Sehnsucht kennt" ("Lied der Mignon"), 23–24, 29, 31, 34, 48, 54, *55*, 58, 76, 158
secondary dominant, 63, 76
semitone motive. *See* motive
sequence, 202
sharp-flat contrast, 47–50, 72. *See also* key characteristics
song cycle, 58, 101, 111
stanza. *See* poetry analysis
stinger (offbeat accent in piano part), 34, 69, 101
strophic form. *See* form
structure (poetic). *See* poetry analysis
subject (in poetry). *See* poetry analysis
sudden shift, 14, 23, 31, 33–34, 38, 50–51, *51*, *53*, 61, 63, 67, 73–75, *75*, 155–56, 164
suspension, 78n14

tempo, 18, 29–31, 35, 37n7, 114, 274
ternary form. *See* form
texture, 18, 35
third relationships, 51, 74–75, 111, 201
through-composed form. *See* form
tonal structure. *See* cadence map
tonicization, 60, 63–67, *65–66*, 77n4, 217

upbeat/downbeat phrases, 18, *28*, 32–33, 35

voice leading, *See* linear motion
vowel patterns. *See* poetry analysis

the wanderer, 15, 101, 181, 185
withholding (of note, chord, or cadence area), 19, 26, 41, 44, 50, 90, 227, 231. *See also* avoidance

www.ingramcontent.com/pod-product-compliance
Lightning Source LLC
Chambersburg PA
CBHW060335010526
44117CB00017B/2839